Britain's
Best
B&Bs

AA Lifestyle Guides

914.106
Bri

 This product includes mapping data licensed from Ordnance Survey® with the permission of the Controller of Her Majesty's Stationery Office. © Crown copyright 2011. All rights reserved. Licence number 100021153.

Maps prepared by the Mapping Services Department of The Automobile Association.

Maps © AA Media Limited 2011.

Advertising Sales:
advertisementsales@theAA.com

Editorial:
lifestyleguides@theAA.com

The contents of this publication are believed correct at the time of printing. Nevertheless, the Publisher cannot be held responsible for any errors or omissions or for changes in the details given in this guide or for the consequences of any reliance on the information provided by the same.

Assessments of AA inspected establishments are based on the experience of the hotel and restaurant inspectors on the occasion of their visit(s) and therefore descriptions given in this guide necessarily dictate an element of subjective opinion which may not reflect or dictate a reader's own opinion on another occasion. We have tried to ensure accuracy in this guide but things do change and we would be grateful if readers would advise us of any inaccuracies they may encounter.

Website addresses are included in some entries and specified by the respective establishment. Such websites are not under the control of AA Media Limited and as such AA Media Limited has no control over them and will not accept any responsibility or liability in respect of any and all matters whatsoever relating to such websites including access, content, material and functionality. By including the addresses of third party websites the AA does not intend to solicit business or offer any security to any person in any country, directly or indirectly.

Typeset by AA Lifestyle Guides

Printed and bound by Graficas, Estella, Spain

Managing Editor: Fiona Griffiths

Cover credits:
Front Cover: Rooks Hill
Back Cover: (t) Trenake Manor Farm;
(c) The Manor
(b) The Print Room

A CIP catalogue record for this book is available from the British Library

ISBN: 978-0-7495-6787-3

Published by AA Publishing, which is a trading name of AA Media Limited, whose registered office is:
Fanum House,
Basing View,
Basingstoke,
Hampshire RG21 4EA
Registered number 06112600

theAA.com/shop

A04569

Britain's Best
B&Bs

Contents

Welcome

Britain's Best B&Bs is a collection of the finest guest houses, farmhouses, inns and restaurants-with-rooms offering bed and breakfast accommodation in England, Scotland, Wales, the Isle of Man and the Channel Islands.

A Place to Stay

This fully revised and updated guide makes it easy to find that special place to stay for a weekend or a longer break. There are more than 400 establishments to choose from, including smart town guest houses, contemporary city B&Bs, accessible country farmhouses and undiscovered gems in hidden-away locations.

Best Quality

Establishments in this book have received either a top star or a highly commended star rating following a visit by an AA inspector. This helps to ensure that you have a friendly welcome, comfortable surroundings, excellent food and great value for money. Further details about the AA scheme, inspections, awards and rating system can be found on pages 8–9.

Before You Travel

Some places may offer special breaks and facilities not available at the time of going to press – it might be worth calling the establishment before you book.

Using the Guide

Britain's Best B&Bs has been created to enable you to find an establishment quickly and efficiently. Each entry provides clear information about the type of accommodation, the facilities available and the local area.

Use page 3 to browse the main gazetteer section by county and the index to find either a location (page 344) or a specific B&B (page 349) by name.

Finding your Way

The main section of the guide is divided into four main parts covering England, the Channel Islands, Scotland and Wales.

The counties within each of these sections are ordered alphabetically as are the town or village locations (shown in capital letters as part of the address) within each county. The establishments are then listed alphabetically under each location name. Town names featured in the guide can also be located in the map section at the back of the guide.

The Old Rectory *sample entry*

★★★★ ⍟ ♨ ⬤ GUEST ACCOMMODATION

Address:	Ash Road, SALISBURY, SA38 2PS
Tel:	00000 300124
Fax:	00000 300128
Email:	info@oldrectory.co.uk
Website:	www.oldrectory.co.uk
Map ref:	3 SZ32

Directions: Next to church at S end of Whitchurch
Rooms: 4 en suite S £85–120, D £95–£120
Parking: 8 Notes: ⊗ on premises ⅻ under 10 Closed: 25–26 Dec

Formerly a rectory and now a stylish and comfortable B&B, the perfect place for relaxing and recharging your batteries, whether staying just for a night or a few days. Guests have use of the spa, hot tub and a gym. Beautifully restored, with its character carefully preserved, The Old Rectory features contemporary furnishings that cleverly complements the spacious internal architecture. The comfortable studio bedrooms all have easy chairs, dining table and chairs, mini-fridges with complimentary fresh milk, fruit juice and yoghurt, hairdryers and remote-controlled TVs. Home cooked meals, including breakfast or a pre-booked evening meal, can be served in the dining room or conservatory.

Recommended in the area

Salisbury Cathedral; New Forest National Park; Stonehenge and Salisbury Plain

❶ Stars and Symbols

All entries in the guide have been inspected by the AA and, at the time of going to press, belong to the AA Guest Accommodation Scheme. Each establishment in the scheme is classified for quality with a grading of one to five stars ★. Each establishment in the Best B&B guide has three, four or five stars and many have a yellow star (highly commended) rating (see page 8 for further details). Establishments with a star rating are given a descriptive category: B&B, GUEST HOUSE, FARMHOUSE, INN, RESTAURANT WITH ROOMS and GUEST ACCOMMODATION. See pages 8–10 for more information on designators and the AA ratings and awards scheme.

continued

Egg cups 🍶 and Pies 🥧 – These symbols denote where the breakfast or dinner are really special, and have an emphasis on freshly prepared ingredients.

Rosette ◎ – This is the AA's food award. See page 9 for further details.

❷ Contact Details

The establishment address includes a locator or place name in capitals (e.g. NORWICH). Within each county, entries are ordered alphabetically first by this place name and then by the name of the establishment.

Telephone and fax numbers, and e-mail and website addresses are given where available. See page 12 for international dialling codes. The telephone and fax numbers are believed correct at the time of going to press but changes may occur. The latest establishment details are on the B&B pages at theAA.com.

❸ Map Reference

Each establishment in this guide is given a map reference for a location which can be found in the atlas section at the back of the guide. It

is composed of the map page number (1–13) and two-figure map reference based on the National Grid.

For example: **Map 05 SU48**
05 refers to the page number of the map section at the back of the guide
SU is the National Grid lettered square (representing 100,000sq metres) in which the location will be found
4 is the figure reading across the top and bottom of the map page
8 is the figure reading down each side of the map page

Maps locating each establishment and a route planner are available at theAA.com.

❹ Directions

Where possible, directions have been given from the nearest motorway or A road.

❺ Room Information

The number of letting bedrooms with a bath or shower en suite are shown. Bedrooms that have a private bathroom adjacent may be included as en suite. Further details on private bathroom and en suite provision may also be included in the description text (see ❾).

It's a good idea to phone in advance and check that the accommodation has the facilities you require.

Prices: Charges shown are per night except where specified. S denotes bed and breakfast per person (single). D denotes bed and breakfast for two people sharing a room (double).

In some cases prices are also given for twin (T), triple and family rooms, also on a per night basis. Prices are indications only, so do check before booking.

❻ Parking

The number of parking spaces available. Other types of parking (on road or Park and Ride) may also be possible; check the descriptions for further information.

Key to symbols

★	Black stars (see page 9)
☆	Yellow stars (Highly commended) (see page 9)
◎	AA Rosette Award (see page 9)
🍶	Breakfast Award
🥧	Dinner Award
3 TQ28	Map reference
S	Single room
D	Double room
T	Twin room
Triple	Triple room
⊗	No dogs allowed (guide dogs for the blind and assist dogs should be allowed)
🚼	No children under age specified
Wi-fi	Wireless network connection

❼ Notes

This section provides specific details relating to:

Smoking policy: Smoking in public areas is now banned in England, Scotland, Wales, the Isle of Man and the Channel Islands.

The proprietor can designate one or more bedrooms with ventilation systems where the occupants can smoke, but communal areas must be smoke-free.

Dogs: Although some establishments allow dogs, they may be excluded from some areas of the property and some breeds, particularly those requiring an exceptional license, may not be acceptable at all. Under the Disability Discrimination Act 1995 access should be allowed for guide dogs and assistance dogs. Please check the policy when making your booking.

Children: No children (👶) means children cannot be accommodated, or a minimum age may be specified, e.g. 👶 under 4 means no children under four years old. The main description may also provide details about facilities available for children.

Establishments with special facilities for children may include additional equipment such as a babysitting service or baby-intercom system and facilities such as a playroom or playground, laundry facilities, drying and ironing facilities, cots, high chairs and special meals. If you have very young children, check before booking.

Other notes: Additional facilities, such as access for the disabled, or notes about other services (e.g. if credit cards are not accepted), may be listed here.

❽ Closed

Details of when the establishment is closed for business. Establishments are open all year unless closed dates/months are shown. Please note that some places are open all year but offer a restricted service in low season.

❾ Description

This is a general overview of the establishment and may include specific information about the various facilities offered in the rooms, a brief history of the establishment, notes about special features and descriptions of the food where an award has been given (see ❶).

❿ Recommended in the Area

This indicates local places of interest, and potential day trips and activities.

7

Best Quality

To achieve one of the highest ratings, an establishment in the AA Guest Accommodation Scheme must provide increased quality standards throughout, with particular emphasis in five key areas: cleanliness, hospitality, food quality, bedrooms and bathrooms.

The AA inspects and classifies more than 3,000 guest houses, farmhouses, inns and restaurants with rooms for its Guest Accommodation Scheme. Establishments recognised by the AA pay an annual fee according to the rating and the number of bedrooms. This rating is not transferable if an establishment changes hands.

Common Standards

A few years ago, the accommodation inspection organisations (The AA, VisitBritain, VisitScotland and VisitWales) undertook extensive consultation with consumers and the hospitality industry which resulted in new quality standards for rating establishments. Guests can now be confident that a star-rated B&B anywhere in the UK and Ireland will offer consistent quality and facilities.

★ Stars

AA Stars classify guest accommodation at five levels of quality, from one at the simplest, to five at the highest level of quality in the scheme. Each rating is also accompanied by a descriptive designator (further explained below).

☆ Highly Commended

Yellow Stars indicate that an accommodation is in the top ten percent of its star rating. Yellow Stars only apply to 3, 4 or 5 star establishments.

The Inspection Process

Establishments applying for AA recognition are visited by a qualified AA accommodation inspector as a mystery guest. Inspectors stay overnight to make a thorough test of the accommodation, food, and hospitality. After paying the bill the following morning they identify themselves and ask to be shown around the premises. The inspector completes a full report, resulting in a recommendation for the appropriate Star rating. After this first visit, the establishment will receive an annual visit to check that standards are maintained. If it changes hands, the new owners must re-apply for a rating.

Guests can expect to find the following minimum standards at all levels:

- Pleasant and helpful welcome and service, and sound standards of housekeeping and maintenance.
- Comfortable accommodation equipped to modern standards.
- Bedding and towels changed for each new guest, and at least weekly if the room is taken for a long stay.
- Adequate storage, heating, lighting and comfortable seating.
- A sufficient hot water supply at reasonable times.
- A full cooked breakfast. (If this is not provided, the fact must be advertised and a substantial continental breakfast must be offered.)

There are additional requirements for an establishment to achieve three, four or five Stars:

- Three Stars and above – access to both sides of all beds for double occupancy.
- Three Stars and above – bathrooms/shower rooms cannot be shared by the proprietor.
- Three Stars and above – a washbasin in every guest bedroom (either in the bedroom or the en suite/private facility).

- Four Stars – half of the bedrooms must be en suite or have private facilities.
- Five Stars – all bedrooms must be en suite or have private facilities.

Designators

All guest accommodation inspected by the AA is given one of six descriptive designators to help potential guests understand the different types of accommodation available in Britain. The following are included in this guide:

B&B: B&B accommodation is provided in a private house run by the owner and with no more than six guests. There may be restricted access to the establishment, particularly in the late morning and the afternoon.

GUEST HOUSE: Provides for more than six paying guests and usually offers more services than a B&B, for example dinner, served by staff as well as the owner. London prices tend to be higher than outside the capital, and normally only bed and breakfast is provided, although some establishments do provide a full meal service. Check on the service offered before booking as details may change during the currency of this guide.

FARMHOUSE: A farmhouse usually provides good value B&B or guest house accommodation and excellent home cooking on a working farm or smallholding. Sometimes the land has been sold and only the house remains, but many are working farms and some farmers are happy to allow visitors to look around, or even to help feed the animals. However, you should always take great care and never leave children unsupervised. The farmhouses are listed under towns or villages, but do ask for precise directions when booking.

INN: Traditional inns often have a cosy bar, convivial atmosphere, good beer and pub food. Those listed in the guide will provide breakfast in a suitable room, and should also serve light meals during licensing hours. The character of the properties vary according to whether they

AA Rosette Awards

Out of the many thousands of restaurants in the UK, the AA identifies around 1,900 as the best. The following is an outline of what to expect from restaurants with AA Rosette Awards. For a more detailed explanation of Rosette criteria please see theAA.com

◉ Excellent local restaurants serving food prepared with care, understanding and skill, using good quality ingredients.

◉◉ The best local restaurants, which aim for and achieve higher standards, better consistency and where a greater precision is apparent in the cooking. There will be obvious attention to the selection of quality ingredients.

◉◉◉ Outstanding restaurants that demand recognition well beyond their local area.

◉◉◉◉ Amongst the very best restaurants in the British Isles, where the cooking demands national recognition.

◉◉◉◉◉ The finest restaurants in the British Isles, where the cooking stands comparison with the best in the world.

are country inns or town establishments. Check arrival times as these may be restricted to opening hours.

RESTAURANT WITH ROOMS: These restaurants offer overnight accommodation with the restaurant being the main business and open to non-residents. The restaurant usually offers a high standard of food and service.

GUEST ACCOMMODATION: This general designator can be chosen by any establishment in the scheme.

Useful Information

There are so many things to remember when embarking on a short trip or weekend break. If you are unsure, always check before you book. Up-to-date information on all B&Bs can be found in the travel section at theAA.com

Codes of practice

The AA encourages the use of The Hotel Industry Voluntary Code of Booking Practice in appropriate establishments. The prime objective of the code is to ensure that the customer is clear about the price and the exact services and facilities being purchased, before entering into a contractually binding agreement. If the price has not been previously confirmed in writing, the guest should be handed a card at the time of registration at the establishment, stipulating the total obligatory charge.

theAA.com

- Go to theAA.com to find more AA listed guest houses, hotels, pubs and restaurants – There are around 12,000 establishments on the site.

- The home page leads to the AA's easy-to-use route planner.

- Simply enter your postcode and the establishment postcode given in this guide and click 'Get Route'. You will have a detailed route plan to take you from door-to-door.

- Use the Travel section to search for Hotels & B&Bs or Restaurants & Pubs by location or establishment name. Scroll down the list of results for the interactive map and local routes.

Fire precautions and safety

Many of the establishments listed in the guide are subject to the requirements of the Fire Precautions Act 1971. This Act does not apply to the Channel Islands or the Isle of Man, where their own rules are exercised. All establishments should display details of how to summon assistance in the event of an emergency at night.

Licensed premises

Whereas inns hold a licence to sell alcohol, not all guest houses are licensed. Some may have a full liquor licence, or others may have a table licence and wine list. Licensed premises are not obliged to remain open throughout the permitted hours, and they may do so only when they expect reasonable trade.

Children

Restrictions for children may be mentioned in the description. Some establishments may offer free accommodation to children when they share their parents' room. Such conditions are subject to change without notice, therefore always check when booking.

Complaints

Readers who have cause to complain are urged to do so on the spot. This should provide an opportunity for the proprietor to correct matters. If the personal approach fails, readers can inform AA Hotel Services, Fanum House, Basingstoke, Hampshire, RG21 4EA.

The AA may at its sole discretion investigate any complaints received from guide users for the purpose of making any necessary amendments to the guide. The AA will not in any circumstances act as a representative or negotiator or undertake to obtain compensation or enter into any correspondence or deal with the matter in any other way whatsoever. The AA will not guarantee to take any specific action.

Booking

Advance booking is always recommended to avoid disappointment. The peak holiday periods in the UK are Easter, and from June to September; public holidays are also busy times. In some parts

Bank and Public Holidays 2011	
New Year's Day	1st January
New Year's Holiday (Scotland)	4th January
Good Friday	22nd April
Easter Monday	25th April
Royal Wedding	29th April
Early May Bank Holiday	2nd May
Spring Bank Holiday	30th May
August Holiday (Scotland)	2nd August
Summer Bank Holiday	29th August
St Andrew's Day (Scotland)	30th November
Christmas Day	25th December
Boxing Day	26th December

of Scotland the winter skiing season is a peak holiday period. Some establishments may only accept weekly bookings from Saturday, and others require a deposit on booking. Guest houses may not accept credit or debit cards. VAT (Value Added Tax) is payable in the UK and in the Isle of Man, on basic prices and additional services. VAT does not apply in the Channel Islands. Always confirm the current price before booking; the prices in this guide are indications rather than firm quotations. It is a good idea also to confirm exactly what is included in the price when booking. Remember that all details, especially prices, may change without notice during the currency of the guide.

Cancellation

Advise the proprietor immediately if you must cancel a booking. If the room cannot be re-let you may be held legally responsible for partial payment. This could include losing your deposit or being liable for compensation. You should consider taking out cancellation insurance.

International Information

If you're travelling from overseas, the following information will provide some useful guidance to help you enjoy your stay in Britain. The individual entries in this book will also give you information regarding travel and the best routes to take.

Money

Some establishments may not accept travellers' cheques, or credit or debit cards, so ask about payment methods when you book. Most European and American credit and debit cards allow you to withdraw cash from British ATMs.

Driving

In the UK you drive on the left and overtake on the right. Seat belts must be worn by every occupant of the car, whether they sit in the front or the rear. Speed limits are displayed in miles per hour.

Visit theAA.com for useful motoring advice, travel information and route planning.

Car rental

You will be required to present your driving licence and credit or debit card. You can also provide an International Driving Permit along with your driving licence. Further identification, such as a passport, may also be required. A minimum age limit will apply.

Trains

The UK has an extensive rail network. To find out about routes, special offers or passes, contact National Rail (www.nationalrail.co.uk, tel: 08457 484950; from overseas +44 20 7278 5240, and international rates apply) or a travel agent.

Medical treatment & health insurance

Travellers who normally take medicines or carry an appliance, such as a hypodermic syringe, should ensure that they have sufficient supply for their stay and a doctor's letter describing the condition and treatment required.

Before travelling ensure you have insurance for emergency medical and dental treatment. Many European countries have reciprocal agreements for medical treatment and require EU citizens to obtain a European Health Insurance Card (EHIC) before travel.

Telephones

Many guest houses have direct dial telephones in the rooms. Always check the call rate before dialling. Payphones usually take cash, credit or debit cards, or phonecards. Phonecards can be purchased from newsagents and post offices.

The telephone and fax numbers in this guide show the area code followed by the subscriber number. When dialling from abroad first dial the international network access code, then the country code (44 for the UK). Omit the first digit of the area code then dial the subscriber number.

For example:
From Europe   00 44 111 121212
From the US   011 44 111 121212

When dialling from the UK, dial the international network access code, then the country code.

Electrical appliances

The British electrical current is 220–240 volts and appliances have square three-pin plugs. Foreign appliances may require an adaptor for the plug, as well as an electrical voltage converter that will allow, for example, a 110-volt appliance to be powered.

Thousands of places to stay throughout the UK & Ireland

ℹ View information on thousands of AA recognised establishments and other accommodation

✓ Access to online booking facilities for selected establishments

▦ Extensive range and choice of accommodation

🢇 Get the most out of your trip with AA Travel

£ Exclusive discounts for AA Members and eligible customers at participating hotels

Terms and conditions apply

ENGLAND

Durdle Door, Dorset

BERKSHIRE

Swans on the River Thames at Windsor

The Crown & Garter

★★★★ ⬢ INN

Address   Great Common, Inkpen, HUNGERFORD,
          RG17 9QR
Tel: 01488 668325
Email: gill.hern@btopenworld.com
Website: www.crownandgarter.com
Map ref: 3 SU36 Directions: 4m SE of Hungerford.
Off A4 into Kintbury, opp corner stores onto Inkpen
Rd, straight for 2m
Rooms: 9 en suite (9 GF) S £69.50 D £99
Notes: Wi-fi ⊗ ⛎ 7yrs Parking: 40

Family owned and run, this 17th-century inn is set in the beautiful Kennet Valley. The bar and restaurant are in keeping with the character of the building, with real ales, wines and a selection of malt whiskies. The restaurant offers an interesting range of country dishes freshly prepared mainly from local produce. The spacious bedrooms are in a courtyard around a pretty cottage garden. Each room has a bath and power shower, a hairdryer, flat-screen TV with Freeview, radio and Wi-fi access, plus hot drinks facilities.
Recommended in the area
Newbury Racecourse; Combe Gibbet; Highclere Castle

The Swan Inn

★★★★ ⬢ ⬢ INN

Address   Craven Road, Inkpen,
          HUNGERFORD, RG17 9DX
Tel: 01488 668326
Fax: 01488 668306
Email: enquiries@theswaninn-organics.co.uk
Website: www.theswaninn-organics.co.uk
Map ref: 3 SU36 Directions: 3.5m SE of
Hungerford. S on Hungerford High St past rail bridge,
left to Hungerford Common, right signed Inkpen
Rooms: 10 en suite (2 fmly rooms) S £70-£85 D £85-£105
Notes: Wi-fi ⊗ Parking: 50 Closed: 25-26 Dec

The peaceful north Wessex downs provide an idyllic setting for this 17th-century inn. Inside there are oak beams, open fires and a warm welcome from the Harris family. The owners are organic farmers, and the restaurant and an adjoining farm shop feature superb produce. The spacious en suite bedrooms are firmly rooted in the 21st century, with direct-dial and internet connections.
Recommended in the area
Combe Gibbet; Kennet and Avon Canal; Avebury stone circle; Newbury Racecourse

Magna Carta

★★★★★ ⌂ GUEST ACCOMMODATION
Address   Thames Side, WINDSOR, SL4 1QN
Tel: 07836 551912
Email: dominic@magna-carta.co.uk
Website: www.magna-carta.co.uk
Map ref: 3 SU36
Directions: M4 junct 5 follow signs to Datchet, then
Windsor. At Windsor & Eton riverside station turn
right & down to river
Rooms: 4 en suite S £100-£140 D £140-£170
Notes: ⊗

Magna Carta has to be Windsor's most unique accommodation. A luxuriously converted Dutch barge moored on the River Thames, it's just a few minutes walk from Windsor town centre and Windsor Castle. The boat has three luxurious double or twin cabins with super-king-size beds and one king-size cabin. All have large en suite shower rooms with heated towel rails, air-conditioning, underfloor heating and DVD players. On the upper deck is a beautiful saloon with library, picture windows (with amazing river views) hi-fi and dining area. Outside, the split-level sun deck has teak furniture and even a hot-tub. Magna Carta is available fully crewed for cruising charters and can also be hired for dinner parties and dinner cruises, etc. Guests are made to feel at home by owner and captain Dominic Read and his crew. The award-winning breakfast is based on fresh, local ingredients, mostly organic and largely from Windsor Farm Shop. The boat is fully licensed and has a bar with an excellent variety of wines and spirits.

Recommended in the area

Windsor Castle; Eton College; Royal Ascot

Windsor Castle

BRISTOL

Clifton Suspension Bridge

Westfield House

★★★★ 🛏 BED & BREAKFAST

Address	37 Stoke Hill, Stoke Bishop, BRISTOL, BS9 1LQ
Tel/Fax:	0117 962 6119
Email:	admin@westfieldhouse.net
Website:	www.westfieldhouse.net
Map ref:	2 ST57
Directions:	1.8m NW of city centre in Stoke Bishop
Rooms:	3 en suite
Notes:	Wi-fi ⊗ 🐾 11yrs
Parking:	5

Set in several acres of private grounds, this large white Georgian-style, family-run guest house makes an ideal retreat from Bristol's city lights. Westfield House is close to Durdham Downs – a vast expanse of open common land, which stretches from Bristol's suburbs to the cliffs of the Avon Gorge – and the Bristol University Halls of Residence. The beautifully decorated and extremely comfortable bedrooms, either single or doubles, are all en suite, and have flat-screen TVs, DVD/CD players, free Wi-fi, fridges and tea- and coffee-making facilities. The living room centres round a cosy fireplace while large bay windows lead onto a large garden terrace. Owner Ann cooks more or less to order using quality local ingredients, and a typical meal may include dishes such as salmon en croûte with puréed spinach and hollandaise sauce accompanied by potatoes dauphinoise, followed by a delicious home-made apple pie – all the better in the summer months when served on the patio overlooking the lovely rear garden. The grounds are also a haven for a variety of wildlife including owls, badgers, newts, falcons, slow worms and hedgehogs. If you still hanker for the bright lights, Westfield House is just a short walk from Bristol city centre. There is ample off-street parking for guests.

Recommended in the area

Clifton Suspension Bridge; SS Great Britain; Bristol Zoo

BUCKINGHAMSHIRE

Coombe Hill and the South Africa Memorial viewed from Beacon Hill

Nags Head Inn & Restaurant

★★★★ ◉ INN

Address	London Road,
	GREAT MISSENDEN, HP16 0DG
Tel:	01494 862200
Fax:	01494 862685
Email:	goodfood@nagsheadbucks.com
Website:	www.nagsheadbucks.com

Map ref: 3 SP80 Directions: N of Amersham on A413, turn left at Chiltern hospital onto London Rd signed Great Missenden
Rooms: 5 en suite (1 fmly rooms) D £90-£120 Notes: Wi-fi
Parking: 40

The delightful Nags Head Inn has served as a location for a number of TV programmes and films, and has played host to many famous names over the years, including prime ministers and the children's author Roald Dahl – the animated film of Dahl's *Fantastic Mr Fox* actually features the inn. Located in the picturesque Chiltern Hills, in the valley of the River Misbourne, the establishment is within walking distance of the lovely village of Great Missenden and close to major road and rail routes. Inside, it has been tastefully refurbished to a high standard and retains its original 15th-century features, including low oak beams and a large inglenook fireplace. This carries through into the individually furnished en suite bedrooms, which are comfortable with a modern twist and come with flat-screen digital TVs and other thoughtful extras, ensuring a home-from-home experience. The gastro pub has a popular reputation locally thanks to its extensive menu of English and French fusion dishes made from high-quality local and organic produce, such as fish smoked on the premises as well as local saddle of lamb and cheeses. There's also an award-winning wine list and a selection of real ales. Ample parking and Wi-fi are available.

Recommended in the area

Hughenden Manor (NT); Bekonscot Model Village; West Wycombe Park (NT)

CAMBRIDGESHIRE

Emmanuel College garden

The Crown Inn

★★★★★ ⍟ INN

Address 8 Duck Street,
ELTON, PE8 6RQ
Tel: 01832 280232
Email: inncrown@googlemail.com
Website: www.thecrowninn.org
Map ref: 3 TL09
Directions: A1 junct 17 onto A605 W. In 3.5m right signed Elton, 0.9m left signed Nassington. On village green
Rooms: 5 en suite (2 fmly rooms) (2 GF)
Notes: Wi-fi **Parking:** 15

Set in the beautiful Cambridgeshire countryside in the exclusive village of Elton, The Crown Inn is a traditional 16th century thatched coaching inn full of old-world charm. The Crown boasts five individually decorated en suite rooms all with modern facilities. There's plenty to do in the area, with lots of pretty villages and the market towns of Oundle and Stamford just on the doorstep. Country walks are a must along the banks of the River Nene, which reputedly inspired Kenneth Grahame to write *The Wind in the Willows*. After a day's exploring, you can enjoy some great gastropub cooking in the Crown's AA Rosetted restaurant, or cosy up in the bar with its inglenook fireplace and try a more traditional bar meal and a pint of Golden Crown ale. In the summer months, relax under the horse-chestnut tree and watch the world go by, or take a seat on the decking surrounded by trees and pretty hanging baskets. Whether your visit is for business or pleasure, you can expect a relaxing and enjoyable stay.

Recommended in the area

Elton Hall; Fotheringhay Church & Castle; Burghley House

CHESHIRE

The City walls in Chester and King Charles' Tower

The Pheasant Inn

★★★★★ ⇔ INN

Address Higher Burwardsley,
BURWARDSLEY, CH3 9PF
Tel: 01829 770434
Fax: 01829 771097
Email: info@thepheasantinn.co.uk
Website: www.thepheasantinn.co.uk
Map ref: 6 SJ55 **Directions:** From A41, left to
Tattenhall, right at 1st junct & left at 2nd Higher
Burwardsley. At post office left, signed
Rooms: 12 en suite (2 fmly rooms) (5 GF) **S** £65-£95 **D** £85-£130 **Notes:** Wi-fi **Parking:** 80

This delightful 300-year-old inn is tucked away in a peaceful corner of rural Cheshire, yet is still within easy reach of the city. It is an ideal stop for walkers and ramblers, sitting high on the Peckforton Hills with views over the Cheshire Plain. Well equipped, comfortable en suite bedrooms are located in an adjacent converted barn or in the main building. Using fresh, local produce, creative dishes are served in the stylish restaurant or the traditional, beamed bar. In summer, guests can dine alfresco.

Recommended in the area

Cheshire Candle Workshops; Beeston Castle; Sandstone Trail

Hilltop Country House

★★★★ GUEST ACCOMMODATION

Address Hilltop, Flash Lane,
PRESTBURY, SK10 4ED
Tel: 01625 829940
Email: enquiries@hilltopcountryhouse.co.uk
Website: www.hilltopcountryhouse.co.uk
Map ref: 7 SJ87 **Directions:** A523 from
Macclesfield to Stockport. At 3rd rdbt turn right to
Bollington. In 40mtrs turn left & follow signs
Rooms: 4 en suite (2 GF) **S** £58.75 **D** £88.12
Notes: Wi-fi ⊗ **Parking:** 50

Approached by a long sweeping drive, 17th century Hilltop Country House lies in 15 acres of private land, with wonderful views towards the Pennines and the Welsh hills. The four en suite rooms exude comfort and style, and all come with fine linen, fluffy towels, Wi-fi, homemade cookies and fruit from the garden. There's a beautiful park right outside the door, and the visitors' book is full of superlatives. Your hosts will be happy to recommend – and give you a lift to – some good local restaurants.

Recommended in the area

Lyme Park (NT); Quarry Bank Mill & Styal Estate (NT); Anson Engine Museum, Poynton

The Bear's Paw

★★★★★ ⬗ INN

Address	School Lane, WARMINGHAM, Sandbach, CW11 3QN
Tel:	01270 526317
Email:	info@thebearspaw.co.uk
Website:	www.thebearspaw.co.uk

Map ref: 5 SJ76 **Directions:** M6 junct 17 onto A534/A533 signed Middlewich/Northwich. Continue on A533, left onto Mill Ln, left onto Warmingham Ln. Right onto Plant Ln, left onto Green Ln

Rooms: 14 en suite (4 fmly rooms) S £75-£90 D £90-£130 Notes: Wi-fi Parking: 75

Located in the heart of Cheshire, this 19th-century gastro inn was totally refurbished in 2009. Today it provides very comfortable and luxurious boutique-style en suite bedrooms, including family rooms. All are well-equipped and feature flat-screen HD televisions and complimentary Wi-fi, along with many thoughtful extras. Imaginative, home-cooked food is served in the friendly open-plan dining room, and there's a choice of inviting lounge areas, as well as a traditional yet stylish bar.

Recommended in the area

Tatton Park; Snugburys Ice Cream; Oulton Park

Wooded escarpment at Alderley Edge.

CORNWALL

Clifftop view of Porthcurno beach

Bangors Organic

★ ★ ★ ★ 🛏 GUESTHOUSE

Address	Poundstock, BUDE, EX23 0DP
Tel:	01288 361297
Email:	info@bangorsorganic.co.uk
Website:	www.bangorsorganic.co.uk
Map ref:	1 SS20
Directions:	4m S of Bude. On A39 in Poundstock
Rooms:	4 en suite (1 GF) D £120-£170
Notes:	Wi-fi ⊗ 🐾 12yrs Parking: 10

Neil and Gill Faiers have created a beautiful and relaxing home which they love sharing with guests who flock to Cornwall's only certified organic bed and breakfast. Spacious, comfortable accommodation combined with a genuine eco-friendly ethos makes this a very special place to stay. All of the food and drink is organic, with evening meals made from fresh seasonal produce, much grown in the Faiers' own garden. The delicious homemade bread is just one of the many culinary delights you can expect during your stay. Bangors Organic is only one mile from the unspoilt north Cornish coast, with its big surfing beaches, spectacular coastal footpath and little fishing coves, making it an ideal place from which to explore by foot, bicycle or car. In fact, if you wish to abandon the car completely, the local bus service stops directly outside the house. The Faiers also offer a free pick up service from Bude for those arriving by public transport. If you can't leave modern technology totally behind during your visit, there is Wi-fi access available, while for cyclists and surfers there's secure storage for bikes and boards. Bangors Organic recently scooped a gold award in the Green Tourism Business Scheme.

Recommended in the area

Clovelly; Boscastle; Tintagel

Cotswold House

★ ★ ★ ★ GUESTHOUSE

Address 49 Melvill Road, FALMOUTH, TR11 4DF
Tel: 01326 312077
Email: info@cotswoldhousehotel.com
Website: www.cotswoldhousehotel.com
Map ref: 1 SW83
Directions: On A39 near town centre & docks
Rooms: 10 en suite (1 fmly rooms) (1 GF)
Notes: ⊗ **Parking:** 10 **Closed:** Xmas

With Falmouth's superb sandy Gyllyngvase Beach and the busy estuary, harbour and yachting marina just a short walk away, this small family-run guest house is ideal for both a holiday or a short break. The smart Victorian property is also close to the picturesque, cobbled town centre with its historic buildings and range of specialist shops. All the bedrooms have a bath or shower room en suite and hospitality trays, and many have lovely views of the sea and the River Fal. Well-cooked traditional cuisine is a feature of a stay here, and the friendly owners offer attentive service. The convivial bar is another plus at this relaxed house, and a popular place for socialising in the evening.

Recommended in the area

Falmouth National Maritime Museum; The Eden Project; Trebah and Glendurgan gardens

The Rosemary

★ ★ ★ ★ GUEST ACCOMMODATION

Address 22 Gyllyngvase Terrace,
FALMOUTH, TR11 4DL
Tel: 01326 314669
Email: stay@therosemary.co.uk
Website: www.therosemary.co.uk
Map ref: 1 SW83
Directions: A39 Melvill Rd signed to beaches & seafront, right onto Gyllyngvase Rd, 1st left
Rooms: 10 en suite (4 fmly rooms)
S £49-£58 **D** £75-£93 **Notes:** Wi-fi **Parking:** 3 **Closed:** mid Dec-Jan

This lovely Edwardian townhouse is tucked away in a peaceful road only 100 metres from Gyllyngvase Beach and five minutes' walk from Falmouth's historic and vibrant town centre. There are glorious views across the bay from most bedrooms, as well as from the light and airy dining room, guest lounge and south facing garden. Rooms are equipped to a high standard, and there are family suites available. Local ingredients feature strongly in the freshly cooked breakfasts, and there's an extensive continental buffet.

Recommended in the area

Pendennis Castle; National Maritime Museum Cornwall; Helford Estuary

Calize Country House

★★★★ ⌂ GUEST ACCOMMODATION
Address   Prosper Hill, Gwithian, HAYLE, TR27 5BW
Tel: 01736 753268
Email: jilly@calize.co.uk
Website: www.calize.co.uk
Map ref: 1 SW53
Directions: 2m NE of Hayle. B3301 in Gwithian at
Red River Inn, house 350yds up hill on left
Rooms: 4 en suite S £55-£65 D £80-£90
Notes: Wi-fi ⊗ 🐾 12yrs Parking: 6

Calize Country House has superb views over St Ives Bay, Godrevy Lighthouse and the countryside.
Your hosts, the Whitakers, run Calize with a natural warmth and friendliness. Homemade cake and
tea are offered on arrival in the comfortable lounge, which has a log burner during the colder months.
Breakfasts are memorable and served around a communal table, with treats including homemade
seeded bread and jams, fresh fruit, and creamy scrambled eggs and smoked salmon. Three miles of
sandy beach are just a short walk away.
Recommended in the area
South West Coast Path; Tate Gallery, St Ives; St Michael's Mount

The Crown Inn

★★★ INN
Address   LANLIVERY, Bodmin, PL30 5BT
Tel: 01208 872707
Fax: 01208 871208
Email: thecrown@wagtailinns.com
Website: www.wagtailinns.com
Map ref: 1 SX05 Directions: Signed from A390,
2m W of Lostwithiel. Inn 0.5m down lane into village,
opposite church Rooms: 9 en suite (7 GF)
Notes: Wi-fi Parking: 50

The historic Crown Inn is one of Cornwall's most iconic country pubs. This black and white painted
Cornish longhouse is a popular stopping point for those walking the famous Saint's Way. The pub oozes
charm with its low-beamed ceilings and open fireplaces, and a welcome absence of piped music or
fruit machines. There are nine comfortable en suite bedrooms, and The Crown serves great traditional
pub meals featuring lots of local produce, including plenty of seafood from the nearby harbour in
Fowey. The pub has a lovely atmosphere, and the hearty Cornish breakfasts are a treat.
Recommended in the area
The Eden Project; St Austell; Fowey

Hurdon Farm

★ ★ ★ ★ ⊜ FARMHOUSE
Address LAUNCESTON, PL15 9LS
Tel: 01566 772955
Map ref: 1 SX38 **Directions:** A30 onto A388 to
Launceston, at rdbt exit for hospital, 2nd right signed
Trebullett, premises 1st on right
Rooms: 6 en suite (1 fmly) (1 GF)
S £34-£38 D £56-£70
Notes: ⊗ **Parking:** 10 **Closed:** Nov-Apr

Hurdon is a 400-acre working farm with cows and pigs, peacefully located at the end of a tree-lined drive. The elegant 18th-century stone and granite farmhouse retains many original features, especially in the kitchen, with its open granite fireplace and original Dutch oven. Bedrooms, including a family room with adjoining children's room, are all en suite and individually furnished. They come with thoughtful extras such as electric blankets, hot-water bottles, bathrobes, hairdryer and even playing cards. Breakfasts (and dinners by prior arrangement) make use of produce from the farm, with the home-made clotted cream a particular treat.

Recommended in the area

The Eden Project; South West Coast Path; Dartmoor and Bodmin Moor

View over Porthzennor Cove towards Mussel Point from Zennor Head

Primrose Cottage

★★★★★ 🛏 BED & BREAKFAST

Address Lawhitton, LAUNCESTON,
          PL15 9PE
Tel: 01566 773645
Email: enquiry@primrosecottagesuites.co.uk
Website: www.primrosecottagesuites.co.uk
Map ref: 1 SX38
Directions: Exit A30 Tavistock, follow A388
through Launceston for Plymouth then B3362,
Tavistock 2.5m
Rooms: 3 en suite (1 GF) S £70-£90 D £80-£130
Notes: ⊗ 🍴 12yrs **Parking:** 5 **Closed:** 23-28 Dec

Set in four acres of gardens and ancient woodland on the banks of the River Tamar, Primrose Cottage is located between Dartmoor and Bodmin Moor, within easy reach of both the north and south Cornish coasts. The three luxury suites – The stable, Tamar View and The garden Room - all enjoy beautiful views across the Tamar valley, and each has its own private entrance, sitting room and en suite facilities. Furnished with designer fabrics, antiques and thoughtful extra touches, every luxury is provided. A bottle of chilled white wine will be waiting for you on arrival, which you can enjoy while admiring the stunning views from your sitting room, or on a warm day you might prefer to choose one of the secluded corners of the garden. A gentle stroll down through the woods to the river might be rewarded with the sight of salmon jumping, or a kingfisher diving. The woodland is an untouched natural haven where wildlife lives undisturbed, and each season brings its own delights. After a day out exploring this beautiful part of the South West, return to Primrose Cottage and enjoy afternoon tea in the garden, or by the log fire in the colder months. Visit the website for details of special breaks.

Recommended in the area

Eden Project; Dartmoor; Tavistock; North Coast

Redgate Smithy

★★★★ 🛏 BED & BREAKFAST

Address Redgate, St Cleer, LISKEARD, PL14 6RU
Tel: 01579 321578
Email: enquiries@redgatesmithy.co.uk
Website: www.redgatesmithy.co.uk
Map ref: 1 SX26 **Directions:** 3m NW of Liskeard.
Off A30 at Bolventor/Jamaica Inn onto St Cleer Rd for
7m, B&B just past x-rds **Rooms:** 3 (2 en suite) (1 pri
facs) **S** £48 **D** £75 **Notes:** Wi-fi 🐾 12yrs
Parking: 3 **Closed:** Xmas & New Year

Redgate Smithy, situated just above Golitha Falls on the southern edge of rugged Bodmin Moor, was built around 200 years ago and makes a great base for exploring the area, especially if you love walking and bird-watching. Guests can relax in the comfortable cottage-style bedrooms, all with digital TV with Freeview, Wi-fi, hairdryer and tea- and coffee-making facilities. There's a lovely woodland garden with a patio, plus a large conservatory. At breakfast tuck into the full Cornish – made from high quality local produce – or perhaps try the 'Redgate Eggs Royale'.

Recommended in the area

Golitha Falls; The Eden Project; Bodmin Moor and The Cheesewring

Trevellas Porth, St Agnes

Barclay House

★ ★ ★ ★ ◉◉ GUEST ACCOMMODATION

Address St Martin's Road, LOOE, PL13 1LP
Tel: 01503 262929
Fax: 01503 262632
Email: reception@barclayhouse.co.uk
Website: www.barclayhouse.co.uk
Map ref: 1 SX25
Directions: 1st house on left on entering Looe from A38
Rooms: 12 en suite (1 fmly room) (1 GF)
S £55-£95 **D** £105-£175 **Notes:** Wi-fi ⊗ **Parking:** 25

High on the hill overlooking the fishing village of Looe, but within walking distance of the town, Barclay House has striking views of the river and the ever-changing countryside beyond. The 12-bedroom Victorian villa, set in six acres of grounds, oozes charm and offers a relaxed atmosphere. Newly enhanced, the smart, contemporary bedrooms provide a refuge from today's hectic pace of life. The award-winning restaurant serves a seasonal menu showcasing the best quality produce including fresh fish landed daily at Looe. The restaurant's French doors open out to the terrace and gardens where you can enjoy a refreshing glass of local wine while watching the sun set. Also available are eight luxury self-catering one-, two- and three-bedroom cottages which feature a split-level design to include en suite bathrooms with jacuzzi-style baths, as well as a barbecue area and private balcony. Visitors can also take advantage of the heated outdoor swimming pool set in a natural sun-trap and a fully fitted, state-of-the-art gym with a sauna; there's also the opportunity for an enjoyable walk along one of the woodland paths.

Recommended in the area

Lost Gardens of Heligan; The Eden Project; Historic fishing villages of Looe and Polperro

Bay View Farm

★ ★ ★ ★ 🏠 FARMHOUSE

Address St Martins, LOOE, PL13 1NZ
Tel: 01503 265922
Fax: 01503 265922
Email: mike@looebaycaravans.co.uk
Website: www.looedirectory.co.uk/bay-view-farm.htm
Map ref: 1 SX25
Directions: 2m NE of Looe. Off B3253 for Monkey
Sanctuary, farm signed
Rooms: 3 en suite (3 GF) **S** £35-£38 **D** £65-£70
Notes: ⊗ ¥ 5yrs **Parking:** 3

A genuine warm Cornish welcome, an air of tranquillity and great food are the hallmarks of Bay View Farm, which is home to a team of prize-winning shire horses. Mrs Elford is a delightful host and it's easy to see why her guests are drawn back to this special place again and again. The renovated and extended bungalow is situated in a truly spectacular spot with ever-changing views across Looe Bay, and is beautifully decorated and furnished throughout to give a light, spacious feel. The three en suite bedrooms each have their own very individual character – one is huge with comfy sofas and a wonderful view, the others smaller but still very inviting. Two of the rooms also have spacious private conservatories. Guests can relax at the end of the day either in the lounge or on the lovely patio and watch the sun set over Looe. Breakfasts at Bay View Farm are substantial and the evening meals feature home-made desserts accompanied by clotted cream. If you do choose to eat out there are numerous restaurants and pubs nearby. The old town of East Looe is a delight of tall buildings, narrow streets and passageways and the fishing industry brings a maritime bustle to the harbour and quayside. West Looe, the smaller settlement, has a lovely outlook across the harbour to East Looe.

Recommended in the area

Lost Gardens of Heligan; The Eden Project; Looe

Bucklawren Farm

★ ★ ★ ★ FARMHOUSE

Address   St Martin-by-Looe, LOOE, PL13 1NZ
Tel: 01503 240738
Fax: 01503 240481
Email: bucklawren@btopenworld.com
Website: www.bucklawren.co.uk
Map ref: 1 SX25
Directions: 2m NE of Looe. Off B3253 to Monkey
Sanctuary, 0.5m right to Bucklawren, farmhouse
0.5m on left
Rooms: 7 (6 en suite) (1 pri facs) (3 fmly rooms) (1 GF) S £37.50-£50 D £64-£75
Notes: Wi-fi ⊗ ⚹ 5yrs Parking: 7 Closed: Nov-Feb

Only half a mile from the coastal path, and a mile from the beach, this spacious 19th-century farmhouse, set in 400 acres, is the perfect place for a holiday. Front-facing rooms have amazing sea and coastal views, and all bedrooms are attractively furnished. The Granary Restaurant, in an adjacent converted barn, is the setting for evening meals prepared from fresh local produce. Jean Henly is a charming hostess.
Recommended in the area
The Eden Project; Lost Gardens of Heligan; fishing villages of Looe & Polperro

Trehaven Manor

★ ★ ★ ★ 🛏 ☕ GUEST ACCOMMODATION

Address   Station Road, LOOE, PL13 1HN
Tel: 01503 262028
Fax: 01503 265613
Email: enquiries@trehavenhotel.co.uk
Website: www.trehavenhotel.co.uk
Map ref: 1 SX25
Directions: In East Looe between railway station &
bridge. Trehaven's drive adjacent to The Globe PH
Rooms: 7 en suite (1 fmly) (1 GF)
Notes: ⊗ Parking: 8

Neil and Ella Hipkiss, the enthusiastic owners of Trehaven Manor, are committed to providing the best service. Bedrooms provide a high level of comfort and style, with quality furnishings and thoughtful extras such as clocks and hairdryers; most overlook the estuary. Guests are welcomed on arrival with home-made scones and local clotted cream in the lounge. Fresh local produce again features at breakfast. Evening meals are available on request, or Neil and Ella can recommend local restaurants.
Recommended in the area
Polperro; Looe town and beach; St Mellion Golf Course

The Old Mill House

★★★★ 🏠 GUESTHOUSE

Address LITTLE PETHERICK, Padstow, PL27 7QT
Tel: 01841 540388
Fax: 01841 540406
Email: enquiries@theoldmillhouse.com
Website: www.theoldmillhouse.com
Map ref: 1 SW97 **Directions:** 2m S of Padstow.
In centre of Little Petherick on A389
Rooms: 7 en suite **S** £80-£120 **D** £80-£120
Notes: ⊗ 🚼 14yrs **Parking:** 20 **Closed:** Nov-Feb

You are assured of a warm welcome in this licensed Grade
II listed mill house just two miles from the popular village of
Padstow. The idyllic converted corn mill and millhouse is next to a pretty stream – you may even spot a kingfisher. The seven comfortable en suite bedrooms are individually decorated, well equipped and all have good views. An extensive breakfast menu is served in the original mill room.

Recommended in the area

The Eden Project; Lost Gardens of Heligan; Camel Trail Cycle Path

Sea through Tintagel Castle archway

Camilla House

★ ★ ★ ★ ★ 🛏 GUESTHOUSE

Address   12 Regent Terrace,
          PENZANCE, TR18 4DW
Tel: 01736 363771
Fax: 01736 363771
Email: enquiries@camillahouse.co.uk
Website: www.camillahouse.co.uk
Map ref: 1 SW43 Directions: A30 to Penzance,
at rail station follow road along harbour front onto
Promenade Rd. Opp Jubilee Bathing Pool, Regent Ter
2nd right Rooms: 8 (7 en suite) (1 pri facs) (1 GF) S £35-£37.50 D £75-£85
Notes: Wi-fi ⊗ Parking: 6

The friendly proprietors of this attractive grade II listed terrace house do their utmost to ensure a comfortable stay. On arrival, guests are served with tea and coffee with 'Thunder and Lightning', a real Cornish treat. Bedrooms and bathrooms are attractively furnished, providing many added extras, such as fluffy towels and bathrobes, refreshment trays with Fairtrade products and Cornish mineral water, flat-screen Freeview TV/DVD, hairdryer, magazines and sweets. Some bedrooms and the dining room also provide delightful sea views over Mount's Bay. Wireless internet connection is available throughout, and there is also access to computers in the stylish, high-ceilinged lounge, which stocks a library of DVDs as well as Cornish Monopoly. A range of breakfast options is on offer in the dining room (home to a well-stocked residents' bar), using home-made or fresh local produce; options include Cornish cheese platters. Evening meals are available by prior arrangement. Camilla House has held the Green Tourism Business Scheme award since 2006 and is committed to operating in an environmentally responsible fashion.

Recommended in the area

Land's End; Lizard Peninsula; South West Coastal Path

Chy-an-Mor

★★★★ GUEST ACCOMMODATION

Address 15 Regent Terrace,
PENZANCE, TR18 4DW
Tel: 01736 363441
Email: reception@chyanmor.co.uk
Website: www.chyanmor.co.uk
Map ref: 1 SW43
Directions: A30 to Penzance, at rail station, follow along harbour front onto Promenade Rd. Pass Jubilee Pool, right at Stanley Guest House
Rooms: 9 en suite **S** £42 **D** £70-£90
Notes: Wi-fi ⊗ ✿ 14yrs **Parking:** 15 **Closed:** 15 Nov-15 Mar

This elegant Grade II listed Regency house has an attractive sea-facing location, overlooking Mount's Bay and the promenade. Chy-an-Mor – the name is Cornish for 'house of sea' – has been refurbished to provide high standards throughout. The impressive entrance leads to spacious, high-ceilinged public rooms, and residents can linger over the changing sea views in the stylish lounge with its comfortable sofas and range of board games. Guests are also welcome to soak up the sun in the pretty south-facing garden, which features benches and a patio area, lit up by fairy lights at night. Inside, each of the en suite bedrooms is individually designed and equipped with thoughtful extras, such as flat-screen digital TVs, Fairtrade tea, coffee and hot chocolate, organic cotton wool and shoe-polishing kits, and many of the rooms enjoy spectacular views. Satisfying breakfasts are served in the large, bright dining room, including vegetarian options and home-made preserves and muffins, all served on tables dressed with crisp white tablecloths and linen napkins. Ample off-street parking is available. A range of in-house beauty treatments is also a draw.

Recommended in the area

St Michael's Mount (NT); The Minnack Theatre; Land's End

Rockpool at Priest's Cove, Cape Cornwall

The Summer House

★★★★★ 🏠 🍽 GUEST ACCOMMODATION

Address Cornwall Terrace, PENZANCE, TR18 4HL
Tel: 01736 363744
Fax: 01736 360959
Email: reception@summerhouse-cornwall.com
Website: www.summerhouse-cornwall.com
Map ref: 1 SW43
Directions: A30 to Penzance, at rail station follow along harbour onto Promenade Rd, pass Jubilee Pool, right after Queens Hotel. Summer House 30yds on left
Rooms: 5 en suite **S** £100-£150 **D** £120-£150
Notes: Wi-fi ⊗ ⛔ 13yrs **Parking:** 6 **Closed:** Nov-Mar

The philosophy of The Summer House is to combine great food and beautiful surroundings with a happy, informal atmosphere, making it the perfect seaside retreat. Close to the seafront and harbour, this stylishly converted, stunning Grade II listed Regency house features a bold decor with polished wood, bright colours, and a curving glass-walled tower that fills the building with light. Fresh flowers are among the thoughtful extras provided in the spacious twin and double en suite bedrooms, which are light, airy and individually decorated, and enhanced by interesting family pieces and collectables. You'll find lots of home comforts to help you relax, including a TV, radio, DVD player, hairdryer, books and magazines. Fresh regional produce is simply prepared, resulting in a memorable dining experience at weekends. Dishes are distinctly Mediterranean in feel, and complemented by good wines. The restaurant opens out onto a walled garden with terracotta pots, sub-tropical planting and attractive blue tables and chairs, where in warmer weather evening drinks and dinner may be enjoyed.

Recommended in the area

St Michael's Mount (NT); Land's End; The Minack Theatre

Ednovean Farm

★★★★★ 🏠 FARMHOUSE

Address   PERRANUTHNOE, TR20 9LZ
Tel: 01736 711883
Email: info@ednoveanfarm.co.uk
Website: www.ednoveanfarm.co.uk
Map ref: 1 SW52
Directions: Off A394 towards Perranuthnoe at
Dynasty Restaurant, farm drive on left on bend
by post box
Rooms: 3 en suite (3 GF) **S** £90-£110 **D** £90-£110
Notes: Wi-fi ⊗ 🐾 16yrs Parking: 4 Closed: 24-28 Dec & New Year

Spectacular sea views over St Michael's Mount and Mount's Bay are a delightful feature of this converted 17th-century farmhouse which stands high above the village in beautiful grounds. The stylish bedrooms are furnished with comfortable beds and quality pieces, chintz fabrics, and thoughtful extras like flowers, magazines and fruit. Guests can relax in the elegant sitting room, the garden room and on several sunny patios. The coastal footpath and the beach and pub are just three minutes away.

Recommended in the area

St Michael's Mount (NT); Godolphin House; Penlee House Gallery (Newlyn School paintings)

Trenake Manor Farm

★★★★ FARMHOUSE

Address   Pelynt, POLPERRO, PL13 2LT
Tel: 01503 220835
Fax: 01503 220835
Email: lorraine@cornishfarmhouse.co.uk
Website: www.cornishfarmhouse.co.uk
Map ref: 1 SX25 Directions: 3.5m N of Polperro.
A390 onto B3359 for Looe, 5m left at small x-rds
Rooms: 3 en suite (1 fmly) **S** £46 **D** £72-£78
Notes: Wi-fi Parking: 10

Situated midway between the historic fishing ports of Looe and Polperro, this welcoming 15th-century farmhouse is surrounded by 300 acres of its own farmland. It has been owned by the same family for five generations and makes a good base for touring Cornwall. En suite bedrooms, including one family room, are spacious and boast elegant Victorian king-sized bedsteads and a number of thoughtful finishing touches. Breakfast is made from local produce and served in the cosy dining room. Guests are welcome to relax on the sunloungers provided in the large, well-kept garden.

Recommended in the area

The Eden Project; Lost Gardens of Heligan; Polperro

Carradale

★★★★ BED & BREAKFAST

Address PORTLOE, Truro, TR2 5RB
Tel: 01872 501508
Email: barbara495@btinternet.com
Map ref: 1 SW93
Directions: Off A3078 into Portloe, B&B 200yds
from Ship Inn
Rooms: 2 en suite (1 fmly) (1 GF)
S £35-£40 D £60-£65
Notes: ⊗ Parking: 5

Carradale, a modern house on the outskirts of the village of Portloe, is an ideal base from which to explore the delights of the idyllic Roseland Peninsula. There are extensive coastal walks, sandy beaches and glorious countryside just minutes away. A stay here offers high levels of peace and comfort. There are two bedrooms to choose from, both en suite, tastefully furnished and equipped with tea- and coffee-making facilities. The room on the ground floor has its own south-facing patio. There's a guest lounge with TV, and breakfast is served at a communal table in the dining room.

Recommended in the area

Eden Project; Lost Gardens of Heligan; National Maritime Museum, Falmouth; boat trips on the Fal

Hunter's Moon

★★★★ GUESTHOUSE

Address Chapel Hill, Polgooth,
         ST AUSTELL, PL26 7BU
Tel: 01726 66445
Email: enquiries@huntersmooncornwall.co.uk
Website: www.huntersmooncornwall.co.uk
Map ref: 1 SX05
Directions: 1.5m SW of town centre. Off B3273 into
Polgooth, pass village shop on left, 1st right
Rooms: 4 en suite (2 fmly) S £52-£56 D £74-£78
Notes: ⊗ ⛄ 14yrs Parking: 5

A friendly welcome awaits at Hunter's Moon – the perfect location for a peaceful holiday. The en suite guest rooms are decorated and furnished to a high standard, and two rooms have super king-sized beds which can be converted into twin beds. There is plenty of space to sit and enjoy the garden and the countryside views, and with its central location this is an ideal touring base for the whole of Cornwall. The Polgooth Inn is just five minutes' walk away and there are many restaurants nearby.

Recommended in the area

The Eden Project; Lost Gardens of Heligan; Charlestown Harbour

Lower Barn

★ ★ ★ ★ ★ 🏠 GUEST ACCOMMODATION

Address Bosue, St Ewe, ST AUSTELL, PL26 6ET
Tel: 01726 844881
Email: janie@bosue.co.uk
Website: www.bosue.co.uk
Map ref: 1 SX05
Directions: 3.5m SW of St Austell. Off B3273 at x-rds signed Lost Gardens of Heligan, Lower Barn signed 1m on right
Rooms: 3 en suite (1 fmly) (1 GF)
Notes: ⊗ Parking: 7 Closed: Jan

Tucked away down a meandering country lane yet with easy access to local attractions, this converted barn has huge appeal. The warm colours and decoration create a Mediterranean feel that is complemented by informal and genuine hospitality from proprietors Mike and Janie Cooksley. It is the attention to detail that places Lower Barn a cut above the rest. The three en suite bedrooms are equipped with a host of extras from fridges and daily fresh towels to tea- and coffee-making facilities. Breakfast is chosen from an extensive menu and served round a large table or on the patio deck overlooking the garden, which also has a luxurious hot tub. You can even collect your own free-range eggs for breakfast. A candlelit dinner, available most nights of the week, is served in the conservatory or on the terrace – and you can bring your own wine. After exploring the many attractions the area has to offer, including Mevagissey, where a bustling harbour shelters a fishing fleet and the narrow streets are lined with colour-washed old houses, galleries and gift shops, you can unwind with a treatment – perhaps a massage – to make your experience at Lower Barn even more memorable.

Recommended in the area

The Eden Project; Lost Gardens of Heligan; Mevagissey; cliff walks; Roseland Peninsula

Penarwyn House

★★★★★ 🏨 GUEST ACCOMMODATION
Address ST BLAZEY, Par, PL24 2DS
Tel/Fax: 01726 814224
Email: stay@penarwyn.co.uk
Website: www.penarwyn.co.uk
Map ref: 1 SX05 **Directions:** A390 W through
St Blazey, left before 2nd speed camera into
Doubletrees School, Penarwyn straight ahead
Rooms: 4 en suite (1 fmly) S £75
D £110-£175 **Notes:** Wi-fi ⊗ 🐾 10yrs **Parking:** 6

True Cornish hospitality and memorable breakfasts are all part of the package at this spacious Victorian house set in tranquil surroundings, yet close to main routes. The owners, Mike and Jan Russell, have restored the house to its original glory, while adding luxury touches and modern facilities. The bedrooms are spacious, delightfully appointed and equipped with tea- and coffee-making facilities, hairdryer, flat-screen TV and DVD/CD player. One room has its own lounge, while some have feature baths and most have separate showers. There's also a snooker room with a 3/4 size snooker table, and Wi-fi access is available.

Recommended in the area

The Eden Project; Lanhydrock (NT); Lost Gardens of Heligan

Edgar's

★★★★ 🏨 GUEST ACCOMMODATION
Address Chy-an-Creet, Higher Stennack,
ST IVES, TR26 2HA
Tel/Fax: 01736 796559
Email: stay@edgarshotel.co.uk
Website: www.edgarshotel.co.uk
Map ref: 1 SW54
Directions: 0.5m W of town centre on B3306,
opp Leach Pottery
Rooms: 8 en suite (2 fmly rooms) (4 GF)
S £50-£80 D £65-£95
Notes: Wi-fi **Parking:** 8 **Closed:** Nov-Feb

Tucked away, surrounded by a border of palms, trees and shrubs and with on-site parking, Edgar's offers an excellent base for exploring picturesque St Ives and farther afield. The well equipped en suite guest rooms are complemented by a spacious breakfast room and comfortable lounge with soft drinks honesty bar. Freshly cooked breakfasts include vegetarian options and fine, locally sourced ingredients.

Recommended in the area

Leach Pottery; Penlee House Gallery; Tate St Ives

The Regent

★★★★ GUEST ACCOMMODATION

Address   Fernlea Terrace,
          ST IVES, TR26 2BH
Tel: 01736 796195
Fax: 01736 794641
Email: keith@regenthotel.com
Website: www.regenthotel.com
Map ref: 1 SW54
Directions: In town centre, near bus & railway station
Rooms: 10 (8 en suite) (1 fmly)
S £36-£58 D £77-£100
Notes: Wi-fi ⊗ 🐾 16yrs Parking: 12

The Regent was established 80 years ago when a local architect purchased Penwyn House from a retired sea captain and converted it into a guest house to provide an interest for his wife and daughter. In 1972 it was bought by the Varnals family, and is today run by the second generation of Varnals, Keith and Sandi Varnals. Sandi, a former lingerie designer, and Keith, an engineer-turned-chef, have modernised the facilities to appeal to today's traveller. All rooms have central heating, TV, radio, and hospitality tray. There are eight en suite double rooms and two economy single rooms which share facilities. Most rooms – plus the two communal lounges – have wonderful views of St Ives historic harbour and the bay beyond. Parking is available for all double rooms, while the bus and rail stations are close by. The Regent is just a short stroll away from the harbour and Porthminster Beach. Breakfasts are a memorable part of a stay here, with a wide range of hot drinks to choose from, plus a choice of cereals, yoghurts and fruit. The cooked selection offers something for everyone and features lots of quality local produce, including locally caught and smoked fish.

Recommended in the area

Tate Gallery; Barbara Hepworth Museum & Sculpture Garden; Leach Pottery

The Rookery

★★★★ GUEST ACCOMMODATION

Address   8 The Terrace,
ST IVES, TR26 2BL
Tel: 01736 799401
Email: therookerystives@hotmail.com
Website: www.rookerystives.com
Map ref: 1 SW54
Directions: A3074 through Carbis Bay, right fork at
Porthminster Hotel, The Rookery 500yds on left
Rooms: 7 en suite (1 GF)
Notes: Wi-fi ⊗ ⊌ 7yrs Parking: 7

Ron and Barbara Rook's friendly establishment stands on an elevated position overlooking the harbour, sandy beaches and St Ives Bay, near the train and bus stations, and only a short walk to the town's shops, galleries and restaurants. The rooms are attractively decorated, and are well equipped with considerate extras such as a chiller to keep soft drinks and wines cool. A choice of full English, continental or vegetarian breakfast is served in the dining room.

Recommended in the area

Tate St Ives; Barbara Hepworth Museum; The Minack Theatre

Tate Gallery, St Ives

The Woodside

★★★★ GUEST ACCOMMODATION

Address   The Belyars,
        ST IVES, TR26 2DA
Tel: 01736 795681
Email: woodsidehotel@btconnect.com
Website: www.woodside-hotel.co.uk
Map ref: 1 SW54
Directions: A3074 to St Ives, left at Porthminster
Hotel onto Talland Rd, 1st left onto Belyars Ln,
Woodside 4th on right
Rooms: 10 en suite (3 fmly rooms)
Notes: ⊗ 🐾 5yrs **Parking:** 12

Suzanne and Chris Taylor are welcoming hosts who diligently attend to their beautiful property. They promise personal attention, ensuring an enjoyable holiday here. Woodside stands in peaceful grounds above St Ives Bay, with fantastic views from most bedrooms and all of the public rooms. Just a five-minute walk away are lovely stretches of golden beaches for bathing and surfing, the picturesque harbour with its traditional fishing fleet, and the narrow cobbled streets lined with artists' studios, galleries and craft shops. The comfortable, spacious en suite bedrooms range from single, double and twin to family rooms, and all are well equipped with colour TV, a radio-alarm clock, hairdryer and a hospitality tray. Guests can relax in the comfortable lounge with a TV and games area, enjoy a drink at the bar, or relish the sea views from the attractive gardens or terrace. Breakfast is another delight: you'll find a hearty choice of full English, continental or vegetarian dishes prepared from fresh, mainly local, produce. A small golf course and a leisure centre with a superb gym and indoor pool are both within a short distance of Woodside.

Recommended in the area

Tate Gallery; Land's End; The Eden Project

New Inn

★★★★ ◉ INN

Address	TRESCO, Isles of Scilly, TR24 0QQ
Tel:	01720 422844 & 423006
Fax:	01720 423200
Email:	newinn@tresco.co.uk
Website:	www.tresco.co.uk
Map ref:	1 SV81
Directions:	By New Grimsby Quay
Rooms:	16 en suite (2 GF)
Notes:	Wi-fi ⊗

With its seaside location, the popular and lively New Inn makes a great base from which to explore Tresco and the Isles of Scilly. The social hub of the island, the New Inn offers a range of bright, comfortably furnished and well-equipped en suite bedrooms, many with splendid sea views. Diners will enjoy a discerning menu of modern and traditional British dishes at lunch and dinner, including daily specials. Quality local ingredients are selected by the New Inn's chef, including Tresco reared beef and seafood from island waters. Meals are served in the bistro-style Pavilion or the popular bar. In fine weather, many guests choose to dine at one of the tables in the garden. The New Inn bar is known for its good selection of real ales – plus its collection of nautical memorabilia – and there are regular live music events and annual ale and cider festivals. There's a quiet lounge area to escape to, as well as a heated outdoor pool. Tresco is by no means just a summer destination though – the New Inn offers a range of special winter breaks.

Recommended in the area

Tresco Abbey subtropical gardens; seal and bird-watching boat trips; unspoilt beaches

CUMBRIA

Rydal Water from Rydal Mount, Lake District National Park

Hall Croft

★★★★ 🏠 BED & BREAKFAST

Address Dufton, APPLEBY-IN-WESTMORLAND,
           CA16 6DB
Tel: 017683 52902
Email: hallcroft@phonecoop.coop
Map ref: 6 NY62 **Directions:** 3m N of Appleby.
In Dufton by village green
Rooms: 3 (2 en suite) (1 pri facs)
Parking: 3 **Closed:** 24-26 Dec

A large Victorian villa situated on the green in the tranquil village of Dufton at the foot of the Pennines with spectacular views in all directions. Owners Frei and Ray Walker extend a warm welcome and do everything to make your stay memorable. Rooms offer high quality facilities with a range of little extras for additional comfort. Substantial cooked breakfasts, including a varied range of home-made produce, are served in the period lounge/dining room; afternoon tea and cakes and packed lunches are also available. Guests can relax in the large gardens and explore the wide network of paths and walks that start from the village.

Recommended in the area

North Pennines (Area of Outstanding Natural Beauty); Northern Lake District; Appleby-in-Westmorland

Swaledale Watch Farm

★★★★ GUEST ACCOMMODATION

Address Whelpo, CALDBECK,
           CA7 8HQ
Tel/Fax: 016974 78409
Email: nan.savage@talk21.com
Website: www.swaledale-watch.co.uk
Map ref: 5 NY34
Directions: 1m SW of Caldbeck on B5299
Rooms: 4 en suite (2 fmly rooms) (4 GF)
Parking: 8 **Closed:** 24-26 Dec

This busy farm is set in idyllic surroundings, with views of the fells and mountains. Just a mile away is the village of Caldbeck, once renowned for its milling and mining, or take a walk through The Howk, a beautiful wooded limestone gorge with waterfalls. Nan and Arnold Savage work hard to make their hospitality seem effortless and to put you at ease. The lounges have TVs, books and games while the bedrooms have bath and shower en suite. Two bedrooms and a lounge are in the converted cowshed, ideal for a group of four. Nan's hearty Cumbrian breakfasts are a highlight.

Recommended in the area

Northern Fells; Howk Walk to Caldbeck village; quality village shops and cafés

Crosthwaite House

★ ★ ★ ★ GUESTHOUSE

Address   CROSTHWAITE, Kendal, LA8 8BP
Tel: 015395 68264
Fax: 015395 68264
Email: bookings@crosthwaitehouse.co.uk
Website: www.crosthwaitehouse.co.uk
Map ref: 6 SD49
Directions: A590 onto A5074, 4m right to
Crosthwaite, 0.5m turn left
Rooms: 6 en suite S £28-£35 D £56-£70
Notes: Wi-fi Parking: 8 Closed: mid Nov-Mar

A sturdy mid 18th-century house, this establishment is in the village of Crosthwaite, at the northern end of the Lyth Valley, famous for its damson orchards. You can see across the valley from the lounge, and from the dining room where guests can enjoy Aga-cooked breakfasts prepared from local ingredients. The spacious en suite bedrooms offer many thoughtful extras, plus tea and coffee facilities. The owners create a relaxed atmosphere, making it easy to feel at home.

Recommended in the area

Lake Windermere; Sizergh Castle and Garden (NT); three golf courses within four miles

Moss Grove Organic

★ ★ ★ ★ ★ 🏠 GUEST ACCOMMODATION

Address   GRASMERE, Ambleside, LA22 9SW
Tel: 015394 35251
Fax: 015394 35306
Email: enquiries@mossgrove.com
Website: www.mossgrove.com
Map ref: 5 NY30
Directions: From S, M6 junct 36 onto A591
signed Keswick, from N M6 junct 40 onto
A591 signed Windermere
Rooms: 11 en suite (2 GF) Notes: Wi-fi 🐾 14yrs Parking: 11 Closed: 24-25 Dec

Located in the centre of Grasmere, this impressive Victorian house has been refurbished using as many natural products as possible, with ongoing dedication to causing minimal environmental impact. The bedrooms are decorated with beautiful wallpaper and natural clay paints, and feature hand-made beds and furnishings. Home entertainment systems, flat-screen TVs and luxury bathrooms add further comfort. Extensive organic Mediterranean breakfasts are taken at the large dining table in the guest lounge.

Recommended in the area

Grasmere Lake; Rydal Water; Dove Cottage & The Wordsworth Museum

The Grange Country Guest House

★ ★ ★ ★ ★ GUESTHOUSE

Address Manor Brow, Ambleside Road,
KESWICK, CA12 4BA
Tel: 017687 72500
Fax: 0707 500 4885
Email: info@grangekeswick.com
Website: www.grangekeswick.com
Map ref: 5 NY22
Directions: M6 junct 40, A66 15m. A591 for 1m,
turn right onto Manor Brow
Rooms: 10 en suite (1 GF) S £75-£95 D £100-£116
Notes: Wi-fi ⊗ 🐾 10yrs **Parking:** 10
Closed: Jan

A stylish Victorian residence, this house stands in beautiful gardens on the outskirts of the lovely market town of Keswick. Here you will be assured of a warm welcome from Mark and Sally and their team. The location with its wonderful views, together with the quality of the facilities and the genuine hospitality, attract many returning guests. The bedrooms are spacious and beautifully decorated, each featuring quality bedding and digital, flat-screen TVs, plus complimentary Fairtrade beverage trays, mineral water and luxury toiletries. Superb, freshly prepared Cumbrian breakfasts are offered along with free Wi-fi, a comfortable lounge, and an outdoor terrace where a nice cold beer or a glass of wine might be enjoyed while watching the sun set behind the fells. Alternatively, guests can settle in the lovely lounge to read or play chess and backgammon. This is the place for a relaxing break in good company – a chance to do lots of walking and sightseeing during the day and to absorb the lovely atmosphere in Keswick in the evenings.

Recommended in the area

Dove Cottage; Theatre by the Lake; Castlerigg Stone Circle

Ees Wyke Country House

★★★★★ ⊗ ⌂ GUESTHOUSE

Address   NEAR SAWREY,
             Ambleside, LA22 0JZ
Tel: 015394 36393
Email: mail@eeswyke.co.uk
Website: www.eeswyke.co.uk
Map ref: 5 SD39
Directions: On B5285 on W side of village
Rooms: 8 en suite (1 GF)
Notes: ⊗ ⛔ 12yrs **Parking:** 12

Visitors to this elegant Georgian country house can enjoy the same views over Esthwaite Water and the surrounding countryside that once drew Beatrix Potter to the area. The thoughtfully equipped en suite bedrooms have all been decorated and furnished with care, and there is a charming lounge with an open fire. In summer, guests can sit on the terrace and spot some of the most well-known fells in the Lake District. Above all, Ees Wyke is renowned for its splendid dining room, where a carefully prepared five-course dinner is served. Breakfasts have a fine reputation due to the skilful use of local produce.

Recommended in the area

Grizedale Forest; Coniston Old Man; Langdale Pikes; Hill Top (Beatrix Potter's Home) (NT)

Hill Crest Country House

★★★★ ⌂ BED & BREAKFAST

Address   Brow Edge, NEWBY BRIDGE,
             Ulverston, LA12 8QP
Tel: 015395 31766
Email: enquiries@hill-crestguesthouse.co.uk
Website: www.hill-crestguesthouse.co.uk
Map ref: 5 SD38 **Directions:** 1m SW of Newby
Bridge. Off A590 onto Brow Edge Rd, house 0.75m
on right **Rooms:** 3 en suite (2 fmly rooms) (1 GF)
S £45-£50 **D** £70-£90
Notes: ⊗ **Parking:** 4 **Closed:** 22-26 Dec

This delightful Lakeland guest house sits at the southern tip of Lake Windermere, and is renowned for quality accommodation, service, and warm hospitality. Guests are welcomed on arrival with fresh scones and tea. Hill Crest is undergoing a major refurbishment at the end of 2010/beginning of 2011, which includes installing contemporary shower rooms and redecorating two bedrooms and the guest lounge. At breakfast, expect plenty of choice and lots of fresh local produce.

Recommended in the area

Lakeside & Haverthwaite Steam Railway; Steam boats on Lake Windermere; Holker Hall

Birks Bridge Rapids in Dunnerdale in the Lake District National Park

Lyndhurst Country House

★ ★ ★ ★ 🛏 GUESTHOUSE

Address   NEWBY BRIDGE, Ulverston, LA12 8ND
Tel: 015395 31245
Email: chris@lyndhurstcountryhouse.co.uk
Website: www.lyndhurstcountryhouse.co.uk
Map ref: 5 SD38
Directions: On junct of A590 & A592 at Newby
Bridge rdbt
Rooms: 3 en suite S £50 D £70-£80
Notes: Wi-fi ⊗ 🐾 8yrs Parking: 3
Closed: 23-28 Dec

Situated at the southern tip of beautiful Lake Windermere and set in its own lovely gardens, Lyndhurst is well located within easy reach of a host of local amenities, such as hotels, restaurants and country inns. The comfortable bedrooms are well equipped and tastefully decorated. Hearty breakfasts here feature local produce as much as possible and are served in the pleasant dining room, which also has a lounge area that opens out onto the garden.

Recommended in the area

Windermere cruises; Hill Top (Beatrix Potter's home, NT); Holker Hall Gardens; Lakeland Motor Museum

---

Brandelhow Guest House

★ ★ ★ ★ GUESTHOUSE

Address   1 Portland Place, PENRITH, CA11 7QN
Tel: 01768 864470
Email: enquiries@brandelhowguesthouse.co.uk
Website: www.brandelhowguesthouse.co.uk
Map ref: 6 NY53
Directions: In town centre on one-way system,
left at town hall
Rooms: 5 (4 en suite) (1 pri facs) (2 fmly rooms)
Notes: Wi-fi ⊗ Closed: 31 Dec & 1 Jan

Situated in the historic market town of Penrith, on the Coast to Coast Walk, this friendly guest house is within easy walking distance of central amenities and is also ideally located for the Lakes and the M6. Guests are welcomed with a hot or cold drink and a selection of home-made cakes, and can relax in the thoughtfully furnished, comfortable bedrooms. Breakfasts utilise ingredients from some of the best Lakeland producers, and are served in a Cumbria-themed dining room overlooking the courtyard garden. Afternoon and cream teas are available by arrangement, as are packed lunches.

Recommended in the area

Hadrian's Wall; Moot Hall, Keswick; Aira Force (NT)

The Coppice

★★★★ 🛏 ☕ GUESTHOUSE

Address	Brook Road, WINDERMERE, LA23 2ED
Tel:	015394 88501
Fax:	015394 42148
Email:	chris@thecoppice.co.uk
Website:	www.thecoppice.co.uk
Map ref:	6 SD49
Directions:	0.25m S of village centre on A5074
Rooms:	9 en suite (2 fmly rooms) (1 GF)
Notes:	Wi-fi Parking: 10

This traditional Lakeland vicarage, built in local stone, retains all its character and charm. It sits in an elevated position between the villages of Windermere and Bowness, close to the Lake, and is perfectly placed for touring, walking or sailing. Hosts Chris and Barbara promise a memorable experience and can provide extras like flowers, chilled champagne and handmade chocolates for your arrival. The bedrooms are all individually designed and have their own charm and character. Some come with spa baths, others with showers, while all have TVs with Freeview and DVD player, Wi-fi access, a mini decanter of sherry and refreshments tray. Excellent Lakeland breakfasts and dinners (available five evenings a week) are served in the light and airy dining room, while pre-dinner drinks can be taken in the comfortable lounge by the coal fire. Menus feature plenty of local and seasonal ingredients, such as local championship sausages, fell-bred beef, pork and lamb, and fish from Fleetwood. In the mornings expect homemade breads, marmalades and jams, award-winning local sausages and fine cured bacon. Vegetarians are catered for, while most special diets can be accommodated with prior notice. Guests can enjoy complimentary access to a nearby health club.

Recommended in the area

Hill Top (Beatrix Potter's home) (NT); Wordsworth's homes – Rydal Mount and Dove Cottage

Fairfield House and Gardens

★ ★ ★ ★ 🏨 GUESTHOUSE

Address   Brantfell Road, Bowness-on-Windermere,
          WINDERMERE, LA23 3AE
Tel: 015394 46565
Fax: 015394 46564
Email: tonyandliz@the-fairfield.co.uk
Website: www.the-fairfield.co.uk
Map ref: 6 SD49
Directions: Into Bowness town centre, turn opp St
Martin's Church & sharp left by Spinnery restaurant,
house 200yds on right
Rooms: 10 en suite (2 fmly rooms) (3 GF) Notes: 🐾 10yrs Parking: 10

Situated close to Bowness Bay, this establishment is the perfect place to take a tranquil break. Owners Tony and Liz Blaney offer genuine hospitality and high standards of personal service at their 200-year-old home, which is set in half an acre of its own beautifully landscaped gardens. All rooms are en suite and there are twin as well as double rooms; the deluxe rooms feature spa baths. The four-poster room has its own wet room with heated floor for that added touch of luxury – the power shower here is big enough for two, and comes with body jets and massage pebbles on the floor. A roof-space penthouse (featured on TV), has a glass shower and spa bath as well as a flat-screen TV and surround-sound. Options are available for guests to have sparkling wine or Belgian chocolates in their room on arrival and, for special occasions, to have rose petals scattered on the bed. Special facilities are available for visitors with mobility requirements. Breakfasts come in hearty or healthy versions, each made with the finest ingredients. There is free internet access via a public terminal or, for those with their own laptops, Wi-fi is available.

Recommended in the area

Blackwell (The Arts & Crafts House); Windermere lake steamers; Wordsworth House (NT)

St Johns Lodge

★ ★ ★ ⌂ GUEST ACCOMMODATION

Address Lake Road, WINDERMERE, LA23 2EQ
Tel: 015394 43078
Fax: 015394 88054
Email: mail@st-johns-lodge.co.uk
Website: www.st-johns-lodge.co.uk
Map ref: 6 SD49
Directions: On A5074 between Windermere & lake
Rooms: 12 en suite (1 fmly)
S £30-£45 D £50-£98
Notes: Wi-fi ⊗ ⚹ 12yrs **Parking:** 3 **Closed:** Xmas

Adult-only, pet-free, eco-friendly St John's Lodge is just 10 minutes' walk from Windermere and the lake, and restaurants, pubs and shops are all nearby. A choice of bedrooms is offered to suit all pockets from budget to premium. All have en suite shower rooms, TVs, Fairtrade tea- and coffee-making facilities and hairdryers. An extensive menu offers over 30 cooked breakfasts and more than 15 vegetarian and vegan options. Gluten free options also available. Free internet access and Wi-fi.

Recommended in the area

Lake Windermere; Beatrix Potter Attraction; Blackwell

Ullswater from Hallin Fell, Lake District National Park

The Willowsmere

★★★★ ≜ GUESTHOUSE

Address   Ambleside Road,
            WINDERMERE, LA23 1ES
Tel: 015394 43575
Fax: 015394 44962
Email: info@thewillowsmere.com
Website: www.thewillowsmere.com
Map ref: 6 SD49
Directions: On A591, 500yds on left after Windermere station, towards Ambleside
Rooms: 12 en suite (1 GF) S £38-£50 D £64-£98
Notes: Wi-fi ⊗ ⼗ 12yrs Parking: 15

Wonderful views of Lake Windermere are available only a few minutes' stroll from this luxuriously renovated gentleman's residence dating from 1850. The town centre and the railway station, too, are just an eight-minute walk away, and ample off-road parking is provided on site. Willowsmere is an imposing property, built from Lakeland stone, set in large, landscaped gardens which have won the titles 'Windermere in Bloom 2010, Best Hotel Garden', and 'Cumbria in Bloom 2010, Best Guest House Garden'. Guests can relax in the secluded gardens during fine weather or in either of the two lounges. The large, comfortable bedrooms are all en suite and include single, twin, double and four-poster rooms. Luxury pocket sprung beds and Egyptian cotton duvets ensure a sound night's sleep. A double ground floor room has wheelchair access and a bathroom with facilities for the disabled. No family rooms are available so only children of 12 years or older can be accommodated. English breakfasts, home cooked to order, are served at individual tables in the stylish dining room.

Recommended in the area

Brockhole Lake District Visitor Centre; Townend; The World of Beatrix Potter

Waterfall on Bonsall Brook, near Cromford in the Peak District, Derbyshire

Dannah Farm Country House

★★★★★ ☰ GUEST ACCOMMODATION

Address   Bowmans Lane, Shottle,
          BELPER, DE56 2DR
Tel: 01773 550273 & 550630
Fax: 01773 550590
Email: reservations@dannah.co.uk
Website: www.dannah.co.uk
Map ref: AA380
Directions: A517 from Belper towards Ashbourne,
1.5m right into Shottle after Hanging Gate pub on
right, over x-rds & right
Rooms: 8 en suite (1 fmly rooms) (2 GF) S £75-£95 D £130-£250
Notes: Wi-fi ⊗ Parking: 20 Closed: 24-26 Dec

Dannah, a Georgian farmhouse on a working farm on the Chatsworth Estate, is home to Joan and Martin Slack and their collection of pigs, hens and cats, and Cracker the very good-natured English Setter. Each bedroom has its own individual character, beautifully furnished with antiques and old pine, and filled with a wealth of thoughtful extras. Some rooms have private sitting rooms, four-poster beds and amazing bathrooms featuring a double spa bath or Japanese-style tubs – the Studio Hideaway suite even has its own private terrace with hot tub. All the bedrooms look out onto green fields and open countryside. The two delightful sitting rooms have open fires on chilly evenings and views over the gardens. The English farmhouse breakfasts are a true delight, served in relaxed and elegant surroundings. Dinner is available by arrangement, alternatively there are excellent pubs and restaurants within easy reach. Footpaths criss-cross the surrounding area in the heart of the Derbyshire Dales, making it an ideal location for walking enthusiasts.

Recommended in the area

Chatsworth; Dovedale; Alton Towers

Buxton's Victorian Guest House

★★★★★ GUESTHOUSE
Address   3A Broad Walk, BUXTON, SK17 6JE
Tel: 01298 78759
Fax: 01298 74732
Email: buxtonvictorian@btconnect.com
Website: www.buxtonvictorian.co.uk
Map ref: 7 SK07 Directions: Signs to Opera House,
proceed to Old Hall Hotel, right onto Hartington Rd,
car park 100yds on right
Rooms: 7 en suite (2 fmly rooms) (1 GF) S £54-£80

D £78-£100 Notes: ⊗ 🐾 4yrs Parking: 9 Closed: 22 Dec-12 Jan

Standing in a prime position overlooking the Pavilion Gardens and boating lake, this delightfully furnished house was built in 1860 for the then Duke of Devonshire. It has been extensively refurbished in recent years and today offers high-quality, comfortable accommodation with its own car park. The en suite bedrooms have individual themes and many extras such as TVs, hairdryers and hospitality trays. Some rooms overlook the Gardens. Excellent breakfasts are served in the Oriental breakfast room.

Recommended in the area

Buxton Opera House; Poole's Cavern; Chatsworth House

Chatsworth House, surrounded by stunning countryside

Roseleigh

★★★★ GUESTHOUSE

Address 19 Broad Walk, BUXTON, SK17 6JR
Tel/Fax: 01298 24904
Email: enquiries@roseleighhotel.co.uk
Website: www.roseleighhotel.co.uk
Map ref: 7 SK07
Directions: A6 to Safeway rdbt, onto Dale Rd, right at lights, 100yds left by Swan pub, down hill & right onto Hartington Rd
Rooms: 14 (12 en suite) (2 pri facs) (1 GF)
S £39-£90 D £76-£90
Notes: Wi-fi ⊗ ♨ 6yrs **Parking:** 9 **Closed:** 16 Dec-16 Jan

Roseleigh is a comfortable and elegant Victorian property that benefits from a prime location overlooking Buxton's 23-acre Pavilion Gardens – the land on which it stands was once owned by the Duke of Devonshire. Built in 1871 and situated on the pedestrianised Broad Walk, it is just a 5-minute walk from the heart of the town and benefits from its own car park. The quality furnishings and decor throughout highlight the house's many original features. Most of the sympathetically furnished bedrooms in this family-run establishment have smart en suite shower rooms; all have TV and tea- and coffee-making facilities, and several have good views over the Pavilion Gardens. The comfortable guest lounge, which overlooks the lake, is the place simply to relax, or you can plan the next day's itinerary by poring over the many books on the Peak District provided by your hosts, Gerard and Maggi. They are knowledgeable about the local area and are happy to advise on suitable pubs, restaurants and activities. The elegant dining room offers a range of breakfast choices, including vegetarian options, from a menu that makes use of local produce where possible. Free internet and Wi-fi access.

Recommended in the area

Buxton Opera House; Chatsworth; Peak District National Park

Bentley Brook Inn

★ ★ ★ INN

Address FENNY BENTLEY, Ashbourne, DE6 1LF
Tel: 01335 350278
Fax: 01335 350422
Email: all@bentleybrookinn.co.uk
Website: www.bentleybrookinn.co.uk
Map ref: 7 SK14 **Directions:** 2m N of Ashbourne at junct of A515 & B5056
Rooms: 11 en suite (1 fmly) (2 GF)
Notes: Wi-fi **Parking:** 100

This popular country inn, located within the Peak District National Park, makes a good base for walkers and those visiting Alton Towers. It is a charming building with an attractive terrace, sweeping lawns and play area. The en suite bedrooms are well appointed, with extras such as TVs, hairdryers and hospitality trays. Overlooking the gardens, the comfortable restaurant offers a wide range of dishes available all day in summer, from snacks through to main meals, using organic and locally sourced ingredients. Food is served in the winter from 12-3pm and 6-9pm. A new function suite is now available.

Recommended in the area

Bakewell; Haddon Hall; Drayton Manor Theme Park

Underleigh House

★ ★ ★ ★ ★ ⌂ GUEST ACCOMMODATION

Address Losehill Lane, off Edale Road, HOPE, Hope Valley, S33 6AF
Tel: 01433 621372
Fax: 01433 621324
Email: info@underleighhouse.co.uk
Website: www.underleighhouse.co.uk
Map ref: 7 SK18 **Directions:** From village church on A6187 onto Edale Rd, 1m left onto Losehill Ln
Rooms: 5 en suite (2 GF) S £65-£85 D £85-£105
Notes: Wi-fi 12yrs **Parking:** 6 **Closed:** Xmas, New Year & 4 Jan-3 Feb

Surrounded by glorious scenery in the heart of the Hope Valley, Underleigh House is a barn and cottage conversion dating from 1873, offering quality accommodation and genuine hospitality. The stone-flagged breakfast room, with its original beams, is where home-made bread, muesli, preserves and top-notch local produce are served at a communal table, and the atmosphere is cosy and warm. It's hardly surprising that owner, Vivienne, was a finalist in the AA's 'Friendliest Landlady' awards in 2009.

Recommended in the area

Castleton Caverns; Chatsworth; Eyam

The Pines

★★★★ BED & BREAKFAST

Address 12 Eversleigh Road, Darley Bridge,
MATLOCK, DE4 2JW
Tel: 01629 732646
Email: info@thepinesbandb.co.uk
Website: www.thepinesbandb.co.uk
Map ref: 7 SK35 **Directions:** From Bakewell or
Matlock take A6 to Darley Dale. Turn at Whitworth
Hotel onto B5057, pass Square & Compass pub &
The 3 Stags Heads, The Pines on right
Rooms: 3 en suite **S** £40-£60 **D** £60-£80 **Notes:** Wi-fi **Parking:** 5

The Pines dates back to 1825 and is full of original features such as open fires and exposed beams.
In recent years the house has been fully refurbished to the highest standards, and offers three en suite
rooms with every modern comfort, including free Wi-fi. Breakfast, served in the delightful breakfast
hall or on the patio during the summer, is a highlight of any stay. At The Pines everyone can expect an
extremely warm welcome, and that extends to children and dogs.

Recommended in the area
Chatsworth House; Haddon Hall; Peak District National Park

Yew Tree Cottage

★★★★ 🏠 BED & BREAKFAST

Address The Knoll, Tansley, MATLOCK, DE4 5FP
Tel: 01629 583862 & 07799 541903
Email: enquiries@yewtreecottagebb.co.uk
Website: www.yewtreecottagebb.co.uk
Map ref: 7 SK35
Directions: 1.2m E of Matlock. Off A615 into
Tansley centre
Rooms: 3 en suite **S** £65-£85
Notes: Wi-fi ⊗ ✦ 12yrs **Parking:** 3

This 18th-century cottage, full of original character and charm and with stunning views, is set in
pretty gardens in the village of Tansley. The cottage is a true home away from home, with outstanding
service and hospitality, and ideally situated for all the Derbyshire Dales and Peak District. The elegantly
furnished and decorated bedrooms have TV/radios, DVD players, bath robes, hairdryers, toiletries
and refreshment trays. Breakfast is a memorable feast of home-made and local produce, and light
refreshments are served in the sitting room where log fires cheer up the cooler days.

Recommended in the area
Chatsworth; Crich Tramway Village; Heights of Abraham cable cars

The Smithy

★★★★★ ⌂ GUEST ACCOMMODATION

Address NEWHAVEN, Biggin, Buxton, SK17 0DT
Tel/Fax: 01298 84548
Email: lynnandgary@
thesmithybedandbreakfast.co.uk
Website: www.thesmithybedandbreakfast.co.uk
Map ref: 7 SK16
Directions: 0.5m S of Newhaven on A515. Next to
Biggin Ln, private driveway opp Ivy House
Rooms: 4 en suite (2 GF) **S** £44-£50 **D** £70-£100
Notes: Wi-fi ⊗ ⛄ **Parking:** 8

Welcoming owners Lynn and Gary Jinks have restored this former drovers' inn and blacksmith's shop
to a high standard with all modern comforts and a very personal service. The well-decorated good-sized
bedrooms are all en suite with hospitality trays and many extras. Flavoursome breakfasts, including
free-range eggs and home-made preserves, are served in the forge, which still has its vast open
hearth, and is adjacent to a cosy lounge. The pleasant gardens are set within 4 acres of meadowland.
Recommended in the area
Chatsworth; Tissington and High Peak Trails (within walking distance); Peak District National Park

View of countryside from rugged Curbar Edge

DEVON

Valley of Rocks, nr Lynton, Exmoor National Park

Greencott

★ ★ ★ ★ GUESTHOUSE
Address   Landscove, ASHBURTON, TQ13 7LZ
Tel: 01803 762649
Map ref: 2 SX77
Directions: 3m SE of Ashburton. Off A38 at
Peartree junct, Landscove signed on slip road,
village green 2m on right, opp village hall
Rooms: 2 en suite **S** £23-£25 **D** £46-£50
Notes: ⊗ Parking: 3 **Closed:** 25-26 Dec

Modern facilities in a traditional atmosphere are offered at this renovated house in the village of
Landscove, which is just three miles from Ashburton. Greencott stands in a garden with lovely country
views. The bedrooms are carefully furnished and well equipped with baths and showers en suite, and
tea and coffee amenities. Television, books, maps and local information are provided in the comfortable
sitting room, and traditional country cooking is served around the oak dining table. The full English
breakfast includes home-made bread, and dinner is available on request. Service is attentive and
caring, and many guests return time and time again.

Recommended in the area

Dartington; Buckfast Abbey; riding, fishing and golf nearby

Bluebells and oak trees, Blackberry Camp, nr Sidmouth

Turtley Corn Mill

★ ★ ★ ★ 🍺 INN
Address AVONWICK, TQ10 9ES
Tel: 01364 646100
Fax: 01364 646101
Email: eat@turtleycornmill.com
Website: www.turtleycornmill.com
Map ref: 2 SX75 **Directions:** From A38, S towards
Avonwick, 0.5m on left **Rooms:** 4 en suite (1 fmly)
S £69-£110 **D** £69-£110
Notes: Wi-fi ⊗ **Parking:** 90 **Closed:** 25 Dec

This fine old mill sits in six acres of grounds complete with a small lake and bordered by the River Glazebrook. Once a working corn mill, it became a pub in the 1970s before undergoing a complete renovation. Today the emphasis is on relaxation, with a light, fresh design and no fruit machines or pool tables. The en suite bedrooms are contemporary in style and come with king-sized beds, Egyptian cotton linen, flat-screen TVs with Freeview, free Wi-fi and powerful showers. The food served here is locally sourced and of a high quality, starting with the hearty cooked breakfasts.

Recommended in the area

Dartmoor National Park; Dartmoor Otter Sanctuary; Salcombe Harbour

Colourful terraced cottages at Clovelly, North Devon

The Pines at Eastleigh

★★★★ 🏠 GUEST ACCOMMODATION

Address The Pines, Eastleigh, BIDEFORD,
EX39 4PA
Tel: 01271 860561 **Fax:** 01271 861689
Email: pirrie@thepinesateastleigh.co.uk
Website: www.thepinesateastleigh.co.uk
Map ref: 2 SS42 **Directions:** A39 onto A386
signed East-the-Water. 1st left signed Eastleigh,
500yds next left, 1.5m to village, house on right
Rooms: 6 en suite (1 fmly) (4 GF) **S** £40-£49
D £70-£89 **Notes:** Wi-fi 🐾 9yrs **Parking:** 20

With a magnificent hilltop position overlooking the Torridge Estuary and Lundy Island, this Georgian house, standing in seven acres, is perfect for a relaxing break. Most of the comfortable bedrooms are in the converted stables around a charming courtyard, and there are two rooms in the main house. Two fully-serviced cottage suites have private sitting rooms and kitchens. Guests can unwind with a drink in the garden-room after a day exploring the beautiful North Devon countryside. Breakfasts are memorable here, featuring lots of local and homemade produce.

Recommended in the area

Instow & Clovelly; cycling and walking the Tarka Trail; Hartland Heritage Coast

Hansard House

★★★★ GUEST ACCOMMODATION

Address 3 Northview Road,
BUDLEIGH SALTERTON, EX9 6BY
Tel: 01395 442773
Fax: 01395 442475
Email: enquiries@hansardhotel.co.uk
Website: www.hansardhousehotel.co.uk
Map ref: 2 SY08
Directions: 500yds W of town centre
Rooms: 12 en suite (1 fmly) (3 GF)
S £46-£57 **D** £84-£99 **Notes:** Wi-fi **Parking:** 11

Set in an ideal situation a short walk from central Budleigh Salterton, Hansard House is just five minutes from the beach and the cliff path of this beautiful part of the East Devon coast. The tastefully decorated en suite bedrooms have TV, tea- and coffee-making facilities and hairdryers, and most have views across the town, to the countryside and estuary beyond. The varied and hearty breakfasts are served in the light and airy dining room. Children and pets are welcome.

Recommended in the area

Otter Estuary Bird Sanctuary; Bicton Park Botanical Gardens

Tor Cottage

★ ★ ★ ★ ★ 🛏 GUEST ACCOMMODATION
Address CHILLATON, Tavistock, PL16 0JE
Tel: 01822 860248
Fax: 01822 860126
Email: info@torcottage.co.uk
Website: www.torcottage.co.uk
Map ref: 1 SX48
Directions: A30 Lewdown exit through Chillaton towards Tavistock, 300yds after Post Office right signed 'Bridlepath No Public Vehicular Access' to end
Rooms: 4 en suite (3 GF) **S** £98 **D** £140–£150
Notes: Wi-fi ⊗ 🐾 14yrs **Parking:** 8 **Closed:** mid Dec-beg Feb

This romantic cottage offers tranquillity and seclusion in 28 acres of grounds. Nothing is too much trouble for Maureen Rowlatt, who has equipped the en suite rooms with everything you could wish for. Each one is individually designed, from the warmth and style of the Art Deco Room to the blue and cream elegance of The Craftsman's Room – both converted from an original craftsman's workshop. One room is in the cottage wing and the others are in converted barns – each has a private terrace/garden and a log fire. Laughing Waters, the garden suite, is nestled in its own private valley. Breakfast is an imaginative range of dishes, and can be taken in the conservatory-style dining room or on the terrace in fine weather. The gardens are a feature in their own right with many private corners, a stream and, in summer, a heated swimming pool. Woodlands cloaking the hillside behind the cottage are home to a variety of wildlife including badgers, pheasants and deer that enjoy the cover of the gorse, while buzzards and the occasional heron can be seen overhead. Special-priced autumn and spring breaks are available.

Recommended in the area

Dartmoor; The Eden Project; National Trust houses and gardens

The New Angel Rooms

★★★★ RESTAURANT WITH ROOMS

Address 51 Victoria Road, DARTMOUTH, TQ6 9RT
Tel: 01803 839425 **Fax:** 01803 839505
Email: info@thenewangel.co.uk
Website: www.thenewangel.co.uk
Map ref: 2 SX85 **Directions:** In Dartmouth take
one-way system, 1st left at NatWest Bank **Rooms:** 6
en suite (2 fmly) **Notes:** ⊗ **Closed:** Jan

The New Angel offers luxurious, stylish
accommodation in the heart of Dartmouth's pretty town centre. Each bedroom has a plasma-screen TV
and DVD player, quality toiletries, soft white towels, a fridge with fresh milk and water, and home-made
shortbread and nibbles, plus there's a lovely guest lounge with an open fire. It's just a short stroll from
here to the picturesque waterfront and the establishment's three-Rosette New Angel restaurant, where
breakfast and dinner are served. The restaurant boasts an open kitchen and a cocktail lounge upstairs
with great views over the Dart Estuary. Guests can also take a leisurely cruise or a fishing trip onboard
the New Angel's fully equipped Sunseeker vessel.

Recommended in the area

Dartmoor National Park; Dartmouth Castle; Bayards Cove Fort

Remains of Wheal Betsy Tin Mine in Dartmoor National Park

Nonsuch House

★ ★ ★ ★ ★ 🏛 🍽 GUEST ACCOMMODATION

Address   Church Hill, Kingswear,
          DARTMOUTH, TQ6 0BX
Tel: 01803 752829
Fax: 01803 752357
Email: enquiries@nonsuch-house.co.uk
Website: www.nonsuch-house.co.uk
Map ref: 2 SX85
Directions: A3022 onto A379 2m before Brixham.
Fork left onto B3205. Left up Higher Contour Rd,
down Ridley Hill, house on bend on left at top of Church Hill

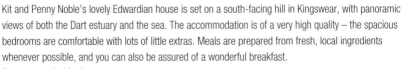

Rooms: 4 en suite (2 GF) S £85-£125 D £110-£150 Notes: Wi-fi ⊗ 🐾 12yrs Parking: 3

Kit and Penny Noble's lovely Edwardian house is set on a south-facing hill in Kingswear, with panoramic views of both the Dart estuary and the sea. The accommodation is of a very high quality – the spacious bedrooms are comfortable with lots of little extras. Meals are prepared from fresh, local ingredients whenever possible, and you can also be assured of a wonderful breakfast.

Recommended in the area

Dartmouth; Brixham; South West Coast Path

A view of landscape around Cadbury Castle, showing the tower of Cadbury village church

Barn

★★★★ GUEST ACCOMMODATION

Address	Foxholes Hill, Marine Drive, EXMOUTH, EX8 2DF
Tel:	01395 224411
Fax:	01395 225445
Email:	exmouthbarn@googlemail.com
Website:	www.barnhotel.co.uk

Map ref: 2 SY08

Directions: From M5 junct 30 take A376 to Exmouth, then follow signs to seafront. At rdbt last exit into Foxholes Hill. Located on right

Rooms: 11 en suite (4 fmly rooms) S £38-£50 D £65-£105

Notes: Wi-fi **Parking:** 30 **Closed:** 23 Dec-10 Jan

Close to miles of sandy beaches, this Grade II listed establishment is set in an impeccable and stunning 2-acre garden, which is sea facing and with spectacular views of the East Devon Heritage Coast. There is a terrace and a swimming pool for summer. The building is a leading example of the Arts and Crafts movement and was built in the early 1900s by Edward Prior, a contemporary of William Morris. The Barn has been sympathetically modernised and furnished in-keeping with its architectural design and has an atmosphere of country-house style. The public rooms and most of the bedrooms have outstanding sea views. The attractively decorated, en suite bedrooms have TV, hospitality tray, hairdryer and direct-dial telephone. Breakfast, featuring freshly squeezed juices and local produce, is served in the bright, airy dining room. Exmouth is 15 minutes' walk away along the tree-lined and landscaped Madeira Walk. There are also several rural and coastal walks in the area and the estuary of the River Exe offers opportunities for birdwatching, sailing, fishing and windsurfing.

Recommended in the area

Crealy Adventure Park; Exeter; Bicton Park Botanical Gardens

Courtmoor Farm

★ ★ ★ ★ FARMHOUSE

Address Upottery, HONITON, EX14 9QA
Tel: 01404 861565
Email: courtmoor.farm@btinternet.com
Website: www.courtmoor.farm.btinternet.co.uk
Map ref: 2 ST10
Directions: 4m NE of Honiton off A30
Rooms: 3 en suite (1 fmly)
S £38-£40 D £64-£68
Notes: Wi-fi ⊗ Parking: 20 Closed: 20 Dec-1 Jan

Rosalind and Bob Buxton welcome you to their spacious farmhouse with marvellous views over the Otter Valley and surrounding countryside. The extensive grounds are home to a flock of sheep, two ponies and Aberdeen Angus cattle. Accommodation is provided in a family room, double room and twin, all equipped with digital TVs, hairdryers, electric blankets, clock radios as well as tea and coffee facilities. There are satisfying full English breakfasts to enjoy, with special diets catered for.
A fitness suite and a sauna are available, plus woodland walks and a nature trail.

Recommended in the area

Honiton antiques shops and Lace Museum; Lyme Regis; Forde Abbey and Gardens

Sea pinks, or thrift, growing on the cliffs at Hope Cove, nr Salcombe

Night In Gails@Kentisbury Mill

★ ★ ★ ★ ☖ GUEST ACCOMMODATION

Address   Kentisbury Mill, KENTISBURY,
        Barnstaple, EX31 4NF
Tel: 01271 883545
Email: info@kentisburymill.co.uk
Website: www.kentisburymill.co.uk
Map ref: 2 SS64
Directions: M5 junct 27 onto A361 towards
Barnstaple, then A399 to Blackmoor Gate. Turn left
at Blackmoor Gate onto A39, then right onto B3229
at Kentisbury Ford, 1m on right
Rooms: 4 en suite S £32.50-£35 D £60-£75
Notes: Wi-fi ⊗ **Parking:** 6 **Closed:** Xmas

Three miles from the coast, bordered by Exmoor National Park and nestling in the north Devon hills, lies Kentisbury Mill. The property sits in two acres of grounds, with lawns sloping down from the old mill leat to the pond, Exmoor stream and summer house where guests can relax and unwind. Originally a thatched cottage dating back to at least 1750, the mill was added in the early 1800s and the west wing in 1923. Your hosts, Gail and Jim Evans, renovated the property in 2007 and it now offers modern, comfortable en suite accommodation while retaining all of its character and charm. Swallow, the largest room, can be used as either a super-king-size or twin room, with a large en suite and double shower. Nuthatch, with a king-size bed, is in the oldest part of the building, as is Wren, a cosy double room. Magpie, a single room, is in the east wing and has a 4ft bed. Breakfast is taken in the 18th century dining room, with the choice including full English, continental, smoked salmon with scrambled eggs (from the mill's own hens) on an English muffin, and smoked haddock, all cooked in the Aga.

Recommended in the area

Arlington Court (NT); Valley of the Rocks; Exmoor National Park

Rock House

★★★★ GUEST ACCOMMODATION

Address	Manor Grounds, LYNMOUTH, EX35 6EN
Tel:	01598 753508
Fax:	0800 7566964
Email:	enquiries@rock-house.co.uk
Website:	www.rock-house.co.uk

Map ref: 2 SS74 **Directions:** On A39, at foot of Countisbury Hill right onto drive, pass Manor green/ play area to Rock House

Rooms: 8 en suite (1 GF)

Notes: Wi-fi **Parking:** 8 **Closed:** 24-25 Dec

Standing alone by the river at the mouth of the harbour, the 18th-century Rock House has wonderful sea views. The bedrooms, some with four-poster beds, are well appointed and furnished to a high standard with en suite facilities, TV/DVD, Wi-fi, hairdryers, alarm clocks and complimentary tea and coffee. They also have superb views of the Lyn Valley, the river or the sea. A choice of menus is offered in the spacious lounge/bar or the Harbour View Restaurant. The large gardens are popular for cream teas in summer.

Recommended in the area

Combe Martin Wildlife & Dinosaur Park; Lyn & Exmoor Museum; Arlington Court

Clapper Bridge over the East Dart River near Postbridge in Dartmoor National Park

Sea View Villa

★★★★★ 🛏 🍽 GUEST ACCOMMODATION

Address 6 Summer House Path, LYNMOUTH, EX35 6ES
Tel: 01598 753460
Fax: 01598 753496
Email: seaviewenquiries@aol.com
Website: www.seaviewvilla.co.uk
Map ref: 2 SS74
Directions: A39 from Porlock, 1st left after bridge, Sea View Villa on right 20yds along path opp church
Rooms: 5 (3 en suite) (1 fmly) **D** £110-£130
Notes: Wi-fi ⊗ 🐾 14yrs **Closed:** Jan

This charming Grade II listed Georgian villa, built in 1721, has been appointed to a high standard by owners Steve Williams and Chris Bissex, who bought the house after moving from London, where they were both involved in the arts as performers and directors. Walking and surfing are popular local pursuits and there are wonderful walks directly from the door, including the Two Moors Walk and Lynton's Valley of the Rocks. Tucked away from the bustle of the main streets, the house provides elegant and peaceful accommodation. The name says it all, and indeed all of the individually decorated bedrooms enjoy impressive views of the harbour and sea. Many thoughtful extras are provided, including Egyptian cotton linen, luxury toiletries and TV/VCR, with a choice of films available to borrow. The proprietors' genuine hospitality assures a relaxed and comfortable stay. Dinner and breakfast are not to be missed, and home-made bread is a speciality here. For guests planning a day out, picnics, hikers' feasts and ploughman's hampers can all be provided. To top it all off, a range of beauty therapies and holistic treatments is available by prior arrangement.

Recommended in the area

Exmoor National Park; Clovelly; Watersmeet Valley

Sunrise from Crockern Tor near Two Bridges, Dartmoor National Park

Victoria Lodge

★ ★ ★ ★ ★ ⌂ GUEST ACCOMMODATION

Address	30-31 Lee Road, LYNTON, EX35 6BS
Tel:	01598 753203
Email:	info@victorialodge.co.uk
Website:	www.victorialodge.co.uk
Map ref:	2 SS74
Directions:	Off A39 in village centre opp Post Office
Rooms:	8 en suite S £59.50-£119 D £70-£140
Notes:	Wi-fi ⊗ 🐾 11yrs Parking: 6
Closed:	Nov-23 Mar

Victoria Lodge is a large, elegant villa, built in the 1880s and conveniently located in the heart of the village of Lynton, a short stroll from a good range of restaurants. Full of character and original features, the house offers luxurious accommodation with quality furnishings and thoughtful extras. The bedrooms are named after Queen Victoria's daughters and daughters-in-law, and reflect the style of the period. Each is individually decorated in rich colours and features coronets, half-testers and four-poster beds. Guests can relax in the gardens, sitting out on the colourful front patio or the pleasant south-facing terrace at the rear of the house. Inside, there are two guest lounges with bay windows, comfortable sofas, and plenty of books, magazines and board games to play. Free Wi-fi is available throughout. An exceptional choice is offered at breakfast, which is served by friendly staff in the sumptuously decorated dining room with its period fireplace and over-mantle. Start with toast and homemade preserves, before moving on to pancakes with maple syrup, eggs Benedict, or 'the full Exmoor works' with egg, sausage, bacon, tomato, mushrooms, hash brown and the Devon delicacy of hog's pudding. Vegetarian and gluten-free options are also offered.

Recommended in the area

Exmoor National Park; Valley of the Rocks; the Tarka Trail

Merritt House B&B

★★★★ 🏠 GUEST ACCOMMODATION

Address 7 Queens Road, PAIGNTON, TQ4 6AT
Tel: 01803 528959
Email: bookings@merritthouse.co.uk
Website: www.merritthouse.co.uk
Map ref: 2 SX86 **Directions:** From Paignton
seafront, turn right onto Torbay Rd, then 1st left onto
Queens Rd, house on right, parking at rear
Rooms: 7 en suite (3 GF) **S** £27-£34 **D** £54-£70
Notes: Wi-fi 🐾 12yrs **Parking:** 4
Closed: 20 Dec-7 Jan

Just a five-minute stroll from the seafront and town centre, this elegant Victorian property is ideally
situated to make the most of the traditional seaside resort of Paignton. The owners take understandable
pride in their establishment, and will assist in any way possible to ensure a relaxed and rewarding
stay. Bedrooms and bathrooms are thoughtfully furnished, comfortable and generously equipped, and
breakfast is a real treat, with plenty of choice and an emphasis on local and homemade produce.
Recommended in the area
Paignton Zoo and Living Coasts; Paignton and Dartmouth Steam Railway; Oldway Mansion

Blue Ball Inn

★★★★ INN

Address Stevens Cross, Sidford,
SIDMOUTH, EX10 9QL
Tel: 01395 514062
Fax: 01395 519584
Email: rogernewton@blueballinn.net
Website: www.blueballinnsidford.co.uk
Map ref: 2 SY18 **Directions:** On A3052,
at Sidford straight over lights. Inn 600yds
Rooms: 9 en suite (2 fmly) (1 GF) **S** £60 **D** £95
Notes: Wi-fi 🚫 **Parking:** 80

Run by the Newton family since 1912, but dating back to 1385, this thatched, cob- and flint-built
old inn was destroyed by fire in 2006 and rebuilt with tremendous care to recapture its original
atmosphere. In the characterful bar – spread across three rooms – you'll find pub food favourites on
the menu and ales served by hand pump. There's an attractive garden, and the eight comfortable,
tastefully furnished en suite bedrooms come with tea- and coffee-making facilities, LCD TVs and Wi-fi.
Recommended in the area
Crealy Adventure Park; Seaton Tramway; South West Coast Path

The Oxenham Arms

★ ★ ★ ★ INN

Address	SOUTH ZEAL, Okehampton, EX20 2JT
Tel:	01837 840244 & 840577
Fax:	01837 840791
Email:	relax@theoxenhamarms.co.uk
Website:	www.theoxenhamarms.co.uk
Map ref:	2 SX69
Rooms:	7 en suite

From the moment you step inside the imposing granite Tudor porch, you know you're about to experience something special. The Oxenham Arms is a truly magnificent 12th century coaching inn nestling right on the edge of Dartmoor in one of Devon's prettiest villages. It's an ideal base for activities like walking, cycling, fishing and horse riding, or for visiting Exeter which is only 20 minutes away. In fact, you can walk from the hotel straight onto the moor or be at the beach within 30 minutes. The Oxenham Arms has been carefully and sympathetically modernised to offer a contemporary restaurant serving great local food, with many of the ingredients supplied by the property's own farm. The home-produced bacon and sausage at breakfast are particularly good. The bar, unchanged for centuries, offers real ale and many interesting wines. It's a lovely place to sit and unwind after a busy day, especially in winter when the fires are lit. All the en suite bedrooms at The Oxenham Arms are individually decorated and many have four-poster beds. Each room has its own character features, enjoyed now by almost 1000 years of travellers.

Recommended in the area

Dartmoor; The Lost Gardens of Heligan; Castle Drogo

Strete Barton House

★★★★★ GUESTHOUSE

Address Totnes Rd, STRETE,
Dartmouth, TQ6 0RU
Tel: 01803 770364
Fax: 01803 771182
Email: info@stretebarton.co.uk
Website: www.stretebarton.co.uk
Map ref: 2 SX85
Directions: Off A379 coastal road into village,
just below church
Rooms: 6 (5 en suite) (1 pri facs) **S** £80-£130 **D** £90-£140 **Notes:** Wi-fi 🐾 8yrs **Parking:** 4

Strete Barton House is a 16th century manor house in extensive grounds in the picturesque village of Strete, near Dartmouth in the South Hams area of Devon. The house enjoys panoramic sea views across Start Bay from Start Point lighthouse to the mouth of the River Dart, and is just 200 yards from the South West Coast Path. Blackpool Sands and Slapton Sands are only a mile away. The contemporary interior offers spacious double bedrooms with king-size beds (one with a super-king, four poster) and twin-bedded rooms. All bedrooms feature luxurious pocket-sprung mattresses, Egyptian cotton sheets and feather down pillows, fluffy towels, wall mounted flat-screen TV with DVD/CD player, Wi-fi access, extensive beverage tray, mineral water and luxury toiletries. There's also a luxurious cottage suite which has its own living room with an inglenook fireplace and log-burning stove. Breakfast is served in the dining room overlooking the garden and includes seasonal fruit, fresh homemade fruit salad, poached fruit and local farm yoghurts as well as a full English using local ingredients. On arrival guests are offered homemade cake and tea or coffee, either in the drawing room with its comfortable sofas and open fireplace, or on the terrace overlooking the sea.

Recommended in the area

Greenway (NT); Blackpool Sands; South West Coast Path

Potters Mooring

★★★★ GUEST ACCOMMODATION
Address   30 The Green, Shaldon,
          TEIGNMOUTH, TQ14 0DN
Tel: 01626 873225 Fax: 01626 872909
Email: info@pottersmooring.co.uk
Website: www.pottersmooring.co.uk
Map ref: 2 SX97 Directions: A38 onto A380 signed
Torquay, B3192 to Teignmouth & Shaldon, over river
signs to Potters Mooring Rooms: 5 (4 en suite) (1 pri
facs) (1 fmly) Notes: Wi-fi Parking: 8

This delightful guest house was formerly a sea captain's residence and dates from 1625 when Shaldon and Teignmouth were small fishing communities. Potters Mooring has been lovingly refurbished to the highest standards, whilst retaining its quiet charm and historic appeal. The five bedrooms have en suite or private bathrooms, TVs, hospitality trays and hairdryers, and most overlook the River Teign or the bowling green. There's also a small cottage, ideal for families. Potters Mooring has Wi-fi access for guests, and all stays include a hearty full English breakfast. Pets are welcome.
Recommended in the area
Dartmoor; Torquay; Dartmouth; Exeter

Thomas Luny House

★★★★★ 🏠 GUEST ACCOMMODATION
Address   Teign Street, TEIGNMOUTH, TQ14 8EG
Tel: 01626 772976
Email: alisonandjohn@thomas-luny-house.co.uk
Website: www.thomas-luny-house.co.uk
Map ref: 2 SX97
Directions: A381 to Teignmouth, at 3rd lights turn right to quay,
50yds turn left onto Teign St, after 60yds turn right through
white archway
Rooms: 4 en suite S £68-£75 D £75-£102
Notes: Wi-fi ⊗ ⚑ 12yrs Parking: 8 Closed: early Jan-mid Feb

This delightful late 18th-century house is run by John and Alison Allan whose relaxed yet attentive approach is much appreciated by their guests. The large drawing room and dining room are beautifully furnished and have French doors opening onto a walled garden with a terraced sitting area. The bedrooms are well equipped and very comfortable. Home-made dishes and a full cooked breakfast are a speciality.
Recommended in the area
Tuckers Maltings; Powderham Castle; Cockington Village

The Cary Arms

★★★★★ INN

Address Babbacombe Beach, TORQUAY, TQ1 3LX
Tel: 01803 327110 Fax: 01803 323221
Email: enquiries@caryarms.co.uk
Website: www.caryarms.co.uk
Map ref: 2 SX96 Directions: A380 at Ashcombe
Cross onto B3192 to Teignmouth. Right at lights
to Torquay on A379, bear left at lights continue to
Babbacombe. Left onto Babbacombe Downs Rd, left
onto Beach Rd Rooms: 8 en suite (1 fmly) (3 GF)
S £100-£200 D £150-£250 Notes: Wi-fi Parking: 15

Known as 'the inn on the beach', The Cary Arms exudes charm, fun and good English pub values along with all the style, comfort and luxury of a top-class boutique hotel. The kitchen serves up the very best of gastropub food, so you can indulge during your stay in hearty breakfasts, long lunches and lazy suppers. The Cary Arms is a place for all seasons; the young are welcomed with their very own fishing net, while the dog friendly rooms come equipped with dog beds and bowls.

Recommended in the area

Babbacombe beaches; South West Coast Path; Living Coasts

The Colindale

★★★★ 🛏 GUEST ACCOMMODATION

Address 20 Rathmore Road, Chelston,
TORQUAY, TQ2 6NY
Tel: 01803 293947
Fax: 01803 231050
Email: rathmore@blueyonder.co.uk
Website: www.colindalehotel.co.uk
Map ref: 2 SX96 Directions: From Torquay station
200yds on left in Rathmore Rd
Rooms: 7 (6 en suite) (1 pri facs)
Notes: Wi-fi ⊗ 🐾 12yrs Parking: 6 Closed: 20 Dec-3 Jan

The Colindale is set in a quiet road overlooking Torre Abbey and close to the seafront and railway station. This elegant establishment, with its antiques and artworks and a library of books, offers attractively co-ordinated en suite bedrooms, some with views over Torbay, and lots of extra touches such as digital TVs, towelling robes and mineral water. Memorable breakfasts are enjoyed in the smart dining room, using local eggs, organic bacon and sausages, and home-made breads and preserves.

Recommended in the area

Paignton Zoo Environmental Park; Babbacombe Model Village; Cockington Village

The Downs

★★★★ GUEST ACCOMMODATION

Address	41-43 Babbacombe Downs Road, Babbacombe, TORQUAY, TQ1 3LN
Tel:	01803 328543
Fax:	01803 317977
Email:	manager@downshotel.co.uk
Website:	www.downshotel.co.uk
Map ref:	2 SX96
Rooms:	12 en suite (4 fmly)

S £45-£59 D £65-£79 **Notes:** Wi-fi **Parking:** 8

The Downs takes its name from its location, perched high above the sea at Babbacombe Downs on the outskirts of Torquay. The house was built in around 1850 by Isaac Singer for his sisters, and forms part of a terrace looking out across a long stretch of common land which boasts the highest seaside promenade in the country. If you book early enough, you might get one of the eight bedrooms (there are 12 in total) that have their own balcony complete with sweeping views across Lyme Bay. The first phase of a refurbishment programme at The Downs has been completed, and all rooms now have 19-inch flat-screen TVs with Freeview, along with free Wi-fi access throughout the building. The Downs is family-run and welcomes young and old, families, couples, singles and dogs. There is a licensed lounge bar, and the accommodation is designed to offer flexibility, with the junior suite and family rooms sleeping up to five. During the summer months, head to the forecourt café for a light lunch, traditional cream tea, a refreshing beer, or a local ice cream. Breakfast can be taken in the spacious restaurant or on your balcony, and evening meals can be provided.

Recommended in the area

Babbacombe Model Village; Kents Cavern; Paignton Zoo

Headland View

★★★★ 🛏 GUESTHOUSE

Address 37 Babbacombe Downs, Babbacombe, TORQUAY,
TQ1 3LN

Tel: 01803 312612 / 07762 960230

Email: reception@headlandview.com

Website: www.headlandview.com

Map ref: 2 SX96

Directions: A379 to Babbacombe, off Babbacombe Rd left onto
Portland Rd & Babbacombe Downs Rd & seafront

Rooms: 6 (4 en suite) (2 pri facs)

S £45-£50 **D** £60-£68 **Notes:** Wi-fi ⊗ 🐾 5yrs **Parking:** 4

This beautiful Victorian guest house, with unobstructed
panoramic views over the World Heritage Coast of Lyme Bay, is a fabulous place to stay. Positioned
directly on the Babbacombe Downs, Headland View has six individually designed bedrooms, most
with French doors opening onto balconies with tables and chairs to sit and relax while taking in the
magnificent vista. Alternatively, some of the rooms have four-poster beds. The property has retained
many of its original Victorian features and architecture, with a spacious guest lounge, a sun lounge and
a pretty dining room where you can enjoy freshly cooked hot breakfasts – anything from a full English to
fruit pancakes, omelettes, scrambled eggs with smoked salmon, or poached eggs on a toasted English
muffin – all accompanied by cereals, fresh fruit, fruit compote and toast with conserves and homemade
marmalade. Your hosts, Craig and Helen, will do their utmost to ensure a relaxing and memorable stay.
Headland View makes a great base for visiting the surrounding area of Torquay, Paignton, Brixham,
Dartmouth and Dartmoor. It is also ideally located for the South West Coast Path and many lovely blue
flag beaches, plus there are lots of great traditional pubs and good restaurants nearby.

Recommended in the area

Dartmoor; South West Coast Path; Oddicombe beach

Millbrook House

★★★★ GUEST ACCOMMODATION

Address 1 Old Mill Road, Chelston,
TORQUAY, TQ2 6AP
Tel: 01803 297394
Email: marksj@sky.com
Website: www.millbrook-house-hotel.co.uk
Map ref: 2 SX96
Rooms: 10 en suite (1 fmly) (2 GF)
Notes: ⊗ Parking: 8 Closed: Nov-Feb

The delightful, personally run Millbrook House is within easy walking distance of Torquay's many attractions and has a friendly and relaxed atmosphere. The well-maintained en suite bedrooms provide many useful facilities; a king-size bed and a four-poster room are available and there is a family room, thoughtfully divided by a partition wall. One room features a sunken bath. There is a cosy bar on the lower ground floor with pool and darts, and the vibrant garden has a summer house for guests to relax in on hotter days. The freshly cooked breakfasts here include local produce as much as possible.

Recommended in the area

Torquay's beaches; Paignton; Brixham

Stover Lodge

★★★★ GUEST ACCOMMODATION

Address 29 Newton Road, TORQUAY, TQ2 5DB
Tel: 01803 297287 **Fax:** 01803 297287
Email: enquiries@stoverlodge.co.uk
Website: www.stoverlodge.co.uk
Map ref: 2 SX96
Directions: Follow signs to Torquay town centre, at station/Halfords left lane. Lodge on left after lights
Rooms: 9 (8 en suite) (1 pri facs) (3 fmly) (2 GF)
S £28-£40 D £50-£56 Notes: Wi-fi ⊗ Parking: 10

Stover Lodge is a comfortable and friendly bed and breakfast just a short walk from Torquay town centre, perfect for business travellers or holidaymakers looking for a relaxing break away. The nine, recently refurbished en suite bedrooms - a mixture of single, double and family rooms - come with tea- and coffee-making facilities, radio-alarm clocks and flat-screen TVs with Freeview. The breakfasts are hearty but also healthy, prepared from high quality ingredients locally sourced where possible. Vegans/ vegetarians and special dietary requirements can be catered for.

Recommended in the area

Paignton Zoo; South West Coast Path; Dartmoor

The Durant Arms

★★★★ 🛏 INN

Address Ashprington, TOTNES,
TQ9 7UP
Tel: 01803 732240
Email: info@durantarms.co.uk
Website: www.durantarms.co.uk
Map ref: 2 SX86
Directions: A381 from Totnes for Kingsbridge,
1m left for Ashprington
Rooms: 8 en suite (2 GF) **S** £50-£55 **D** £80-£85
Notes: 🐾 **Parking:** 8 **Closed:** 25-26 Dec evenings

This beautifully kept inn with well-tended shrubs and plants is a focal point in the picturesque village of Ashprington, deep in the heart of Devon's South Hams district. Owners Eileen and Graham Ellis proudly offer their own brand of hospitality and provide attractive accommodation in either the main building or the Old Coach House. The bedrooms are individually designed to a very high standard, using stylish furnishings, and include a host of thoughtful touches to help ensure a memorable stay. Each room has a luxurious well-appointed en suite bathroom. The inn is renowned locally for its delicious home cooking. A blackboard menu is available in the character bar or the smart dining room, both furnished in rich red velvets. All dishes are freshly cooked to order, offering fresh vegetables and a wide variety of meat and fish; seasonal local produce is used whenever possible. Packed lunches are also available. To complement your meal there is a good choice of real ales, beers and wines, some from the local Sharpham Vineyard, just a 15-minute walk away and open to the public for visiting and wine tasting. There are stunning views of the River Dart too, making The Durant Arms the perfect place to stay.

Recommended in the area

Historic Totnes; The Eden Project; Sharpham Vineyard

DORSET

Hengistbury Head

Druid House

★★★★★ 🛏 GUEST ACCOMMODATION

Address 26 Sopers Lane,
CHRISTCHURCH, BH23 1JE
Tel: 01202 485615 **Fax:** 01202 473484
Email: reservations@druid-house.co.uk
Website: www.druid-house.co.uk
Map ref: 3 SZ19 **Directions:** A35 exit Christchurch
main rdbt onto Sopers Ln, establishment on left
Rooms: 8 en suite (3 fmly rooms) (4 GF)
Notes: ⊗ **Parking:** 8

Overlooking the park, this delightful family-run bed and breakfast is just a short stroll from the high street, Christchurch Priory and the quay. The bedrooms are furnished to the highest standard and come with tea- and coffee-making facilities, flat-screen TVs with Freeview, and thoughtful extras like CD players, iPod docks, and soft, fluffy bathrobes. Some rooms have balconies or private patios, and a number have their own lounge. There is a pleasant rear garden, guests' conservatory and a licensed bar. Expect a warm welcome and an excellent breakfast prepared from locally sourced produce.

Recommended in the area
Christchurch Priory; New Forest National Park; Bournemouth beaches

Baytree House Dorchester

★★★★ BED & BREAKFAST

Address 4 Athelstan Road, DORCHESTER, DT1 1NR
Tel: 01305 263696
Email: info@baytreedorchester.com
Website: www.bandbdorchester.co.uk
Map ref: AA2102
Directions: 0.5m SE of town centre
Rooms: 3 en suite **S** £35 **D** £65
Notes: ⊗ **Parking:** 3

In 2006 owners Nicola and Gary Cutler completely refurbished Baytree House, creating a stylish place to stay, with spacious and light rooms, contemporary decor and luxurious fittings. Although it is set in a quiet residential area, it's just a 10-minute stroll to the historic centre of Dorchester and a short drive to many of rural Dorset's attractions. The bedrooms offer either en suite shower rooms or private bathrooms with a shower and bath. The Cutlers also own the Walnut Grove Restaurant and Coffee shop in the town centre, and employ the same high standards of cooking at Baytree House. Guests are offered a 15 per cent discount on meals at the Walnut Grove.

Recommended in the area
Thomas Hardy's Cottage; Monkey World; Jurassic Coast

The Acorn Inn

★★★★ ◎ INN

Address EVERSHOT, Dorchester, DT2 0JW
Tel: 01935 83228
Fax: 01935 83707
Email: stay@acorn-inn.co.uk
Website: www.acorn-inn.co.uk
Map ref: 2 ST50
Directions: 0.5m off A37 between Yeovil &
Dorchester, signed Evershot & Holywell
Rooms: 10 en suite (2 fmly rooms) S £65-£130
D £95-£130 Notes: Wi-fi Parking: 40

This 16th-century coaching inn was immortalised as the Sow and Acorn in Thomas Hardy's *Tess of the D'Urbervilles*. It stands at the heart of the village of Evershot, in an Area of Outstanding Natural Beauty, with walking, fishing, shooting and riding all nearby. Inside are two oak-panelled bars – one flagstoned, one tiled – with logs blazing in carved hamstone fireplaces, and a cosy restaurant. There's also a skittle alley in what was once the stables, and it's rumoured that the residents' sitting room was once used by Hanging Judge Jeffreys as a court room. The en suite bedrooms are all individually styled, and each named after a character from Hardy's novel – several feature interesting four-poster beds. All of the rooms, including two family rooms, have a TV, free Wi-fi, a beverage tray and hairdryers. Irons are available on request. Fresh, local produce is included on the varied and interesting menu, with most of the food sourced from within a 15-mile radius, including local fish and game, and bolstered by blackboard specials. Bar snacks and lighter meals are also available, accompanied by a selection of real ales and a comprehensive wine list. Plenty of parking spaces are available.

Recommended in the area

Evershot village; Forde Abbey; Lyme Regis

Farnham Farm House

★★★★★ GUEST ACCOMMODATION

Address   FARNHAM, Blandford Forum, DT11 8DG
Tel: 01725 516254
Fax: 01725 516306
Email: info@farnhamfarmhouse.co.uk
Website: www.farnhamfarmhouse.co.uk
Map ref: 2 ST91 **Directions:** Off A354 Thickthorn
x-rds into Farnham, continue NW from village centre
T-junct, 1m bear right at sign
Rooms: 3 en suite (1 fmly)
S £70-£80 **D** £80-£90 **Notes:** ⊗ **Parking:** 7 **Closed:** 25-26 Dec

Farnham Farm House, with its flagstone floors, open log fires and magnificent views, dates back to the 1850s. Guests can walk around the 350-acre working farm, part of a private estate owned by the descendants of archaeologist General Pitt-Rivers. Facilities include a heated outdoor swimming pool, and the Sarpenela Natural Therapy Centre for therapeutic massage. Delicious Aga-cooked breakfasts are served in the attractive dining room. Local produce is used whenever possible.

Recommended in the area

Cranborne Chase; Kingston Lacey (NT); Larmer Tree Gardens

View from Durdle Door to Bat's Head

Longpuddle

★ ★ ★ ★ BED & BREAKFAST

Address 4 High Street, PIDDLEHINTON, DT2 7TD
Tel: 01300 348532
Email: ann@longpuddle.co.uk
Website: www.longpuddle.co.uk
Map ref: 2 SY79
Directions: From Dorchester (A35) take B3143,
after entering village 1st thatched house on left after
village cross
Rooms: 2 en suite (2 fmly rooms)
S £40-£50 D £80-£100 **Notes:** Wi-fi **Parking:** 3

Set in the Piddle Valley, midway between the abbey town of Sherborne and the county town of Dorchester, Longpuddle is well placed for exploring Thomas Hardy's Dorset and the Jurassic Coast. The 400-year-old thatched cottage overlooks the embryo River Piddle, which runs between the large garden and paddocks, and off-road parking is available. Guest accommodation comprises two spacious, tastefully decorated rooms ideal for an extended stay; one double and one twin, both with en suite facilities. A third bed can be made available if required for a child. Guests have the use of a spacious, comfortable drawing room with a TV and views over the garden and paddocks. Breakfast consists of local produce personally cooked by proprietor, Ann, including homemade marmalade. Individual tastes and vegetarians are catered for. The name Longpuddle was used by Thomas Hardy, collectively, for the villages of the Piddle Valley, where there are several pubs serving local food and the excellent Abbots Tea Room. For a special meal there are some excellent restaurants within a 40-minute drive. Well-behaved pets are welcome by prior arrangement.

Recommended in the area

Cerne Abbas Giant; Maiden Castle; Sherborne

The Piddle Inn

★★★★ ⬭ INN

Address PIDDLETRENTHIDE, Dorchester, DT2 7QF
Tel: 01300 348468
Fax: 01300 348102
Email: piddleinn@aol.com
Website: www.piddleinn.co.uk
Map ref: 2 SY79
Directions: 7m N of Dorchester on B3143 in middle
of Piddletrenthide **Rooms:** 3 en suite (1 fmly)
S £55-£60 **D** £75-£85 **Notes:** Wi-fi **Parking:** 15

In the heart of rolling Dorset downland in the unspoilt Piddle Valley, this 18th century pub takes its name from the river flowing through the beer garden. It's a welcoming place, popular for its traditional bar where real ales are served straight from the barrel, and its good food which can be ordered from the bar or a la carte menu. There's plenty of choice including locally sourced, chargrilled meats, fresh fish and homemade puddings. The Piddle Inn has three beautifully refurbished bedrooms, all with power showers in the en suite bathrooms, and two with lovely river views.

Recommended in the area

Dorchester; Jurassic Coast; Salisbury Cathedral

Offley Bed & Breakfast

★★★★ GUEST ACCOMMODATION

Address Looke Lane, PUNCKNOWLE,
          Dorchester, DT2 9DB
Tel: 01308 897044 & 07792 624977
Map ref: 2 SY58
Directions: Off B3157 into village centre, left after
Crown Inn onto Looke Ln, 1st house on right
Rooms: 3 (2 en suite) (1 pri facs) **S** £45-£60 **D** £70
Parking: 3

Magnificent valley views are one of the many highlights of a stay at this delightful bed and breakfast. The house is furnished with many period pieces, giving it a warm and homely feel which is completed by the homemade cake and tea served on arrival, and roaring log fires in winter. The bedrooms are well equipped with TVs and hairdryers, and there's a garden and patio for guests to use in the warmer months. Breakfast is a real treat, featuring lots of homemade and local produce. Offley Bed and Breakfast is in the heart of some great walking country, as well as being within easy reach of the historic town of Dorchester and the swannery at Abbotsbury.

Recommended in the area

South West Coast Path; Horse riding and golf; Abbotsbury Swannery

La Fleur de Lys Restaurant with Rooms

★ ★ ★ ★ ◉◉ RESTAURANT WITH ROOMS
Address   Bleke Street, SHAFTESBURY, SP7 8AW
Tel: 01747 853717
Fax: 01747 853130
Email: info@lafleurdelys.co.uk
Website: www.lafleurdelys.co.uk
Map ref: 2 ST82 Directions: 0.25m off junct of
A30 with A350 at Shaftesbury towards town centre Rooms: 7 en suite (2 fmly rooms) (1 GF)
S £75-£90 D £100-£175 Notes: Wi-fi ⊗ Parking: 10 Closed: 3rd wk Jan

This long-established restaurant with rooms occupies a former girls boarding school. There are seven well-appointed en suite rooms and a lovely, peaceful courtyard garden to relax in. In the winter you can curl up by one of the open fires in the lounge/bar. Dining at La Fleur de Lys, which holds two AA Rosettes, is a real treat, with quality local produce used to good effect in the French-inflected cooking.
Recommended in the area
Stonehenge; Bath; Jurassic Coast

Avalon Townhouse

★ ★ ★ ★ BED & BREAKFAST
Address   South Street, SHERBORNE, DT9 3LZ
Tel: 01935 814748
Email: enquiries@avalontownhouse.co.uk
Website: www.avalontownhouse.co.uk
Map ref: 2 ST61
Directions: A30 from Shaftesbury, towards
Sherborne town centre, left onto South St
Rooms: 3 en suite S £70-£80 D £80-£90
Notes: Wi-fi ⊗ ⚑ 18yrs

Avalon is a spacious and comfortable Edwardian townhouse in the heart of historic Sherborne, close to the railway station. The building, recently refurbished to a high standard, retains many original features, such as the open fire in the lounge, and the small garden has been redesigned to create a feeling of space. All of the en suite bedrooms have Freeview flat-screen TVs, free Wi-fi, power showers and luxurious towels and toiletries. A freshly prepared breakfast starts the day around a large oak table in the farmhouse-style kitchen, and there is a real commitment to using locally sourced ingredients.
Recommended in the area
Sherborne Abbey; Sherborne Castle; Jerram Gallery

The Kings Arms

★★★★★ ⬤ INN

Address	Charlton Horethorne, SHERBORNE, DT9 4NL
Tel:	01963 220281
Fax:	01963 220496
Email:	admin@thekingsarms.co.uk
Website:	www.thekingsarms.co.uk

Map ref: 2 ST61 **Directions:** From A303 follow signs for Templecombe & Sherborne onto B3145 to Charlton Horethorne

Rooms: 10 en suite (1 fmly) S £105 D £105 **Notes:** Wi-fi **Parking:** 30

Situated in the heart of the pretty village of Charlton Horethorne, the Kings Arms has benefited from a total refurbishment, resulting in impressive standards throughout. Behind the imposing Edwardian façade, the atmosphere remains that of a traditional English country pub, but with all modern facilities and conveniences. Indeed, the experienced owners have created something for everyone with a convivial bar, snug and choice of dining environments, including the garden terrace with lovely countryside views. There's also a croquet lawn beside the terrace. All of the bedrooms possess individuality, quality and style, with marble bathrooms, robes and powerful showers, as well as Wi-fi and flat-screen TVs and DVD players. Some of the rooms are in the newly-built part of the house, while others are found in the older part of the building. Three have lift as well as stair access, and one room is specially adapted for wheelchair users. The food, which has won an AA Dinner Award, is taken seriously here, with assured cooking from a menu majoring on quality local produce. Much is cooked and prepared on the premises – from the fresh-baked bread to the home-made ice cream and pasta. It's no wonder The Kings Arms was named 'Best Dining Pub' in the 2010 Taste of Somerset Awards.

Recommended in the area

Fleet Air Arm Museum; Sherborne Old Castle; Haynes International Motor Museum; Stourhead (NT)

The Alendale Guest House

★ ★ ★ GUESTHOUSE

Address 4 Waterloo Place, WEYMOUTH, DT4 7NX
Tel: 01305 788817
Email: bowie538@aol.com
Website: www.thealendale.com
Map ref: 2 SY67 **Directions:** Turn left at clock tower, through 2nd set of lights, Alendale 20mtrs on left **Rooms:** 5 en suite (2 fmly rooms)
S £34-£44 D £60-£70 **Notes:** Wi-fi ⊗ **Parking:** 6

The Alendale Guest House is a warm and comfortable grade II listed Georgian building in the beautiful seaside town of Weymouth. Situated at the end of the esplanade, The Alendale is just a short walk away from the town centre and harbour area. The guest house offers comfortable, en suite accommodation, with all rooms featuring memory foam mattresses, iPod docking stations/radios, flat-screen TVs with Freeview, and free Wi-fi access. Breakfast is served in the delightful dining room and the menu offers plenty of choice. As a member of Direct from Dorset, The Alendale sources all of its breakfast produce locally were possible.

Recommended in the area

Jurassic Coast; Monkey World; Bovington Tank Museum

Les Bouviers Restaurant with Rooms

★★★★★ ◎◎ RESTAURANT WITH ROOMS

Address Arrowsmith Road, Canford Magna,
WIMBORNE MINSTER, BH21 3BD
Tel: 01202 889555
Fax: 01202 639428
Email: info@lesbouviers.co.uk
Website: www.lesbouviers.co.uk
Map ref: 2 SZ09 **Directions:** A31 onto A349. In 0.6m turn left. In approx 1m right onto Arrowsmith Rd. Establishment approx 100yds on right
Rooms: 6 en suite (4 fmly rooms) S £110-£185 D £130-£215 **Notes:** Wi-fi **Parking:** 50

Ideally located in over five acres of peaceful, landscaped grounds, this house gives the feeling of being deep in the country yet is close to Wimborne, Poole and Bournemouth. Each of the en suite bedrooms has been individually designed with many little luxuries and home comforts such as supremely comfortable beds, in-room coffee systems and Wi-fi. Impressive food, accompanied by wines from an extensive cellar, is a highlight of any stay here, as is the friendly, attentive service.

Recommended in the area

Wimborne Model Town; Purbeck Hills; Poole Harbour

ESSEX

Exterior of the parish church at Saffron Walden

The Chudleigh

★★★★ GUEST ACCOMMODATION

Address 13 Agate Road, Marine Parade West,
CLACTON-ON-SEA, CO15 1RA
Tel: 01255 425407 **Fax:** 01255 470280
Email: chudleighhotel@btconnect.com
Website: www.chudleighhotel.com
Map ref: 4 TM11 **Directions:** 250yds W of pier, off
Marine Pde West **Rooms:** 10 en suite (2 fmly rooms)
(2 GF) **S** £50 **D** £80-£85
Notes: Wi-fi ✿ 1yr ☛ allowed **Parking:** 7

This family-run B&B stands out from the crowd near Clacton seafront with its unusual architecture, sunny front terrace and masses of colourful flowers spilling out of window boxes, tubs and hanging baskets. The pier and main shopping centre are just a short distance away, making The Chudleigh the ideal stopover for both business and leisure guests, yet it's also a peaceful place, run for more than four decades with dedication and enthusiasm by Carol and Peter Oleggini. As you can probably tell from the name, Carol and Peter can converse fluently with Italian, and also French, speaking guests. The Olegginis manage to strike the right balance between pleasantly informal service and attention to detail, with high standards of housekeeping, so it's hardly surprising that many guests return time and time again. The en suite bedrooms are attractively furnished, with comfortable beds and armchairs, digital televisions, direct-dial telephones, free wireless internet, and hospitality trays. There are some spacious family bedrooms and two bedrooms on the ground floor, along with a residents' lounge with digital TV. An extensive breakfast menu is offered in the attractively refurbished dining room, where guests eat at separate tables.

Recommended in the area

Sandy beaches of the Essex Sunshine Coast; Colchester; Beth Chatto Gardens; John Constable country at Flatford Mill

GLOUCESTERSHIRE

Arlington Row, Bibury

The Old Passage Inn

★ ★ ★ ★ ◉◉ 🍴 RESTAURANT WITH ROOMS

Address Passage Road, ARLINGHAM, GL2 7JR
Tel: 01452 740547
Fax: 01452 741871
Email: oldpassage@ukonline.co.uk
Website: www.theoldpassage.com
Map ref: 2 SO71
Directions: A38 onto B4071 through Arlingham.
House by river
Rooms: 3 en suite **S** £40-£130 **D** £60-£130
Notes: Wi-fi **Parking:** 30 **Closed:** 25 & 26 Dec

This restaurant with rooms is delightfully located on the very edge of the River Severn. The en suite bedrooms are decorated in contemporary style and welcoming extras include air-conditioning, mini-bars and tea- and coffee-making equipment. In the restaurant the fresh water crayfish is local, and pride is taken in using sustainably sourced fish and shellfish, with lobster fresh from the tanks, and freshly shucked oysters and fruits de mers as house specialities.

Recommended in the area

Dean Heritage Centre; Lydney Park Gardens; Edward Jenner Museum

The Devil's Chimney, Leckhampton Hill on the Cotswold Way

Beaumont House

★ ★ ★ ★ ★ GUEST ACCOMMODATION

Address	56 Shurdington Road, CHELTENHAM, GL53 0JE
Tel:	01242 223311
Fax:	01242 520044
Email:	reservations@bhhotel.co.uk
Website:	www.bhhotel.co.uk
Map ref:	2 SO92
Directions:	S side of town on A46 to Stroud
Rooms:	16 en suite (3 fmly rooms)

S £69-£80 D £89-£249

Notes: Wi-fi ⊗ Parking: 16

Historic Beaumont House, birthplace of Captain Anketell Moutray Read VC, was built in the 1850s. It has been sympathetically renovated and converted into a very special five-star guest house set in a pleasant and spacious garden. Beaumont House is conveniently situated within walking distance of Cheltenham town centre and the fashionable Montpellier quarter, with plenty of shops, restaurants and pubs a five-minute stroll away. Bedrooms are beautifully designed and have free Wi-fi access and flat-screen televisions with Sky Sports. There are several luxury and themed rooms, some en suite with whirlpool baths. Room service evening meals are available from Monday to Thursday until 8pm (excluding public holidays). The excellent freshly cooked breakfasts have achieved a recognition award from Enjoy England, and you can expect friendly and efficient service. There's a lovely lounge for guests to relax in, complete with an honesty bar, and a comfortable conservatory where you can help yourself to complimentary hot drinks and biscuits. Beaumont House guests also benefit from free parking.

Recommended in the area

The Cotswolds Area of Outstanding Natural Beauty; Sudeley Castle; Gloucester Cathedral; Corinium Museum

Cleeve Hill House

★★★★★ GUEST ACCOMMODATION
Address   Cleeve Hill, CHELTENHAM, GL52 3PR
Tel: 01242 672052 Fax: 01242 679969
Email: info@cleevehill-hotel.co.uk
Website: www.cleevehill-hotel.co.uk
Map ref: 2 SO92
Directions: 3m N of Cheltenham on B4632
Rooms: 10 en suite (1 GF) S £50-£60
D £80-£95 Notes: Wi-fi ⊗ ⛄ 8yrs Parking: 11

This large Edwardian property sits near the top of Cleeve Hill, the highest point in the Cotswolds, and backs onto Cleeve Common. It has spectacular views across to the Malvern Hills. The en suite bedrooms are comfortably furnished with many welcome extras such as plasma-screen TVs with DVD players, tea- and coffee-making facilities and complimentary Wi-fi (laptops can be provided on request). Some have four-poster beds and one has a private lounge. Downstairs, there's a comfortable guest lounge and a 24-hour honesty bar. Breakfast is served in the light and airy conservatory and includes a good selection of hot and cold options.

Recommended in the area
Cheltenham Spa; Snowshill Manor (NT); Stratford-upon-Avon

Westonbirt Arboretum

Lypiatt House

★★★★★ GUEST ACCOMMODATION

Address Lypiatt Road,
CHELTENHAM, GL50 2QW
Tel: 01242 224994
Fax: 01242 224996
Email: stay@lypiatt.co.uk
Website: www.lypiatt.co.uk
Map ref: 2 SO92
Directions: M5 junct 11 to town centre. At Texaco
petrol station mini-rdbt take exit signed Stroud. Fork
right, pass shops, turn sharp left onto Lypiatt Rd
Rooms: 10 en suite (2 GF)
Notes: Wi-fi ⊗ 🐾 10yrs **Parking:** 10

Close to Cheltenham's exclusive and fashionable Montpellier area, Lypiatt House is within walking distance of the main shopping centre, restaurants and theatres, as well as being well located for the many festivals that take place in the town. A very fine house, built in typical Victorian style, it is set in its own grounds and provides ample residents' parking. Inside, the atmosphere is intimate and tranquil, with contemporary decor enhancing the building's traditional features. Guests are welcome to relax in the spacious and elegant drawing room or in the conservatory, with the latter featuring an honesty bar. The bedrooms and bathrooms, all en suite, come in a range of shapes and sizes, but all of the rooms are decorated and maintained to a high standard and include a range of welcome extras, such as TVs, beverage trays, direct-dial telephones and free Wi-fi; two of the rooms are on the ground floor. Full English breakfasts are served, and a laundry service is available. All in all, this makes a relaxing base for a stay in Cheltenham, whether travelling on business or for pleasure.

Recommended in the area

Pittville Pump Room; Gloucester Cathedral; Gloucestershire Warwickshire Steam Railway

Stone wall and landscape near Chedworth

Hare & Hounds

★★★★ ◉ INN

Address   Fosse-Cross, Chedworth,
           CIRENCESTER, GL54 4NN
Tel: 01285 720288
Email: stay@hareandhoundsinn.com
Website: www.hareandhoundsinn.com
Map ref: 3 SP00
Directions: 4.5m NE of Cirencester. On A429 by
speed camera
Rooms: 10 en suite (2 fmly rooms) (8 GF)
Notes: Wi-fi ⊗ Parking: 40

This country inn is close to the historic Fosse Way and perfectly situated for visiting nearby Cirencester and the Cotswolds. The smart bedrooms surround a peaceful courtyard and have full disabled access. Guests can dine outside on warm summer days, in the orangerie, or in one of the three elegant dining areas in the main pub. The home-cooked food, prepared by chef Gerry Ragosa, an advocate of Cotswold produce, is highly regarded.

Recommended in the area

Chedworth Roman Villa (NT); Cheltenham; Cotswold Wildlife Park

Aston House

★★★★ BED & BREAKFAST

Address   Broadwell, MORETON-IN-MARSH,
           GL56 0TJ
Tel: 01451 830475
Email: fja@astonhouse.net
Website: www.astonhouse.net
Map ref: 3 SP12
Directions: A429 from Stow-on-the-Wold towards
Moreton-in-Marsh, 1m right at x-rds to Broadwell,
Aston House 0.5m on left Rooms: 3 (2 en suite)
(1 pri facs) (1 GF) D £70-£80 Notes: Wi-fi ⊗ ◆ 10yrs Parking: 3 Closed: Nov-Feb

Aston House's enthusiastic owner has thought of everything when it comes to comfort, with armchairs in all the rooms, electric blankets and fans, TVs, radios and hairdryers, tea- and coffee-making facilities, bedtime drinks and biscuits, and quality toiletries in the en suite bathrooms. Although the rooms are not suitable for wheelchair users, there is a stairlift for those with limited mobility. A full English breakfast is served and there is a good pub within walking distance.

Recommended in the area

Cotswolds villages; Blenheim Palace; Hidcote Manor Gardens; Warwick Castle

1 Woodchester Lodge

★★★★ ⊜ BED & BREAKFAST

Address Southfield Road, North Woodchester,
STROUD, GL5 5PA
Tel: 01453 872586
Email: anne@woodchesterlodge.co.uk
Website: www.woodchesterlodge.co.uk
Map ref: 2 SO80 **Directions:** A46 onto Selsley Rd,
take 2nd left, 200yds on left
Rooms: 3 (1 en suite) (2 pri facs) (1 fmly)
S £45-£48 **D** £65-£70
Notes: Wi-fi ⊗ **Parking:** 4 **Closed:** Xmas & Etr

This large, late Victorian house is situated in the peaceful village of North Woodchester. Spacious bedrooms offer king-size beds, TVs, hospitality trays and comfortable chairs. The colourful gardens are well tended, and guests can enjoy the patio in warmer weather; otherwise, the comfortable lounge/dining room offers an open fire, books, magazines and games. Excellent breakfasts and meals, prepared by a qualified chef, use fruit and vegetables from the garden and freshly laid eggs.

Recommended in the area

Woodchester Mansion and grounds; WWT Slimbridge; Westonbirt Arboretum

Hailes Abbey, near Winchcombe

HAMPSHIRE

HMS Victory, the flagship of Admiral Horatio Nelson, Portsmouth

The Woolpack Inn

★★★★ @ INN

Address Totford, NORTHINGTON,
Alresford, SO24 9TJ
Tel: 01962 734184
Fax: 0845 293 8055
Email: info@thewoolpackinn.co.uk
Website: www.thewoolpackinn.co.uk
Map ref: 3 SU53
Directions: M3 junct 6 take A339 towards Alton,
turn right onto A3046. In Totford on left
Rooms: 7 en suite (1 fmly room) (4 GF) **S** £85-£105 **D** £85-£105 **Notes:** Wi-fi **Parking:** 20

Located in a tranquil village setting, yet within easy reach of the main transport routes, this traditional listed establishment has benefited from an extensive refurbishment. Throughout, it skilfully balances contemporary styling with traditional features, and the en suite bedrooms include many extras, such as plasma-screen TV with DVD, and mini-bar. The award-winning dining room showcases local produce, while breakfast features options such as kippers and home-made muesli, as well as full English.
Recommended in the area
Winchester Cathedral; Watercress Line Steam Railway; Alresford

The Cottage Lodge

★★★★★ GUEST ACCOMMODATION

Address Sway Road, BROCKENHURST, SO42 7SH
Tel: 01590 622296
Fax: 01590 623014
Email: enquiries@cottagelodge.co.uk
Website: www.cottagelodge.co.uk
Map ref: 3 SU30
Directions: Off A337 opp Careys Manor Hotel
onto Grigg Ln, 0.25km over x-rds, cottage next to
war memorial
Rooms: 12 en suite (6 GF) **S** £50-£90 **D** £50-£180
Notes: Wi-fi ⚑ 10yrs **Parking:** 12 **Closed:** Xmas & New Year

Owners David and Christina welcome guests to their cosy, award-winning 17th-century B&B with tea or coffee, served in front of the roaring fire. Brockenhurst is one of the few New Forest settlements where grazing ponies and cattle still have right of way. Conveniently close to the high street and the open forest. The individually furnished bedrooms are en suite and a local New Forest breakfast is served.
Recommended in the area
National Motor Museum, Beaulieu; Exbury Gardens; walking, cycling and horse riding

Ravensdale

★★★★ BED & BREAKFAST

Address   19 St Catherines Road,
           HAYLING ISLAND, PO11 0HF
Tel: 023 9246 3203 & 07802 188259
Email: phil.taylor@tayloredprint.co.uk
Website: www.ravensdale-hayling.co.uk
Map ref: 3 SU70 **Directions:** From A27 onto A3023
at Langstone, cross Hayling Bridge, 3m to mini rdbt,
right into Manor Rd 1m. Right by Barley Mow into
Station Rd, 3rd left into St Catherines Rd **Rooms:** 3 (2
en suite) (1 pri facs) **S** £40-£42 **D** £66-£68
Notes: ⊗ ✝ 8yrs **Parking:** 4 **Closed:** last 2wks Dec

A warm welcome awaits at Ravensdale, where Phil and Jane will make you feel at home in a relaxed
and friendly environment. Situated in a quiet, tree-lined road close to the beach and golf course, the
house offers tastefully decorated, comfortable accommodation, attractive bedrooms, home cooking
and evening meals on request.

Recommended in the area

Chichester Cathedral; Portsmouth Historic Dockyard; walking on the South Downs

Temple Lodge

★★★★ 🏠 GUEST ACCOMMODATION

Address   2 Queens Road, LYNDHURST, SO43 7BR
Tel: 023 8028 2392 **Fax:** 023 8028 4910
Email: templelodge@btinternet.com
Website: www.templelodge-guesthouse.com
Map ref: 3 SU30 **Directions:** M27 junct 2/3 onto
A35 to Ashurst/Lyndhurst, Temple Lodge on 2nd
corner on right, opposite forest
Rooms: 6 en suite (2 fmly rooms) **D** £60-£120
Notes: Wi-fi ⊗ ✝ 12yrs **Parking:** 6

Temple Lodge is a beautiful Victorian residence, lovingly restored by its present owners and retaining
many original features. The six spacious bedrooms all have en suite facilities, generous hospitality
trays, TVs/DVDs and mini fridges. The attractive guest lounge has a good selection of books and
magazines and comfortable leather sofas. There is a wide choice at breakfast, ranging from continental
to full English, with everything freshly prepared from local ingredients and served in the elegant dining
room overlooking the well-stocked gardens.

Recommended in the area

National Motor Museum; Exbury Gardens; Buckler's Hard; Lymington; Bournemouth; Christchurch

The Festing Grove Guest House

★ ★ ★ GUEST ACCOMMODATION

Address 8 Festing Grove, Southsea, PORTSMOUTH, PO4 9QA
Tel: 023 9273 5239
Email: thefestinggrove@ntlworld.com
Map ref: 3 SU60 **Directions:** E along seafront to South Parade Pier, after pier sharp left, around lake, 3rd left & 2nd right
Rooms: 6 (1 en suite) (1 pri facs) (2 fmly rooms)
S £25-£40 D £40-£58 **Notes:** Wi-fi ⊗

Situated in one of the quieter areas of the seaside resort of Southsea and within three minutes' walk of the seafront and pier, this long-established and well-presented property makes an ideal base for visiting Portsmouth's maritime attractions, plus the shops and restaurants at Gunwharf Quay. A continual programme of upgrading ensures that the bedrooms, two of which are family rooms, enjoy a high standard of decor and comfort. Breakfast is served in the homely dining room, and there is a well-appointed lounge for guests' use. On street parking is available and bus routes to all parts of the city pass close to the front door.

Recommended in the area

Isle of Wight; Portsmouth Historic Dockyard; Royal Marines Museum, Southsea

Watership Down

Moortown Lodge

★ ★ ★ ★ GUEST ACCOMMODATION

Address 244 Christchurch Road,
RINGWOOD, BH24 3AS
Tel: 01425 471404
Fax: 01425 476527
Email: enquiries@moortownlodge.co.uk
Website: www.moortownlodge.co.uk
Map ref: 3 SU10
Directions: 1m S of Ringwood. Off A31 at Ringwood
onto B3347, signs to Sopley, Lodge next to David
Lloyd leisure club
Rooms: 7 en suite (3 fmly rooms) (2 GF) **D** £86-£96 **Notes:** Wi-fi **Parking:** 9

Moortown Lodge is a charming, family-run Georgian property in the attractive market town of Ringwood, the western gateway to the New Forest, where there is a wide range of unusual shops, traditional pubs and lovely restaurants. It offers guests a warm welcome and luxury grade B&B accommodation with many of the features found in a good class hotel. The seven elegantly furnished en suite rooms include one with a romantic four-poster bed and two easy access ground-floor rooms. All suites have digital TV and DVD, free broadband connection and free national direct-dial phones. Generous traditional breakfasts are cooked to order with lighter and vegetarian breakfast options available. Wherever possible fresh New Forest produce is used in the cooking. The peace and tranquillity of the open forest as well as the unspoilt water meadows of the River Avon are only minutes away. Moortown Lodge is the ideal stopover for business people as well as an excellent base for touring and leisure visitors. There are special arrangements for guests wishing to use the bar, restaurant and outstanding recreational facilities at the adjacent private David Lloyd leisure club.

Recommended in the area

Bournemouth; New Forest National Park; Stonehenge

A lone Scots pine stands amongst a sea of pink - Rockford Common, New Forest National Park

Greenvale Farm

★ ★ ★ ★ BED & BREAKFAST

Address Melchet Park, Sherfield English,
ROMSEY, SO51 6FS

Tel: 01794 884858

Email: suebrown@greenvalefarm.com

Website: www.greenvalefarm.com

Map ref: 3 SU32

Directions: 5m W of Romsey. On S side of A27
through red-brick archway for Melchet Court,
Greenvale Farm 150yds on left, left at slatted barn

Rooms: 1 en suite (1 GF) **Notes:** Wi-fi ⊗ ⛫ 14yrs **Parking:** 10

Greenvale Farm in Melchet Park is located on the Hampshire/Wiltshire border, just four miles from the New Forest, near the historic market town of Romsey. The cathedral cities of Salisbury and Winchester are also within easy reach for days out. Greenvale Farm offers spacious, self-contained, ground floor accommodation with a twin or double room, en suite facilities, television and Wi-fi access. A hearty breakfast is served to set you up for the day and, if you're lucky, you can have freshly-laid eggs.

Recommended in the area

The Hillier Arboretum; Mottisfont Abbey and Gardens; Florence Nightingale's Grave

A lone fallow deer stands alert on the plains near Stoney Cross, New Forest National Park

White Star Tavern, Dining and Rooms

★★★★★ ◎◎ INN

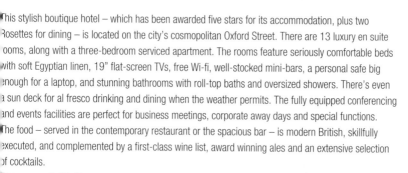

Address	28 Oxford Street, SOUTHAMPTON, SO14 3DJ
Tel:	023 8082 1990
Fax:	023 8090 4982
Email:	reservations@whitestartavern.co.uk
Website:	www.whitestartavern.co.uk
Map ref:	3 SU41
Directions:	M3 junct 14 onto A33, towards Ocean Village
Rooms:	13 en suite S £89-£109 D £89-£169
Notes:	Wi-fi ⊗

This stylish boutique hotel – which has been awarded five stars for its accommodation, plus two Rosettes for dining – is located on the city's cosmopolitan Oxford Street. There are 13 luxury en suite rooms, along with a three-bedroom serviced apartment. The rooms feature seriously comfortable beds with soft Egyptian linen, 19" flat-screen TVs, free Wi-fi, well-stocked mini-bars, a personal safe big enough for a laptop, and stunning bathrooms with roll-top baths and oversized showers. There's even a sun deck for al fresco drinking and dining when the weather permits. The fully equipped conferencing and events facilities are perfect for business meetings, corporate away days and special functions. The food – served in the contemporary restaurant or the spacious bar – is modern British, skillfully executed, and complemented by a first-class wine list, award winning ales and an extensive selection of cocktails.

Recommended in the area

Hall of Aviation; Maritime Museum; Southampton Art Gallery

Giffard House

★★★★★ GUESTHOUSE

Address 50 Christchurch Road,
WINCHESTER, SO23 9SU

Tel: 01962 852628

Fax: 01962 856722

Email: giffardhotel@aol.com

Website: www.giffardhotel.co.uk

Map ref: 3 SU42

Directions: M3 junct 11, at rdbt 3rd exit onto A333
St Cross road for 1m. Pass BP garage on right, take
next left then 2nd right. 150mtrs on left

Rooms: 13 en suite (1 fmly) (4 GF) S £69 D £89-£135

Notes: Wi-fi ⊗ **Parking:** 13 **Closed:** 24 Dec-2 Jan

Visitors to this stunning 19th-century Victorian house, located a ten-minute walk from Winchester town centre, with its many amenities and points of interest, will find the recently refurbished establishment maintained to a high standard. Conference facilities are available, making it a good choice for business as well as leisure travellers. Inside, it combines elegance with comfort, and the well-equipped en suite bedrooms come with crisp white bed linen, luxurious bathrooms, beverage trays, direct-dial telephones and TV and radio facilities as standard. A family room and ground-floor rooms are available – one room is large enough for wheelchair users and grab rails can be provided – and for special occasions there is a suite. Guests are welcome to make use of Giffard House's garden, as well as the fully licensed bar, which is set in the elegant conservatory. Traditional breakfasts are served in the dining room and a self-service continental option is also on offer. Special diets can be catered for by arrangement. Wi-fi access is available, and there is ample free parking in the car park.

Recommended in the area

Winchester Cathedral; St Cross Hospital; Winchester City Mill (NT)

River Wye at Hereford

Somerville House

★★★★★ GUEST ACCOMMODATION

Address 12 Bodenham Road, HEREFORD, HR1 2TS
Tel: 01432 273991
Fax: 01432 268719
Email: enquiries@somervillehouse.net
Website: www.somervillehouse.net
Map ref: 2 SO53
Directions: A465, at Aylestone Hill rdbt towards city centre, left at Southbank Rd, leading to Bodenham Rd
Rooms: 12 en suite (2 fmly rooms) (1 GF) S £50-£55 D £65-£99 **Notes:** Wi-fi ⊗ **Parking:** 10

An imposing Victorian villa set in a quiet tree-lined road, Somerville House is run by Bill and Rosie, who provide modern boutique-style accommodation. The house is just a short walk from the railway station, bus station and Hereford city centre shops, restaurants and main attractions, and off-street parking is available within the grounds. To relax after a busy day, guests can sit with a drink on the terrace or in the lovely lounge with its open fire and later, perhaps, take a stroll around the garden. A mixture of large, luxury and smaller character bedrooms all have high quality en suite bathrooms, Wi-fi access, flat-screen Freeview televisions, ironing equipment, hairdryers, hospitality trays and mini bars. Luxury rooms are more spacious and have large beds, CD and DVD players. Flavours of Herefordshire are supported in-house, so enjoy locally produced drinks and snacks, such as Lulham Court wine and Tyrrell's crisps. The dining room has contemporary appeal, and here the full English breakfast is a speciality, using quality, locally sourced, organic produce with vegetarian options. There are also delicious local organic yoghurts, fruit juices, cereals, muesli and fresh fruit. Continental breakfast and healthy options are also offered. Special breaks are available.

Recommended in the area

Hereford Cathedral, Mappa Mundi & Chained Library; Hereford Museum; beautiful country walks

Bluebells in Wintergreen Wood, Knebworth Country Park

Farmhouse B&B

★★★★★ BED & BREAKFAST

Address Hawkins Grange Farm, Hawkins Hall Lane,
DATCHWORTH, Knebworth, SG3 6TF
Tel: 01438 813369
Email: mail@hawkinsgrangefarm.com
Website: www.hawkinsgrangefarm.com
Map ref: 3 TL21 **Directions:** A1(M) junct 7 onto A602
(Hertford). From Bragbury End right onto Bragbury Ln, 1m, 50yds
on left after phone box **Rooms:** 3 (2 en suite) (1 pri facs)
S £35-£45 D £70 **Notes:** Wi-fi ⊗ **Parking:** 8

This extensively refurbished house is set amid beautiful
countryside, yet is within easy reach of Hertford, Stevenage and
Welwyn Garden City. The tastefully designed bedrooms are comfortably furnished and come with an
abundance of thoughtful extras. All have good views over the open countryside. Jane's locally sourced
organic breakfasts offer full English, vegetarian/vegan and continental choices, including Braughing
sausages and Datchworth honey.

Recommended in the area

Hertford; Datchworth Museum; Welwyn

Knebworth House

ISLE OF MAN

Cashtal-Yn-Ard burial chamber

Aaron House

★ ★ ★ ★ ★ ⛫ GUESTHOUSE

Address The Promenade,
PORT ST MARY, Isle of Man, IM9 5DE
Tel: 01624 835702
Fax: 01624 837731
Website: www.aaronhouse.co.uk
Map ref: 5 SC26
Directions: Follow signs for South & Port St Mary, left at Post Office. House in centre of Promenade
Rooms: 4 (3 en suite) (1 pri facs) **D** £70-£118
Notes: ⊗ 🐾 12yrs **Closed:** 21 Dec-3 Jan

Overlooking Chapel Bay's stunning harbour, this family-run establishment lovingly recreates the property's original Victorian style, with exquisite interior design, cast-iron fireplaces in the public rooms and sparklingly polished period furniture. Delicious home-made cakes are served on arrival and the luxurious bedrooms have a hot water bottle placed in your bed at night. Breakfast is a treat and evening meals are offered in the winter only (Monday–Friday). There is free parking 70 yards away.

Recommended in the area

Cregneash Folk Village; Victorian Steam Railway; Sound and Calf of Man (bird sanctuary)

Santon, Isle of Man

ISLE OF WIGHT

View to The Needles from the rocket testing site

The Old House

★★★★ 🛏 BED & BREAKFAST

Address Gotten Manor, Gotten Lane, CHALE,
Ventnor, PO38 2HQ
Tel: 01983 551368 & 07746 453398
Email: aa@gottenmanor.co.uk
Website: www.gottenmanor.co.uk
Map ref: 3 SZ47 **Directions:** 1m N of Chale. Turn right off
B3399 onto Gotten Ln (opp chapel), house at end
Rooms: 2 en suite **S** £70-£90 **D** £80-£100
Notes: Wi-fi ⊗ 🚫 12yrs **Parking:** 3

The Old House is the original part of Gotten Manor, a country
house dating back around 1,000 years, which sits well off
the beaten track beneath St Catherine's Down. It is run today as a two-bedroom, self-contained bed
and breakfast, surrounded by a walled garden full of fruit trees. The bedrooms have wooden floors
and cast-iron baths and the sitting room has an open fire. Breakfast – made from local and organic
produce, along with homemade preserves – is served in the old creamery.

Recommended in the area

Blackgang Chine; St Catherine's Down; Ventnor

Early morning views over Sandown from Culver Down

The Lawns

★★★★ GUEST ACCOMMODATION

Address 72 Broadway, SANDOWN,
         PO36 9AA
Tel: 01983 402549
Email: lawnshotel@aol.com
Website: www.lawnshotelisleofwight.co.uk
Map ref: 3 SZ58
Directions: On A3055 N of town centre
Rooms: 13 en suite (2 fmly rooms) (2 GF)
S £40-£50 D £68-£90
Notes: Wi-fi ⊗ Parking: 13
Closed: Nov-Jan

A warm welcome always awaits you at The Lawns, which has been lovingly upgraded by owners Nick and Stella to provide every home comfort. The Lawns was built in 1865 and stands in its own southwest-facing gardens offering ample parking. Situated in the pleasing area of Sandown, it is just a short walk away from a blue-flag beach, public transport and the town centre, with its restaurants and shops, and is an ideal base from which to explore the rest of the island. Other local attractions on offer include the pier, go-karting, crazy golf and the Tiger and Big Cat Sanctuary, as well as many opportunities to take part in water sports. The Lawns has a comfortable lounge, with Freeview TV and a selection of games available, as well as a bar. Evening meals are available by arrangement. Service is friendly and attentive, and the bedrooms, two of which are on the ground floor, include three superior rooms. All are comfortably equipped with flat-screen TVs and hospitality trays. All bathrooms are of a very high standard and include wall-mounted hairdryers.

Recommended in the area

Isle of Wight Zoo; Dinosaur Isle; Sandown Pier

The Leconfield

★ ★ ★ ★ ★ ◎ ⌂ GUEST ACCOMMODATION

Address   85 Leeson Road, Upper Bonchurch, VENTNOR,
          PO38 1PU
Tel: 01983 852196
Email: enquiries@leconfieldhotel.com
Website: www.leconfieldhotel.com
Map ref: 3 SZ57
Directions: On A3055, 3m from Old Shanklin village
Rooms: 11 en suite (3 GF) S £45-£180 D £80-£220
Notes: Wi-fi ⊗ 🐾 16yrs
Parking: 14 Closed: 24-26 Dec & 3-27 Jan

Paul, Cheryl and their small team welcome you to their delightful
Victorian house. The Leconfield is elevated 400-feet above sea level and nestles into St Boniface Down
in an Area of Outstanding Natural Beauty. There are views of the sea from nearly all the bedrooms,
the sitting rooms, dining room, conservatory and garden. The Leconfield is on the island's south side
and its unique micro climate is perfect for a break in the quieter winter months, while in the summer
months guests can enjoy the heated outdoor swimming pool in the delightful gardens; a strictly
adults-only oasis. Luxurious, individually designed bedrooms, some at ground-floor level, are equipped
with en suite facilities, TVs with DVD players, hairdryers, hospitality trays, bathrobes and quality
complimentary toiletries. A hearty breakfast prepared from local produce and free-range eggs is served
in the Seascape Dining Room with its panoramic sea views. After a day of exploring the island's many
treasures you'll be welcomed back to an AA Rosette standard evening meal with your choice from a
wide selection of wines and other drinks. Your only distraction from the relaxing ambience might be the
coming and going of ships on the open seas.

Recommended in the area

Ventnor Gardens; Carisbrooke Castle; Osborne House

St Maur

★★★★ GUEST ACCOMMODATION

Address Castle Road,
VENTNOR, PO38 1LG
Tel: 01983 852570 & 853645
Fax: 01983 852306
Email: sales@stmaur.co.uk
Website: www.stmaur.co.uk
Map ref: 3 SZ57
Directions: Exit A3055 at end of Park Av onto
Castle Rd, premises 150yds on left
Rooms: 9 en suite (2 fmly rooms) **D** £80-£140
Notes: ⊗ ⛄ 5yrs **Parking:** 9 **Closed:** Dec

Built in 1876, this Victorian villa has been run as a guest house by the same family since 1966. St Maur occupies an elevated position overlooking Ventnor Park in one of the prettiest parts of the island, with sandy beaches, idyllic countryside, quaint villages and a variety of entertainment on the doorstep. The large sub-tropical gardens are a delight, with a profusion of colour and wonderful floral fragrances all year round. In summer the lawn provides the perfect place for soaking up the sun. Most of the ample bedrooms – with double, twin or queen-size beds – have been refurbished and all have good size bathrooms, TVs, tea- and coffee-making facilities, clock radios, complimentary toiletries and hairdryers. Some rooms have sea views and balconies or decking. A spacious lounge on the grand Victorian scale overlooks the garden and provides a quiet place to sit and relax. Alternatively there is a cosy licensed bar where you can enjoy a drink before or after your six-course dinner. A comprehensive full English breakfast gets the day off to a satisfying start. Special breaks including car ferry are available, plus there's a 10 per cent discount for over 55s on stays of a week or more during the summer.

Recommended in the area

Appuldurcombe House; Blackgang Chine Fantasy Park; Ventnor Botanic Gardens

KENT

Canterbury Cathedral

Boys Hall

★★★★★ GUEST ACCOMMODATION

Address Boys Hall Road, ASHFORD, TN24 0LA
Tel: 01233 633772
Fax: 01233 631447
Email: enquiries@boyshall.co.uk
Website: www.boyshall.co.uk
Map ref: 4 TR04
Rooms: 8 (6 en suite) (2 pri facs) (1 fmly)
S £87-£169 D £99-£199
Notes: Wi-fi ⊗ Parking: 42

Boys Hall is one of the most beautiful buildings in Ashford. Built in the 17th century, it is a Grade II listed property which retains many of its original Jacobean features, sitting in over three acres of glorious landscaped gardens. All the bedrooms at Boys Hall are individually designed and have tea- and coffee-making facilities, TVs and DVD players, and lovely garden views. Free Wi-fi is available throughout the house. Boys Hall Manor is just a short drive from junction 10 of the M20, while Ashford International railway station is less than 10 minutes away.

Recommended in the area

Leeds Castle; Canterbury Cathedral; Sissinghurst Castle Garden

House of Agnes

★★★★ GUEST ACCOMMODATION

Address 71 Saint Dunstans Street,
         CANTERBURY, CT2 8BN
Tel: 01227 472185 Fax: 01227 470478
Email: info@houseofagnes.co.uk
Website: www.houseofagnes.co.uk
Map ref: 4 TR15
Directions: On A290 between London Rd & Orchard St, 300mtrs from West Gate
Rooms: 8 en suite (1 fmly) S £60-£90
D £75-£130 Notes: Wi-fi ⊗ 🐾 5yrs Parking: 8 Closed: 24-25 Dec

The original charm and character of this 14th-century property, just a short stroll from the city centre, remains after a refurbishment to create luxury accommodation. Each of the individually themed rooms benefits from high-quality bed linen, flat-screen TV and DVD player and free Wi-fi. MP3 docking stations and a DVD library are also available. A heritage garden adds to the appeal of this historically significant property, which features in Charles Dickens's novel *David Copperfield*.

Recommended in the area

Canterbury Cathedral; Whitstable; Herne Bay

Magnolia House

★★★★★ GUEST ACCOMMODATION

Address   36 St Dunstan's Terrace,
              CANTERBURY, CT2 8AX
Tel: 01227 765121 & 07776 236459
Fax: 01227 765121
Email: info@magnoliahousecanterbury.co.uk
Website: www.magnoliahousecanterbury.co.uk
Map ref: 4 TR15 **Directions:** A2 E onto A2050 for
city centre, 1st rdbt left signed University of Kent. St
Dunstan's Ter 3rd right
Rooms: 6 en suite (1 GF) **Notes:** Wi-fi ⊗ ⛵ 12yrs **Parking:** 5

This charming late Georgian property, set in a quiet residential street just 10 minutes' stroll from Canterbury town centre, provides superbly appointed en suite bedrooms. Each is equipped with digital TV and Wi-fi, as well as a fridge containing complimentary wine, mineral water and fresh milk. Generous breakfasts based on fresh local produce are served in the dining room overlooking the attractive walled garden. Guests may relax in the sitting room or garden.

Recommended in the area

Wingham Wildlife Park; Herne Bay; Canterbury Castle

Court Lodge B&B

★★★★ GUEST ACCOMMODATION

Address   Court Lodge, Church Road, Oare,
              FAVERSHAM, ME13 0QB
Tel/Fax: 01795 591543
Email: d.wheeldon@btconnect.com
Website: www.faversham.org/courtlodge
Map ref: 4 TR06 **Directions:** A2 onto B2045, left
onto The Street, right onto Church Rd, 0.25m on left
Rooms: 2 (1 en suite) (1 pri facs) **S** £50 **D** £70
Notes: Wi-fi ⊗ **Parking:** 10 🐾

This sympathetically restored 16th-century listed farmhouse stands in 1.5 acres of gardens amid arable farmland – the perfect place to relax. The spacious rooms have private bathrooms, TV, and tea- and coffee-making facilities. Breakfast is served in the farmhouse kitchen, using the best of local produce including fish and home-made preserves. Court Lodge is ideal for those visiting Oare Creek or walking the Saxon Shore Way. Several pubs and restaurants are only a short distance away. Ample parking is available.

Recommended in the area

Faversham; Canterbury; Whitstable

Botany Bay

The Relish

★★★★★ GUEST ACCOMMODATION

Address   4 Augusta Gardens,
          FOLKESTONE, CT20 2RR
Tel: 01303 850952
Fax: 01303 850958
Email: reservations@hotelrelish.co.uk
Website: www.hotelrelish.co.uk
Map ref: 4 TR23
Directions: Off A2033 (Sandgate Rd)
Rooms: 10 en suite (2 fmly rooms)
S £69 D £95-£145 Notes: Wi-fi ⊗ Closed: 22 Dec-2 Jan

You will get a warm welcome at this stylish Victorian property overlooking Augusta Gardens in the fashionable West End of town. On arrival you will be greeted with a complimentary glass of wine or beer, while fresh coffee, tea and home-made cakes are available throughout your stay. The bedrooms feature lovely coordinated fabrics, great showers and all have DVD players. Public rooms include a modern lounge-dining room and a terrace where breakfast is served during summer.

Recommended in the area

Dover Castle; Romney, Hythe and Dymchurch Railway; Canterbury

Seabrook House

★★★★ GUEST ACCOMMODATION

Address   81 Seabrook Road, HYTHE, CT21 5QW
Tel: 01303 269282
Fax: 01303 237822
Email: seabrookhouse@hotmail.co.uk
Website: www.seabrook-house.co.uk
Map ref: 4 TR13
Directions: 0.9m E of Hythe on A259
Rooms: 13 en suite (4 fmly rooms) (4 GF) S £30-£40
D £55-£65 Notes: ⊗ Parking: 13

This striking Victorian property, easily recognised by the heavily timber-framed frontage and pretty gardens, is conveniently located for the M20 and Eurotunnel. Many of the art-deco style bedrooms have lovely sea views. These spacious en suite rooms, with their attractive decor and furnishings, also have hospitality trays, TV and hairdryers. A memorable full English breakfast sets you up for the ferries from Folkestone or Dover or for sightseeing in the local area, and there are plenty of comfortable spots for relaxation, including a sunny conservatory and an elegant lounge.

Recommended in the area

Romney, Hythe and Dymchurch Railway; Dover Castle; Port Lympne Animal Park; Royal Military Canal

Merzie Meadows

★ ★ ★ ★ ★ BED & BREAKFAST
Address Hunton Road, MARDEN, TN12 9SL
Tel: 01622 820500 & 07762 713077
Fax: 01622 820500
Email: pamela@merziemeadows.co.uk
Website: www.merziemeadows.co.uk
Map ref: 4 TQ74
Directions: A229 onto B2079 for Marden, 1st right
onto Underlyn Ln, 2.5m large Chainhurst sign, right
onto drive
Rooms: 2 en suite (1 suite) (2 GF) S £80 D £90-£100
Notes: Wi-fi ⊗ ✦ 15yrs Parking: 4 Closed: mid Dec-mid Feb

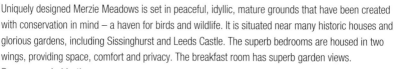

Uniquely designed Merzie Meadows is set in peaceful, idyllic, mature grounds that have been created with conservation in mind – a haven for birds and wildlife. It is situated near many historic houses and glorious gardens, including Sissinghurst and Leeds Castle. The superb bedrooms are housed in two wings, providing space, comfort and privacy. The breakfast room has superb garden views.
Recommended in the area
Sissinghurst Castle Garden (NT); Leeds Castle; The Hop Farm Country Park; Yalding Organic Gardens

Danehurst House

★ ★ ★ ★ ★ 🛏 BED & BREAKFAST
Address 41 Lower Green Road, Rusthall,
            TUNBRIDGE WELLS, TN4 8TW
Tel: 01892 527739
Fax: 01892 514804
Email: info@danehurst.net
Website: www.danehurst.net
Map ref: 4 TQ53
Directions: 1.5m W of Tunbridge Wells in Rusthall.
Off A264 onto Coach Rd & Lower Green Rd
Rooms: 4 en suite (1 fmly)
Notes: ⊗ ✦ 8yrs Parking: 6 Closed: Xmas

Angela and Michael Godbold's spacious Victorian home stands just west of the historic spa town of Tunbridge Wells. There is a comfortable, relaxing drawing room, and the Victorian-style conservatory is a delightful setting for breakfast, whether full English, fish, cold meats or continental. The four cosy bedrooms are en suite, and have a wealth of thoughtful extras and notably comfortable beds. No pets.
Recommended in the area
Groombridge Place; Hever Castle; Chartwell (NT)

LANCASHIRE

View towards Totridge in the Forest of Bowland

Bona Vista

★★★★ GUEST ACCOMMODATION

Address 104-106 Queens Promenade,
BLACKPOOL, FY2 9NX
Tel: 01253 351396
Fax: 01253 594985
Email: enquiries@bonavistahotel.com
Website: www.bonavistahotel.com
Map ref: 5 SD33
Directions: 0.25m N of Uncle Toms
Cabin & Castle Casino
Rooms: 19 (17 en suite) (4 fmly rooms) **S** £27-£35 **D** £54-£70
Notes: Wi-fi Parking: 16

The Bona Vista has a seafront location on Queens Promenade north of the town centre. It's a peaceful spot only minutes away from the attractions of the town, which can easily be reached by tram thanks to a new tram stop right opposite the guest house. You can expect all the usual facilities at The Bona Vista, along with a delightful sun lounge running the full width of the building which is ideal for viewing the Illuminations. Meals are available in the modern and airy dining room, with menus changing daily and personal dietary requirements catered for. If you prefer a lighter meal, snacks are served in the cosy bar. A major benefit of staying at The Bona Vista, particularly during Illuminations time, is the on-site, off-street parking. The owners strive to create a relaxed and friendly environment for all guests – from single people and couples through to families – but do not welcome hen and stag parties, which are more associated with the town centre.

Recommended in the area

Blackpool Tower; North Pier; Blackpool Pleasure Beach

Blackpool Tower

Bradgate Country Park

The Manners Arms

★★★★ ◎ RESTAURANT WITH ROOMS

Address Croxton Road, KNIPTON,
          Grantham, NG32 1RH
Tel: 01476 879222
Fax: 01476 879228
Email: info@mannersarms.com
Website: www.mannersarms.com
Map ref: 3 SK83 **Directions:** Off A607 into Knipton
Rooms: 10 en suite (1 fmly)
Notes: Wi-fi **Parking:** 60

This delightful country house is the perfect place to enjoy a break in the picturesque Vale of Belvoir. It was originally built for the 6th Duke of Rutland as a hunting lodge in the 1880s, and remained in the duke's family until the 1950s when it was converted into a hotel and restaurant. There is plenty to recommend at the Manners Arms, not least the blazing fire in the cosy bar, the beautiful garden with its stunning countryside views, the light and airy conservatory, and the stylish restaurant with its lovely atmosphere and good food. The Manners Arms is also fully licensed for civil ceremonies.

Recommended in the area

Belvoir Castle; countryside walks; Barnsdale Gardens

Foxton Locks

LINCOLNSHIRE

Saltfleet Haven

The Brownlow Arms

★★★★★ ⊛ INN

Address	High Road, HOUGH-ON-THE-HILL, Grantham, NG32 2AZ
Tel:	01400 250234
Fax:	01400 271193
Email:	paulandlorraine@thebrownlowarms.com
Website:	www.thebrownlowarms.com

Map ref: 8 SK94 **Rooms:** 4 en suite **S** £65-£70 **D** £96-£110 **Notes:** Wi-fi ⊗ ⚑ 12yrs **Parking:** 20 **Closed:** 25-27 Dec & 31 Dec-20 Jan

This 17th-century country inn enjoys a peaceful location in the heart of a picturesque village. Once owned by Lord Brownlow, today it offers tranquillity and relaxation alongside exceptional modern comforts and country hospitality. It is tastefully decorated throughout, and all the comfortable bedrooms are en suite with LCD flat-screen TVs and power/drench showers. The friendly bar serves real ales, while chef Paul Vidic works with premium local produce to create some imaginative modern British dishes. There's also a luxurious lounge and a landscaped terrace.

Recommended in the area

Belton House; Belvoir Castle; Lincoln Cathedral

All Saints Church on the Viking Way in Walesby

Winteringham Fields

★ ★ ★ ★ ★ ◎◎ 🛏 RESTAURANT WITH ROOMS

Address 1 Silver Street, WINTERINGHAM, DN15
9ND
Tel/fax: 01724 733096 / 733898
Email: reception@winteringhamfields.co.uk
Website: www.winteringhamfields.co.uk
Map ref: 8 SE92
Directions: In village centre at x-rds
Rooms: 11 en suite (2 fmly) (3 GF)
S £115-£145 **D** £145-£220
Parking: 14 **Closed:** 25 Dec for 2 wks, last wk Oct, 2 wks Aug

This highly regarded restaurant-with-rooms is housed in a 16th-century manor house with a cellar that dates back to the 1300s. Its location, deep in the countryside in a quiet village, gives it a real feeling of seclusion, yet it is just six miles west of the Humber Bridge, which can be seen from the pretty, rambling grounds. Here, guests can enjoy a peaceful aperitif or afternoon tea. The public rooms and bedrooms, some housed in renovated barns and cottages, are delightfully cosseting and styled with real flair and individuality. Some of the bedrooms have been recently refurbished, and all have their own special design features, including walk-in wardrobes, beamed ceilings, roll-top or aromatherapy baths, four-posters and fully fitted kitchens. The pièce de résistance, chef-patron Colin McGurran's award-winning food, is modern European in style and artfully presented. Served in the lavish, richly decorated restaurant, which has a stained-glass dome in the ceiling and smart, well-spaced tables, it emphasises the sourcing of fresh, local produce: fish is delivered daily, game in season comes from nearby shoots, and herbs and vegetables are grown in the restaurant's own garden. As well as a six-course 'Menu surprise', there is an ever-changing a la carte.

Recommended in the area

The Deep, Hull; Humber Bridge Country Park; Sewerby Hall & Gardens

LONDON

St Paul's Cathedral and the Millennium Bridge

The New Inn

★★★ INN

Address 2 Allitsen Road, St Johns Wood,
LONDON, NW8 6LA
Tel: 020 7722 0726
Fax: 020 7722 0653
Email: thenewinn@gmail.com
Website: www.newinnlondon.co.uk
Map ref: 3 TQ38
Directions: Off A41 by St Johns Wood tube station
onto Acacia Rd, last right, to end on corner
Rooms: 5 en suite S £85 D £85 **Notes:** Wi-fi ⊗

Built in 1810, this traditional inn is located in a leafy suburb just a stroll from Regents Park, and close to many central London places of interest. The en suite bedrooms are appointed to a high standard and are popular with business and leisure guests alike. Rooms are equipped with TVs, free Wi-fi, hairdryers and tea- and coffee-making facilities. A good choice of English ales, continental beers, wines and spirits is served alongside Thai and English cuisine in the bar lounge. Live music is played at weekends.
Recommended in the area
Madame Tussaud's; London Zoo; Lord's Cricket Ground; Camden Market

San Domenico House

★★★★★ GUEST ACCOMMODATION

Address 29-31 Draycott Place, LONDON, SW3 2SH
Tel: 020 7581 5757
Fax: 020 7584 1348
Email: info@sandomenicohouse.com
Website: www.sandomenicohouse.com
Map ref: 3 TQ38
Rooms: 13 en suite
Notes: ⊗ on premises

This newly extended and redesigned property, located in the heart of fashionable Chelsea, just a short walk from Sloane Square underground, offers luxurious accommodation and friendly, personalised service. The individually styled bedrooms and suites, all with antique and period pieces and rich soft furnishings, feature well-appointed marble en suites complete with Italian toiletries and bathrobes. An extensive room-service menu is available, and there is a sumptuous drawing room where guests can relax and enjoy works of art. Breakfast is served either in guests' bedrooms or in the elegant lower ground-floor dining room.
Recommended in the area
Shopping in Sloane Street; King's Road; Royal Hospital Chelsea

The Cottage

★★★★ GUEST ACCOMMODATION

Address   150-152 High Street, CRANFORD,
          Hounslow, TW5 9WB
Tel: 020 8897 1815
Email: info@the-cottage.eu
Website: www.the-cottage.eu
Map ref: 3 TQ17
Directions: M4 junct 3, A312 towards Feltham,
left at lights, left after 1st pub on left
Rooms: 20 en suite (4 fmly rooms) (12 GF)
S £75 D £95
Notes: Wi-fi ⊗ Parking: 20 Closed: 24-26 Dec & 31 Dec-1 Jan

This lovely 19th-century family-run property is just a few minutes' drive from Heathrow Airport, yet it benefits from a peaceful location. Guests here can rely on a friendly atmosphere combined with spacious and comfortable accommodation. The en suite bedrooms are tastefully decorated in a country style, using neutral colours and wooden furniture, and all come with a range of home comforts such as hospitality tray, TV, free Wi-fi, alarm clock and hairdryer. Some of the rooms in the main house, which include family rooms, are on the ground floor. There are now six newer bedrooms located at the rear of the landscaped garden, where guests will find fruit trees, shrubs and flowerbeds. These rooms are connected to the main building by a covered walkway overlooking the stunning courtyard, and all have beamed ceilings, fridges, ironing facilities and luxury bathrooms with power showers. Breakfast, cooked or continental, is served in the stylish dining room, which opens on to a conservatory overlooking the garden. Fully secure CCTV-covered parking is free for those in residence. Be sure to mention the AA when booking at The Cottage for a good discount.

Recommended in the area

Hampton Court Palace; Legoland; Kew Gardens

Eros Statue in Piccadilly Circus

NORFOLK

Thurne Mill beside the River Thurne, Norfolk Broads National Park

Shrublands Farm

★ ★ ★ ★ FARMHOUSE

Address   Church Street, Northrepps,
          CROMER, NR27 0AA
Tel/Fax: 01263 579297
Email: youngman@farming.co.uk
Website: www.shrublandsfarm.com
Map ref: 4 TG24
Directions: Off A149 to Northrepps, through village,
past Foundry Arms, cream house 50yds on left
Rooms: 2 (1 en suite) (1 pri facs)
S £43-£47 D £66-£74 Notes: ⊗ 🐾 12yrs Parking: 5

Shrublands is a working farm set in mature gardens amid 300 acres of arable farmland, an ideal base for exploring the coast and countryside of rural north Norfolk. Traditional hospitality is a distinguishing feature at the 18th-century farmhouse, with good cooking using home-grown and fresh local produce. Breakfast is served at a large table in the dining room, and there is also a cosy lounge, with a log fire, books and a television. The bedrooms have TVs, radio alarms and tea and coffee facilities. No pets.

Recommended in the area

Blickling Hall and Felbrigg Hall (NT); Sandy beaches at Cromer and Overstrand; Blakeney Point

Kadina

★ ★ ★ ★ BED & BREAKFAST

Address   Warren Close, High Kelling,
          HOLT, NR25 6QX
Tel: 01263 710116 & 07900 928729
Fax: 01263 710116
Email: enquiries@kadinanorfolk.co.uk
Website: www.kadinanorfolk.co.uk
Map ref: 4 TG03 Directions: Turn off A148 onto
Bridge Rd, turn right onto Warren Rd. Right again
onto Warren Close, Kadina fourth on left
Rooms: 2 en suite (1 GF) S £50-£55 D £70-£75 Notes: ⊗ 🐾 Parking: 5

A warm welcome and a homely, peaceful atmosphere is guaranteed at Kadina, set in the wooded village of High Kelling. A stay at Kadina begins with afternoon tea and homemade cake, and a chance to pick up some tips from owner Allison Graves on the many coastal and countryside attractions on the doorstep. Kadina has two spacious double en suite rooms, tastefully decorated to a high standard and with many thoughtful extras. High quality evening meals are served by request Monday to Thursday.

Recommended in the area

The Poppyline, North Norfolk Steam Railway; Felbrigg Hall; North Norfolk Wildlife Trust Reserve at Cley

Edmar Lodge

★★★ GUEST ACCOMMODATION

Address   64 Earlham Road, NORWICH, NR2 3DF
Tel: 01603 615599
Fax: 01603 495599
Email: mail@edmarlodge.co.uk
Website: www.edmarlodge.co.uk
Map ref: 4 TG20 Directions: Off A47 S bypass onto
B1108 Earlham Rd, follow university and hospital
signs Rooms: 5 en suite (1 fmly)
S £38-£45 D £45-£50 Notes: Wi-fi Parking: 6

Located just a ten-minute walk from the city centre, this friendly, family-run guest house boasts a convenient location and ample private parking. The individually decorated en suite bedrooms, including one family room, are smartly appointed and well equipped, and there are DVD players and a collection of films that guests may borrow. Freshly prepared breakfasts offer great choice and are served in the cosy dining room. A microwave and refrigerator along with plates and utensils are provided for those who wish to bring in food later. Guests are also welcome to enjoy the pretty garden.

Recommended in the area

Norwich Cathedral; Norfolk Broads; Norwich Castle

Gothic House Bed & Breakfast

★★★★ GUEST ACCOMMODATION

Address   King's Head Yard, Magdalen Street,
              NORWICH, NR3 1JE
Tel: 01603 631879
Email: charvey649@aol.com
Website: www.gothic-house-norwich.com
Map ref: 4 TG20 Directions: Follow signs for A147,
turn off at rdbt past flyover into Whitefriars. Right again
onto Fishergate, at end, right onto Magdalen St
Rooms: 2 (2 pri facs) S £65 D £95
Notes: Wi-fi ⊗ ⛶ 18yrs Parking: 2 Closed: Feb

Set in a quiet courtyard in the heart of the most historic part
of Norwich, Gothic House is a Grade II listed building barely five minutes' walk from the cathedral. The area has a wealth of gracious Georgian and earlier architecture. Gothic House has been lovingly restored and retains much of its original character. With Wi-fi access available, the bedrooms are spacious, individually decorated and stylishly presented. Breakfast is served in the elegant dining room.

Recommended in the area

Norwich Castle; Norwich Aviation Museum; Norwich Gallery

A field of lavender in West Newton

Old Thorn Barn

★ ★ ★ ★ GUEST ACCOMMODATION

Address	Corporation Farm, Wymondham Road, Hethel, NORWICH, NR14 8EU
Tel:	01953 607785 & 07894 203208
Fax:	01953 601909
Email:	enquires@oldthornbarn.co.uk
Website:	www.oldthornbarn.co.uk
Map ref:	4 TG20

Directions: 6m SW of Norwich. Follow signs for Lotus Cars from A11or B1113, on Wymondham Rd
Rooms: 7 en suite (7 GF) Notes: Wi-fi ⊗ Parking: 12

Reconstruction of a group of derelict buildings has resulted in this delightful conversion. The substantial 17th-century barns and stables feature a stylish open-plan dining room, where you can linger over breakfast around individual oak tables. At the other end of the room there is a cosy lounge area with a wood-burning stove. Antique pine furniture and smart en suites are a feature of the spacious bedrooms which have tea and coffee trays, trouser presses and hairdryers.

Recommended in the area

Fairhaven Woodland and Water Garden; Pettitts Animal Adventure Park; Wolterton Park

Holly Lodge

★ ★ ★ ★ ★ 🛏 BED & BREAKFAST

Address	The Street, THURSFORD, NR21 0AS
Tel/Fax:	01328 878465
Email:	info@hollylodgeguesthouse.co.uk
Website:	www.hollylodgeguesthouse.co.uk
Map ref:	4 TF93

Directions: Off A148 into Thursford, village green on left. 2nd driveway on left past green
Rooms: 3 en suite (3 GF) S £70-£110 D £90-£120
Notes: Wi-fi ⊗ 🚭 14yrs Parking: 5 Closed: Jan

This 18th-century property is situated in a picturesque location surrounded by open farmland. The lovely landscaped gardens include a large sundeck, which overlooks the water gardens, providing a great place to relax. The lodge and its guest cottages have been transformed into a splendid guest house, with stylish ground-floor bedrooms that are individually decorated and beautifully furnished. En suite bathrooms, TVs and lots of thoughtful extras make for a pleasant stay. The attractive public areas are full of character, with flagstone floors, oak beams and open fireplaces.

Recommended in the area

North Norfolk Coast; Thursford Museum; Walsingham

NORTHUMBERLAND

A section of Hadrian's Wall seen from Highshield Crags, Northumberland National Park

Ivy Cottage

★ ★ ★ ★ ★ 🏠 GUEST ACCOMMODATION

Address	1 Croft Gardens, Crookham, CORNHILL-ON-TWEED, TD12 4ST
Tel/Fax:	01890 820667
Email:	stay@ivycottagecrookham.co.uk
Website:	www.ivycottagecrookham.co.uk
Map ref:	10 NT83 **Directions:** 4m E of Cornhill. Off A697 onto B6353 into Crookham

Rooms: 3 (1 en suite) (2 pri facs) (1 GF)
S £47-£55 **D** £70-£88 **Notes:** 🐕 8yrs **Parking:** 2

This pristine stone-built modern cottage is testament to the many years spent in the hospitality industry by owner Doreen Johnson, and guests soon feel the benefit of her experience and dedication. Set in delightful gardens, the summerhouse provides a welcome spot in which to take tea on fine afternoons. Inside, everything is bright and spotless, and the three spacious bedrooms offer a choice of furnishings – the downstairs room is smart and modern, one room upstairs is beautifully done out in antique pine, and the new Premier Room has a spacious layout with a huge bed. Each room has fresh flowers, crisp embroidered bedding, home-baked biscuits and tea-making facilities, plus its own private bathroom with a deep tub, Crabtree & Evelyn toiletries, huge terry towels and bathrobes. Breakfasts, served in the formal dining room or in the farmhouse-style kitchen, with its Aga cooking range, are splendid. Whichever room is used, the feast always includes local free-range eggs, organic produce where possible, home-made preserves, freshly squeezed orange juice and home-baked bread made from stone-ground flour from nearby Heatherslaw Mill. The sumptuous guests' sitting room has a log burning stove in the winter. Ivy Cottage is perfectly located for exploring the Northumberland coast and the Cheviot Hills.

Recommended in the area

Holy Island; Alnwick Castle & Gardens; Flodden Battlefield

Pheasant Inn

★★★★ INN

Address Stannersburn, HEXHAM, NE48 1DD
Tel: 01434 240382
Fax: 01434 240382
Email: stay@thepheasantinn.com
Website: www.thepheasantinn.com
Map ref: 6 NY78
Directions: 1m S of Falstone. Off B6320 to Kielder
Water, via Bellingham or via Hexham A69 onto
B6320 via Wall-Wark-Bellingham
Rooms: 8 en suite (1 fmly) (5 GF) **S** £50-£55 **D** £90-£95
Notes: ⊗ **Parking:** 40 **Closed:** Xmas

Set close to the magnificent Kielder Water, this classic country inn, built in 1624, has exposed stone
walls, original beams, low ceilings, open fires and a display of old farm implements in the bar. Run
by the welcoming Kershaw family since 1985, the inn was originally a farmhouse and has been
refurbished to a very high standard. The bright, modern en suite bedrooms, some with their own
entrances, are all contained in stone buildings adjoining the inn and are set round a pretty courtyard.
All the rooms, including one family room, are spotless, well equipped, and have tea and coffee facilities,
hairdryer, colour TV and radio-alarm clock; all enjoy delightful country views. Delicious home-cooked
breakfasts and evening meals are served in the bar or in the attractive dining room, or may be taken
in the pretty garden courtyard if the weather permits. Irene and her son Robin are responsible for
the traditional home cooking using local produce and featuring delights such as game pie and roast
Northumbrian lamb, as well as imaginative vegetarian choices. Drying and laundry facilities are
available and, for energetic guests, cycle hire can be arranged.

Recommended in the area

Hadrian's Wall; Scottish Borders region; Northumberland's castles and stately homes

Peth Head Cottage

★★★★ 🛏 BED & BREAKFAST

Address	Juniper, HEXHAM, NE47 0LA
Tel:	01434 673286
Fax:	01434 673038
Email:	peth_head@btopenworld.com
Website:	www.peth-head-cottage.co.uk
Map ref:	7 NY96

Directions: B6306 S from Hexham, 200yds fork right, next left. Continue 3.5m, house 400yds on right after Juniper sign

Rooms: 2 en suite S £30 D £60

Notes: ⊗ Parking: 2

This lovingly maintained rose-covered cottage dates back to 1825 and is popular for its warm welcome, idyllic setting, and home comforts. Tea and hand-made biscuits are offered on arrival, and the delicious home cooking is enjoyed at breakfast too, along with freshly baked bread and delicious homemade preserves. The inviting sandstone cottage is set in peaceful, well-kept gardens. There are two bright, south-facing bedrooms, both overlooking the garden, with shower rooms en suite, a hairdryer, TV, radio alarm and hospitality trays. The relaxing lounge is heavily beamed and furnished with comfortable chairs. Peth Head Cottage is ideally situated for visiting Durham and Newcastle as well as nearby Roman sites, and there are plenty of opportunities for walking and cycling in the area. A wide range of tourist information and maps are on hand for visitors to browse through and plan the day. The owner, Joan Liddle, is an excellent host who knows how to ensure her guests have an enjoyable stay. There is private off-road parking.

Recommended in the area

Beamish Open Air Museum; Hadrian's Wall; the Northumberland coast; Durham Cathedral; Finchale Priory; Lanercost Priory

Warkworth Castle

The Old Manse

★ ★ ★ ★ ★ 🛏 GUEST ACCOMMODATION

Address New Road, Chatton,
ALNWICK, NE66 5PU
Tel: 01668 215343 & 07811 411808
Email: chattonbb@aol.com
Website: www.oldmansechatton.co.uk
Map ref: 10 NT92
Directions: 4m E of Wooler. On B6348 in Chatton
Rooms: 3 en suite (1 GF) S £45-£75 D £85-£110
Notes: Wi-fi 🐾 14yrs **Parking:** 4 **Closed:** Nov-Feb

Built in 1875 and commanding excellent views over the open countryside, this imposing former manse stands on the edge of the pretty village of Chatton between the Cheviot Hills and the scenic North Northumberland Heritage Coast. The Old Manse is approached by a sweeping gravel drive bordered with lawns, roses and evergreen trees. Guests can relax in the secluded rear garden, with its patio, large fish pond, summerhouse and beautiful countryside views. Christine and Tony Lummis are welcoming hosts who do their utmost to ensure that The Old Manse feels like a home from home for all guests. The en suite accommodation is spacious, comfortable and well-equipped, and ranges from the Rosedale Suite with a four-poster bed, to the Buccleuch garden suite which has a sitting room and private patio, to the Mansfield Room with a king-size bed and slightly more contemporary decor. There's a lovely lounge with a stove for the colder months, and hearty breakfasts made from locally sourced produce are served in the elegant conservatory. When the weather is fine, tea and cake can be enjoyed outside on the decked terrace.

Recommended in the area

Alnwick Garden; Chillingham Castle and wild cattle; Bamburgh Castle

OXFORDSHIRE

View from the White Horse

Burford House

★ ★ ★ ★ ★ 🔔 GUEST ACCOMMODATION

Address 99 High Street, BURFORD, OX18 4QA
Tel: 01993 823151
Fax: 01993 823240
Email: stay@burfordhouse.co.uk
Website: www.burfordhouse.co.uk
Map ref: 3 SP21 **Directions:** Off A40 onto A361, on right half way down hill
Rooms: 8 en suite (1 fmly) (1 GF) **S** £124-£186.50 **D** £159-£199
Notes: Wi-fi ⊗

Set in picturesque Burford, a famous Cotswolds market town with many specialist shops, this charming 17th-century house is a landmark on the High Street. Marked by its half-timbered and stone exterior, it is a beautiful building in a great location, offering guests quality, space and comfort. The en suite bedrooms, including one family suite and some rooms with four-posters, are individually decorated and furnished to a very high standard. The host of thoughtful extras includes Witney pure wool blankets, fine cotton bed linen, flat-screen TV/DVDs, bathrobes, Penhaligon's toiletries and complimentary mineral water. Wi-fi is available in all rooms. Guests are invited to make use of the two comfortable lounges, one furnished in contemporary style with a wood-burning stove and the other bright and airy with traditional furnishings and doors leading out to the wisteria-clad courtyard garden. Using fine-quality local produce, wonderful lunches and afternoon teas are available daily in the Centre Stage restaurant, with its theatre posters and pictures, while dinner is also available on Thursday, Friday and Saturday evenings. Morning coffee and afternoon tea may also be enjoyed in the lounges. A full bar service is available, and the house has a fine array of malt whiskies, cognacs and wines.

Recommended in the area

Ashmolean Museum; Batsford Arboretum; Blenheim Palace

Chowle Farmhouse Bed & Breakfast

★★★★ FARMHOUSE

Address FARINGDON, SN7 7SR
Tel: 01367 241688
Email: info@chowlefarmhouse.co.uk
Website: www.chowlefarmhouse.co.uk
Map ref: 3 SU29
Directions: From Faringdon rdbt on A420,
2m W on right. From Watchfield rdbt 1.5m E on left
Rooms: 4 en suite (1 GF) **S** fr £65 **D** fr £85
Notes: Wi-fi **Parking:** 10

This friendly establishment makes an ideal base for visiting the Thames Valley and surrounding area. All four bedrooms are very well equipped with tea- and coffee-making facilities, flat-screen TV, hairdryer, a spacious en suite bathroom (with either a bath or power shower) and complimentary toiletries. Breakfast is prepared to order using fresh, locally sourced ingredients – home-made preserves, the farm's own eggs and family reared bacon – and is served at private tables. Guest facilities include a heated pool, hot tub, sauna, a large garden, a patio area and secure parking.

Recommended in the area

Blenheim Palace; Kelmscott Manor; Buscot Park

Blenheim Palace, Woodstock

The Miller of Mansfield

★★★★★ ⑧ RESTAURANT WITH ROOMS
Address High St, GORING, RG8 9AW
Tel: 01491 872829 **Fax:** 01491 873100
Email: reservations@millerofmansfield.com
Website: www.millerofmansfield.com
Map ref: 3 SU68 **Directions:** M40 junct 7,
S on A329 towards Benson, A4074 towards
Reading, B4009 towards Goring. Or M4 junct 12,
S on A4 towards Newbury. 3rd rdbt onto A340 to
Pangbourne. A329 to Streatley, right at lights onto
B4009 into Goring **Rooms:** 13 en suite (2 fmly rooms) **Notes:** Wi-fi **Parking:** 2

The newly renovated Miller of Mansfield occupies a quiet Thames-side village setting, overlooking the Chiltern Hills. Inside, this former coaching inn offers sumptuous en suite rooms and suites, all distinctively and individually styled and with all the home comforts guests could want, and more. There are flat-screen digital TVs, marble bathrooms, free-standing stone resin baths and/or high-pressure showers, fluffy robes, Egyptian cotton linen, organic latex mattresses and luxurious REN toiletries. Residents in some rooms can enjoy a good night's sleep in stunning antique French beds. The award-winning restaurant, which enjoys views over the terrace gardens, aims to provide an informal and enjoyable eating experience. Diners can expect impressive modern British cuisine featuring local, free-range and organic produce, home-cured and smoked fish and meats, hand-rolled pasta, home-made breads, ice creams and sorbets, coupled with an exciting wine list – with many wines available by the glass – and a selection of local real ales in the bar. From breakfast, light meals and afternoon tea through to three-course dinners, the menus at the Miller change regularly to reflect the best of seasonal produce. Free high-speed internet access is available at the Wi-fi hotspot and there are also fully equipped meeting facilities for business travellers.

Recommended in the area

Basildon Park (NT); Beale Wildlife Park and Gardens; Henley-on-Thames

Kelmscott Manor grounds

Radcliffe Observatory, Oxford

The Bell at Hampton Poyle

★★★★★ INN

Address   11 Oxford Road,
          HAMPTON POYLE, OX5 2QD
Tel: 01865 376242
Email: contactus@thebelloxford.co.uk
Website: www.thebelloxford.co.uk
Map ref: 3 SP51
Directions: From N, turn off A34 signed Kidlington,
0.25m; From S, N from Kidlington Sainsburys rdbt,
with Sainsburys on left, on left 0.25m

Rooms: 9 en suite (3 GF) S £75-£145 D £75-£155 Notes: Wi-fi 🐾 5yrs Parking: 31

This privately-owned historic inn has been recently renovated and reopened as a gastropub with rooms.
It has all of its original old-world charm along with a contemporary restaurant with an open kitchen, and
nine superb bedrooms with walk-in rain showers and roll-top baths. Each room is individually designed,
but all have large beds with Egyptian linen, flat-screen TVs with Freeview, broadband internet, tea- and
coffee-making facilities, fluffy towels and L'Occitane bathroom products.

Recommended in the area

Bicester Village retail park; Blenheim Palace; Oxford

Corn Croft Guest House

★★★★ GUEST ACCOMMODATION

Address   69-71 Corn Street, WITNEY, OX28 6AS
Tel: 01993 773298
Fax: 01993 773298
Email: richardturner4@btconnect.com
Website: www.corncroft.co.uk
Map ref: 3 SP31 Directions: A40 to town centre,
from Market Square onto Corn Street, 400mtrs on left
Rooms: 9 en suite (1 fmly) (2 GF)
Notes: Wi-fi Closed: 24-26 Dec

Corn Croft Guest House occupies a handsome old building in the quieter end of the town of Witney,
though only two minutes' walk from the centre. It's a great base for visiting the Cotswolds and Oxford,
which is only seven miles away. The friendly staff will make you feel at home, as will the comfortable,
well-equipped accommodation. All nine en suite bedrooms are furnished with Queen Anne and
Jacobian-style pieces, and come with tea- and coffee-making facilities and flat-screen TVs. Substantial
breakfasts based on local produce are served in the spacious dining room.

Recommended in the area

Oxford; Blenheim Palace; The Cotswolds

Heather, Long Mynd

Caro's Bed & Breakfast

★ ★ ★ BED & BREAKFAST

Address 1 Higher Netley, DORRINGTON,
Shrewsbury, SY5 7JY

Tel: 01743 718790 & 07739 285263

Email: info@carosbandb.co.uk

Website: www.carosbandb.co.uk

Map ref: 2 SJ40

Directions: 1m SW of Dorrington. Off A49 in
Dorrington signed Picklescott, 1m left onto driveway
by stone bridge, signed Higher Netley

Rooms: 2 en suite **S** £40-£55 **D** £55-£90 **Notes:** Wi-fi ⊗ **Parking:** 4 **Closed:** 21-28 Dec

This charming cottage bed and breakfast in the foothills of Long Mynd is a perfect base for walking
holidays. The cottage has lovely views across open countryside, a pretty garden, and a roaring log fire
for warming yourself up when you return from a day's exploring. There are two en-suite rooms with
king-size beds, one of which connects to a children's room. Breakfasts are based on locally sourced
and homemade produce, and packed lunches and frozen homemade meals are available on request.

Recommended in the area

Ironbridge Gorge Museum; Stokesay Castle; Medieval towns of Shrewsbury and Ludlow

Broseley House

★ ★ ★ ★ GUESTHOUSE

Address 1 The Square, Broseley,
IRONBRIDGE, TF12 5EW

Tel: 01952 882043 & 07790 732723

Email: info@broseleyhouse.co.uk

Website: www.broseleyhouse.co.uk

Map ref: 2 SJ60 **Directions:** 1m S of Ironbridge in
Broseley town centre

Rooms: 6 en suite (1 fmly) (1 GF) **S** £45-£50 **D** £70-
£80 **Notes:** Wi-fi ❤ 5yrs

This impressive and lovingly restored Georgian house prides itself on being 'the friendly place to stay'. It
offers high-quality decor throughout, and the thoughtfully and individually furnished en suite bedrooms,
one of which is a family room, all come with homely extras such as TV with DVD/CD/video (with a free
borrowing library) hairdryer, radio alarm, bathrobes and beverage tray. Self-catering accommodation is
also available. Comprehensive breakfasts, ranging from full English to lighter alternatives, are freshly
cooked from local produce and served in the elegant dining room.

Recommended in the area

Benthall Hall; Blists Hill Victorian Town; Buildwas Abbey

The Library House

★★★★★ 🏠 GUEST ACCOMMODATION

Address   11 Severn Bank, IRONBRIDGE,
          Telford, TF8 7AN
Tel: 01952 432299
Email: info@libraryhouse.com
Website: www.libraryhouse.com
Map ref: 2 SJ60
Directions: 50yds from Iron Bridge
Rooms: 4 en suite S £65-£75 D £75-£100
Notes: Wi-fi ⊗ 🐾

Located just 60 yards from the famous Iron Bridge, this Grade II listed Georgian building is tucked away in a peaceful thoroughfare yet is close to good pubs and restaurants. Hanging baskets and window boxes enhance the creeper-covered walls of the former library, and in the spring and summer the gardens are immaculate. All of the bedrooms have a television with DVD player and a hospitality tray. Excellent breakfasts are served in the pine-furnished dining room.

Recommended in the area

Ironbridge World Heritage Site; Telford International Exhibition Centre; Blists Hill Victorian Town

The Clive Bar & Restaurant with Rooms

★★★★★ ◉◉ RESTAURANT WITH ROOMS

Address   Bromfield, LUDLOW, SY8 2JR
Tel: 01584 856565
Fax: 01584 856661
Email: info@theclive.co.uk
Website: www.theclive.co.uk
Map ref: 2 SO57 Directions: 2m N of Ludlow on

A49 in village of Bromfield Rooms: 15 en suite (9 fmly rooms) (11 GF) S £65-£90 D £90-£115
Notes: Wi-fi ⊗ Parking: 100 Closed: 25-26 Dec

A stylish makeover of a former farmhouse has given The Clive a smart contemporary look. The well-known restaurant has an emphasis on fresh produce ranging from local meats to Cornish fish. The spacious en suite bedrooms, situated in period outbuildings, have been tastefully refurbished to provide well-equipped, modern accommodation. A family suite and room with disabled facilities is available.

Recommended in the area

Stokesay Castle, Craven Arms; Ludlow Food Hall; Ludlow Race Course and Golf Club; Offa's Dyke

De Greys of Ludlow

★★★★★ GUESTHOUSE

Address   5-6 Broad Street, LUDLOW, SY8 1NG
Tel: 01584 872764
Fax: 01584 879764
Email: degreys@btopenworld.com
Website: www.degreys.co.uk
Map ref: 2 SO57
Directions: Off A49, in town centre, 50yds beyond clock tower
Rooms: 9 en suite (1 GF)
Notes: ⊗ Closed: 26 Dec & 1 Jan

This 16th-century timber-framed property houses De Grey's Tea Rooms, a well-known establishment in Ludlow town centre. It now also provides high-quality accommodation with luxurious modern facilities. All of the individually decorated and spacious bedrooms – including two suites and one room on the ground floor – have been carefully renovated, the design of each governed by the labyrinth of historic timbers that comprise this Tudor building. Sporting evocative names such as The Buttercross, Valentines View, Castle View and Market View, all the rooms have en suite facilities, and some feature stunning bathrooms with roll-top baths and large, powerful showers; one even has 'his and hers' bathrooms separated by a 4-foot beam. Furnishings are tasteful, with lots of lush fabrics used throughout and four-poster beds in some rooms. Combined with the latest in entertainment technology, this creates a successful fusion of past and present, and guests are encouraged to return to their rooms, unwind and relax with a bottle of wine. Breakfast, taken in the adjacent tearoom/restaurant and bakery shop, and served by smartly dressed waitresses, includes award-winning breads and pastries freshly made on the premises.

Recommended in the area

Ludlow Castle; Long Mynd; Cardin Mill Valley

Ludlow Castle and Dinham Bridge

Number Twenty Eight

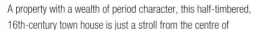 BED & BREAKFAST

Address 28 Lower Broad Street, LUDLOW, SY8 1PQ
Tel: 01584 875466
Email: enquiries@no28ludlow.co.uk
Website: www.no28ludlow.co.uk
Map ref: 2 SO57
Directions: In town centre. Over Ludford Bridge onto Lower Broad St, 3rd house on right
Rooms: 2 en suite S £65-£75 D £80-£90
Notes: Wi-fi ⊗ 🐾 16yrs **Closed:** Nov-May

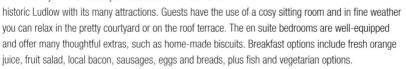

A property with a wealth of period character, this half-timbered, 16th-century town house is just a stroll from the centre of historic Ludlow with its many attractions. Guests have the use of a cosy sitting room and in fine weather you can relax in the pretty courtyard or on the roof terrace. The en suite bedrooms are well-equipped and offer many thoughtful extras, such as home-made biscuits. Breakfast options include fresh orange juice, fruit salad, local bacon, sausages, eggs and breads, plus fish and vegetarian options.

Recommended in the area
Berrington Hall; Stokesay Castle; Ironbridge World Heritage Site

Riseholme

★★★★ BED & BREAKFAST

Address 4 Hampton Road,
OSWESTRY, SY11 1SJ
Tel: 01691 656508
Email: ssparnell1234@googlemail.com
Map ref: 5 SJ22
Rooms: 3 en suite (1 fmly)
Notes: Wi-fi 🐾 12yrs
Parking: 5

Riseholme is located in a residential area of Oswestry, a pretty market town that sits close to the Welsh border. The house is within easy walking distance of the town centre, taking in the attractive memorial gardens en route. Inside this attractive home, the comfortable bedrooms, which all provide tea- and coffee-making facilities, are complemented by smart, modern en suite bathrooms; one room is suitable for families. Comprehensive breakfasts are taken in a cosy dining room and a spacious guest lounge is also available.

Recommended in the area
Whittington Castle; Park Hall Farm; Erddig Hall (NT)

Fieldside Guest House

★ ★ ★ ★ GUESTHOUSE

Address 38 London Road, SHREWSBURY, SY2 6NX
Tel: 01743 353143
Fax: 01743 354687
Email: robrookes@btinternet.com
Website: www.fieldsideguesthouse.co.uk
Map ref: 2 SJ41
Directions: A5 onto A5064, premises 1m on left
Rooms: 8 (5 en suite) (3 pri facs)
Notes: Wi-fi Parking: 8

Fieldside, which dates back to 1835, is just one mile from the centre of Shrewsbury and a 5-minute walk from Shrewsbury Abbey. This delightful house is attractively furnished and decorated and offers both single and double/twin rooms. The bedrooms feature period-style furniture and are equipped with tea and coffee facilities. Breakfast is served at individual tables in the spacious dining room. Traditional English or vegetarian or lighter options are available. There is ample private parking.

Recommended in the area

Shrewsbury Castle and Abbey; Attingham Park (NT); Ironbridge Gorge and museums

The Union Canal near Colemere Country Park

Soulton Hall

★ ★ ★ ★ 🍽 GUEST ACCOMMODATION

Address Soulton, WEM, SY4 5RS
Tel: 01939 232786
Fax: 01939 234097
Email: enquiries@soultonhall.co.uk
Website: www.soultonhall.co.uk
Map ref: 6 SJ52 **Directions:** A49 between
Shrewsbury & Whitchurch turn onto B5065 towards
Wem. Soulton Hall 2m E of Wem on B5065
Rooms: 7 en suite (2 fmly rooms) (3 GF)
Notes: Wi-fi **Parking:** 50

The Ashton family can trace their tenure of this impressive manor house back to the 1400s and 1500s, and much evidence of the building's age remains. The family and their staff offer excellent levels of personal service, with the care of guests given utmost importance. The welcoming entrance lounge leads into the well-stocked bar on one side and an elegant dining room on the other. Here, a good range of freshly prepared dishes, using local produce wherever possible, are served in a friendly and relaxed setting. After a meal, guests can retire to the lounge hall to enjoy coffee and liqueurs in front of a blazing log fire (the house has central heating as well as log fires during the winter). The bedrooms at Soulton Hall reflect the character of the house, with features like mullioned windows, exposed timbers and wood panelling. The converted carriage house across the garden offers ground-floor accommodation in two spacious double rooms, each with spa baths. Standing in its own grounds beyond the walled garden, Cedar Lodge provides a choice of a peaceful four-poster suite, or more modest family accommodation. Soulton Hall stands in 500 acres of open farmland, parkland and ancient oak woodland, which guests are welcome to explore.

Recommended in the area

Blists Hill Victorian Town, Ironbridge; China museum and ironworks, Ironbridge; Shrewsbury

Gough's Caves, Cheddar Gorge

Brooks Guesthouse

★ ★ ★ ★ 🛏 GUEST ACCOMMODATION

Address 1 & 1A Crescent Gardens, Upper Bristol Road, BATH, BA1 2NA
Tel: 01225 425543
Fax: 01225 318147
Email: info@brooksguesthouse.com
Website: www.brooksguesthouse.com
Map ref: 2 ST76 **Directions:** On A4, 350yds W of Queens Square, before Royal Victoria Park
Rooms: 21 en suite (4 fmly rooms) (7 GF) S £65-£85 D £75-£115 **Notes:** Wi-fi ⊗ **Closed:** 25 Dec

Conveniently located just a few minutes' stroll from the centre of Bath, Brooks Guesthouse offers a relaxed atmosphere and upgraded en suite accommodation. The bedrooms and bathrooms are well decorated, with pocket-sprung mattresses, goose-down duvets and flat-screen TVs. There's an open fire in the guest living room and an honesty bar, while the breakfasts – which emphasise local suppliers – are a highlight of any stay.

Recommended in the area
Jane Austen Centre; Stonehenge; The Grand Pump Room

Cheriton House

★ ★ ★ ★ ★ GUEST ACCOMMODATION

Address 9 Upper Oldfield Park, BATH, BA2 3JX
Tel: 01225 429862
Fax: 01225 428403
Email: info@cheritonhouse.co.uk
Website: www.cheritonhouse.co.uk
Map ref: 2 ST76
Directions: A36 onto A367 Wells Rd, 1st right
Rooms: 11 en suite (2 fmly rooms) (2 GF)
Notes: Wi-fi ⊗ 🐾 12yrs **Parking:** 11

This grand Victorian house has panoramic views over Bath and is only a short walk from the city centre. Expect a friendly welcome from the proprietors who work hard to achieve a relaxed atmosphere. The carefully restored en suite bedrooms are charmingly individual, and include a two-bedroom suite in a converted coach house. All rooms have a TV and a well-stocked hospitality tray. A substantial breakfast is served in the large conservatory overlooking beautifully manicured gardens. Plan your day in the comfortable lounge, where you can browse the brochures and guide books.

Recommended in the area
The Abbey & many museums in Bath; Cheddar Gorge; Wells; Longleat

Devonshire House

★★★★ GUEST ACCOMMODATION

Address 143 Wellsway, BATH, BA2 4RZ
Tel: 01225 312495
Email: enquiries@devonshire-house.uk.com
Website: www.devonshire-house.uk.com
Map ref: 2 ST76 Directions: 1m S of city centre.
A36 onto A367 Wells Rd & Wellsway
Rooms: 4 en suite (1 fmly) (1 GF) S £50-£88 D £70-£98
Notes: Wi-fi ⊗ Parking: 6

Located within walking distance of the city centre, this charming
house, built in 1880, maintains its Victorian style. The attractive
en suite bedrooms, all appointed to a high standard, have TVs
and tea- and coffee-making facilities. There is a small lounge area. Continental breakfast choices
are abundant and English breakfast is available at a supplement; all are served in the pleasant dining
room, which was originally a Victorian grocer's shop. Secure parking is in the walled courtyard, and the
proprietors make every effort to ensure your stay is pleasant and memorable.

Recommended in the area

Roman Baths; Longleat House and Safari Park; Wells Cathedral

Royal Crescent in Bath

Dorian House

★★★★★ GUEST ACCOMMODATION

Address 1 Upper Oldfield Park, BATH, BA2 3JX
Tel: 01225 426336
Fax: 01225 444699
Email: info@dorianhouse.co.uk
Website: www.dorianhouse.co.uk
Map ref: 2 ST76 **Directions:** A36 onto A367 Wells Rd,
right onto Upper Oldfield Park, 3rd building on left
Rooms: 13 en suite (4 fmly rooms) (2 GF)
S £59-£99 **D** £65-£165
Notes: Wi-fi ⊗ **Parking:** 9 **Closed:** 25 & 26 Dec

This elegant Victorian property, built from Bath stone around
1880, has stunning views over the city. The house is just 10 minutes' walk from the centre and is also
close to many fine gardens and pretty villages, making it a good base. Dorian House is owned by Tim
Hugh, Principal Cellist with the London Symphony Orchestra, and his wife Kathryn. Music influences
the overall character and ambience of the property, with bedrooms bearing names such as Vivaldi,
Gershwin and Rossini. The house was extensively refurbished in 2009 and one new room, which
contains a beautiful four-poster, has been named Slava in honour of the Russian cellist Rostropovich.
Each of the en suite bedrooms, which feature opulent fabrics and stunning decor, have good views over
Bath's famous Georgian Royal Crescent or the well-tended gardens. All provide a range of extras such
as marble bathrooms with high-pressure showers, crisp cotton sheets, fluffy towels and hairdryers.
The attractive lounge has an open fireplace, large comfortable sofas, a bar and views of the terraced
gardens. Delicious breakfasts offer treats such as freshly baked croissants and fresh fruit juices,
as well as the traditional full English. Parking is on a very steep incline but free.

Recommended in the area

Thermae Bath Spa; Bath Abbey; Westonbirt Arboretum

Marlborough House

★★★★ GUEST ACCOMMODATION

Address	1 Marlborough Lane, BATH, BA1 2NQ
Tel:	01225 318175 **Fax:** 01225 466127
Email:	mars@manque.dircon.co.uk
Website:	www.marlborough-house.net

Map ref: 2 ST76 **Directions:** 450yds W of city centre, at A4 junct with Marlborough Ln
Rooms: 6 en suite (2 fmly rooms) (1 GF)
S £75-£110 **D** £85-£135
Notes: Wi-fi **Parking:** 3 **Closed:** 24-26 Dec

This enchanting Victorian town house, within walking distance of Bath's major attractions, is run in a friendly and informal style by owner Peter Moore. The house is large and impressive, with well proportioned bedrooms elegantly furnished with antiques, including some antique four-poster or king-size beds. All rooms are fully en suite and feature free Wi-fi, flat-screen TV with Freeview, and complimentary organic toiletries. A hospitality tray is provided, too, complete with organic teas and coffees and a decanter of sherry.

Recommended in the area

Roman Baths; Abbey Tower Tour; Thermae Bath Spa

Whittles Farm

★★★★ FARMHOUSE

Address	BEERCROCOMBE, TA3 6AH
Tel/Fax:	01823 480301
Email:	djcm.mitchem@btinternet.com
Website:	www.whittlesfarm.co.uk

Map ref: 2 ST32
Directions: Off A358 through Hatch Beauchamp to Beercrocombe, keep left through village, Whittles Farm 1st lane on right, no through road
Rooms: 2 en suite S £42-£46 **D** £70-£74
Notes: ⊗ 🐾 12yrs **Parking:** 4 **Closed:** Dec & Jan

This 200-year-old farmhouse, with lots of character and luxurious furnishings, is ideally set on a no-through road, with lovely walks nearby. The en suite bedrooms, with zip-link beds, are light and spacious, and guests have their own cosy lounge with an inglenook fireplace, and a dining room with a large table where excellent breakfasts are served. Owners John and Claire Mitchem have been receiving guests here for more than 25 years, and their friendly hospitality is the highlight of any stay.

Recommended in the area

Montacute House; Forde Abbey; Barrington Court (NT)

School Cottages Bed & Breakfast

★ ★ ★ ★ BED & BREAKFAST

Address The Street, Near Bath, FARMBOROUGH,
Bath, BA2 0AR

Tel: 01761 471167 & 07989 349428

Email: tim@schoolcottages.co.uk

Website: www.schoolcottages.co.uk

Map ref: 2 ST66 **Directions:** Off A39 in
Farmborough onto The Street, 1st left opp village
school **Rooms:** 3 en suite S £50-£60 D £70-£90
Notes: Wi-fi 🐾 10yrs **Parking:** 3

This tastefully renovated country house sits in lovely gardens in the pretty village of Farmborough.
The en suite accommodation is contemporary and stylish, equipped with Wi-fi and TVs with Freeview.
There's a cosy guest lounge with log fires, and School Cottages is within walking distance of the village
pubs serving good food. Good food is certainly what you'll get at breakfast in the charming conservatory
overlooking the garden. There's an extensive choice and it's all made from locally sourced ingredients,
including freshly laid eggs from the B&B's own hens, as well as homemade preserves.

Recommended in the area

The Roman Baths, Bath; Thermae Bath Spa; Longleat Safari Park

Cannards Grave Farmhouse

★ ★ ★ ★ GUEST ACCOMMODATION

Address Cannards Grave,
SHEPTON MALLET, BA4 4LY

Tel: 01749 347091

Fax: 01749 347091

Email: sue@cannardsgravefarmhouse.co.uk

Website: www.cannardsgravefarmhouse.co.uk

Map ref: 2 ST64

Directions: On A37 between Shepton Mallet and The
Bath & West Showground, 100yds from Highwayman
pub towards showground on left

Rooms: 5 en suite (2 fmly rooms) (1 GF) **Notes:** Wi-fi ⊗ **Parking:** 6

Charming host Sue Crockett offers quality accommodation at this welcoming 17th-century farmhouse.
The bedrooms are delightful and have thoughtful touches such as hospitality trays, mineral water,
biscuits and mints. One room has a four-poster bed and a fridge with fresh milk. Delicious breakfasts
are served in the garden conservatory and there is a comfortable lounge to relax in.

Recommended in the area

Bath and West Showground; Historic Wells; Glastonbury Tor; City of Bath

Tarr Steps clapper bridge and the River Barle, Exmoor National Park

Greyhound Inn

★★★★ ⇔ INN

Address STAPLE FITZPAINE, Taunton, TA3 5SP
Tel: 01823 480227
Fax: 01823 481117
Email: thegreyhound-inn@btconnect.com
Website: www.thegreyhoundinn.biz
Map ref: 2 ST21 **Directions:** M5 junct 25, A358
signed Yeovil. In 3m turn right, signed Staple
Fitzpaine **Rooms:** 4 en suite
Notes: Wi-fi ⛙ 10yrs **Parking:** 40

Set in the heart of Somerset in the Blackdown Hills, this creeper-clad 16th century village inn has great atmosphere and character, complete with flagstone floors and open fires. An imaginative choice of freshly-prepared seasonal dishes, making the most of locally sourced ingredients, is offered on the ever-changing menu, along with award-winning ales. The delightful bedrooms are spacious, comfortable and well-equipped. The Greyhound's rural setting makes it the perfect country retreat, yet it is only four miles south of Taunton and the M5.

Recommended in the area

Hestercombe Gardens; Fleet Air Museum; Taunton Racecourse

Lower Farm

★★★★ FARMHOUSE

Address Thornfalcon, TAUNTON, TA3 5NR
Tel: 01823 443549
Email: doreen@titman.eclipse.co.uk
Website: www.thornfalcon.co.uk
Map ref: 2 ST22
Directions: M5 junct 25, 2m SE on A358, left opp
Nags Head pub, farm signed 1m on left
Rooms: 11 (8 en suite) (3 pri facs) (2 fmly rooms)
(7 GF) **S** £45-£50 **D** £70-£80
Notes: Wi-fi ⊗ ⛙ 5yrs **Parking:** 10

This charming thatched 15th-century longhouse is full of character, and surrounded by lovely gardens and open farmland. Beamed ceilings and inglenook fireplaces testify to its age. The bedrooms include some in a converted granary and byre, and all are en suite or have private facilities, and are furnished to a high standard. A hearty breakfast, using local bacon and sausages, and eggs from the proprietor's own hens, is cooked on the Aga and served in the farmhouse kitchen.

Recommended in the area

Hestercombe Gardens; Willow & Wetlands Visitor Centre; Quantock Hills; Barrington Court; Forde Abbey

Crown & Victoria

★★★★ ⊛ INN

Address Farm Street, TINTINHULL,
Yeovil, BA22 8PZ
Tel: 01935 823341
Fax: 01935 825786
Email: info@thecrownandvictoria.co.uk
Website: www.thecrownandvictoria.co.uk
Map ref: 2 ST41
Directions: Off A303, signs for Tintinhull Gardens
Rooms: 5 en suite
Notes: Wi-fi **Parking:** 60

The Crown and Victoria country inn stands in the heart of the pretty village of Tintinhull. In days gone by, as well as being the village pub, the inn was also a private school – lessons took place where the existing bar is situated. Today, above the new restaurant, the unfussy bedrooms are light and airy and very well equipped with hairdryers, TVs with DVD players, tea- and coffee-making facilities, and wireless broadband internet access. The staff ensure you are well cared for. The contemporary bar and restaurant offers a successful combination of traditional pub atmosphere and quality dining. Carefully presented dishes are available for lunch and dinner under the direction of head chef, Stephen Yates. The menu ranges from traditional English dishes such as steak and ale pie to the more elaborate pan-roasted breast of duck on a bed of spinach with a potato rösti, plum and port jus. The extensive wine list includes 10 fine house wines and there is a choice of local real ales. When the weather is kind, guests can relax in the garden with a drink or a light meal or enjoy a candlelit dinner in the conservatory with lovely garden views.

Recommended in the area

Tintinhull House Garden (NT); Montacute House (NT); Barrington Court (NT); Yeovil; Fleet Air Arm Museum, Yeovilton

Double-Gate Farm

★ ★ ★ ★ FARMHOUSE

Address Godney, WELLS, BA5 1RX
Tel: 01458 832217
Fax: 01458 835612
Email: doublegatefarm@aol.com
Website: www.doublegatefarm.com
Map ref: 2ST54 **Directions:** A39 from Wells towards Glastonbury, at Polsham right signed Godney/Polsham. 2m to x-rds, continue to farmhouse on left after inn **Rooms:** 7 en suite (4 fmly rooms) (4 GF) **S** £60-£75 **D** £70-£100 **Notes:** ⊗ **Parking:** 5 **Closed:** 22 Dec-5 Jan

A special welcome awaits you, not just from the owners but from Jasper and Paddy, the friendly retrievers, at this lovely old farmhouse situated on the banks of the River Sheppey on the Somerset Levels. There are good views of Glastonbury Tor and the Mendip Hills, as well as fishing at the bottom of the garden, and cycle rides from the farm on the quiet roads which abound with birds and wildlife. There's even a resident barn owl in the chimney! Guests can play table tennis or snooker in the games room, or watch their own DVDs in the well-equipped en suite bedrooms. There is free internet access in the guest lounge. New to Double-Gate Farm are some luxury riverside suites (£45-50pppn) suitable for two to four guests, with spacious bedrooms with fridges, ceiling fans, mood lighting and access onto an extensive patio. Each of these large suites can be adapted for disabled use (NAS 3). Double-Gate Farm is well-known for its beautiful summer flower garden and home-grown tomatoes and fruit. Excellent breakfasts are served in the dining room with its panoramic views of the garden and meadow. The options are extensive – take your pick from cereals, juices, yoghurts, compotes, local cheeses, home-made bread, a full farmhouse breakfast, kippers and freshly-made pancakes.

Recommended in the area

Wells Cathedral and Bishop's Palace; Cheddar Gorge; Bath; Glastonbury

9 The Park

★★★★★ GUEST ACCOMMODATION

Address	9 Ellenborough Park Road,
	WESTON-SUPER-MARE, BS23 1XJ
Tel:	01934 415244
Email:	info@9theparkbandb.co.uk
Website:	www.9theparkbandb.co.uk

Map ref: 2 ST36

Directions: A370 towards town centre, through 5 rdbts, at next 1st exit onto Station Approach. Pass station onto Neva Rd, left onto Ellenborough Park Rd, 40mtrs on left

Rooms: 3 en suite (2 fmly rooms) **S** £60 **D** fr £85 (fmly fr £95)

Notes: Wi-fi ⊗ **Parking:** 4

9 The Park is a luxurious, non-smoking bed and breakfast situated a stone's throw away from the seafront at Weston-Super-Mare. It sits opposite a lovely park and next to the Victorian Ellenborough Crescent in a quiet residential area which is only a short distance away from the railway and coach stations. 9 The Park has been lovingly restored to its former glory and converted from an 11-bed nursing home into a stunning bed and breakfast which provides a peaceful and comfortable stay for all guests, whether travelling on business or for a leisure break. The en suite rooms are all tastefully decorated and well-equipped with flat-screen TVs and wireless internet. There's a lounge area for relaxing and a mature garden with a private area for guests to enjoy. At breakfast you can look forward to homemade bread and a menu based on mainly local produce. Ample off-street parking behind electric gates ensures peace of mind while staying at 9 The Park.

Recommended in the area

Weston beach; Cheddar Gorge; Wells Cathedral

STAFFORDSHIRE

Stowe Pool, Lichfield

The Church Farm

★★★★ FARMHOUSE

Address   Holt Lane, KINGSLEY,
              Stoke-on-Trent, ST10 2BA
Tel: 01538 754759
Email: thechurchfarm@yahoo.co.uk
Website: www.bandbatthechurchfarm.co.uk
Map ref: 7 SK04
Directions: Off A52 in Kingsley onto Holt Ln,
150mtrs on right opposite school drive
Rooms: 3 en suite S £30 D £50-£55
Notes: Wi-fi ⊗ Parking: 6

The Church Farm, a listed 18th-century farmhouse situated in the quaint village of Kingsley, is still a working dairy farm and family home. It sits amid 100 acres of farmland and makes a good base for exploring the Potteries and the Peak District. Inside, it provides friendly, relaxed accommodation in a number of beautiful, individually decorated rooms, complete with original antique furniture. There's a lounge with a log fire where guests can put their feet up during the winter season and relax. The thoughtfully equipped en suite bedrooms within the main house contain stylish furnishings, and guests are provided with a range of little extras. Breakfast is not to be missed, as you will be offered a hearty Staffordshire farmhouse plate of locally sourced produce, including free-range eggs from the owners' hens, all served at individual tables overlooking the cottage gardens. Church Farm's scented garden is a haven for birds and butterflies during the summer, and you can wander down the paths that lead from the house to the beautiful Churnet Valley.

Recommended in the area

Alton Towers; Peak District National Park; Churnet Valley Steam Railway

Netherstowe House

★ ★ ★ ★ 🛏 GUESTHOUSE

Address Netherstowe Lane,
LICHFIELD, WS13 6AY
Tel: 01543 254270
Fax: 01543 254270
Email: reservations@netherstowehouse.com
Website: www.netherstowehouse.com
Map ref: 3 SK10 **Directions:** A38 onto A5192,
0.3m on right, turn onto Netherstowe Ln. Take 1st
left & 1st right down private drive

Rooms: 20 en suite (2 fmly rooms) (5 GF) **Notes:** Wi-fi ⊗ **Parking:** 35

Netherstowe House is a charming boutique guest house set in a beautiful country estate – the perfect retreat for leisure and business guests alike. The house is a stunning Georgian grade II listed building, surrounded by tranquil formal grounds, resplendent in verdant shades at any time of the year. Netherstowe has the elegance of a fine old country house, along with every modern luxury you could possibly desire. Guests can enjoy the many stylishly decorated public rooms, conference facilities, gardens, gym, restaurant, cheese and wine cellar and bar throughout their stay. All the guest accommodation at Netherstowe House is en suite, with lots of little extra touches to make you feel welcome, such as complimentary Wi-fi, flat-screen TVs with Freeview, luxury toiletries, memory foam pillows, and a superb selection of refreshments including home-made biscuits. The bedding is of the highest quality, and fresh fluffy towels await you after a refreshing shower or bath. There's secure private parking, and a well-appointed gymnasium. The restaurant is delightfully elegant and formal, with crisp white linen and efficient yet discreet service. Breakfast and dinner are a real treat, with a wide range of delicacies prepared from fine local and seasonal produce.

Recommended in the area

Lichfield Cathedral; The National Forest; Fradley Junction

Haywood Park Farm

★ ★ ★ ★ FARMHOUSE

Address Shugborough, STAFFORD, ST17 0XA
Tel: 01889 882736
Fax: 01889 882736
Email: haywood.parkfarm@btopenworld.com
Website: www.haywoodparkfarm.co.uk
Map ref: 7 SJ92
Directions: 4m SE of Stafford off A513. Brown signs to Shugborough, on right 400yds past estate exit
Rooms: 2 en suite **S** £60-£80 **D** £70-£90
Notes: ⊗ 📵 14yrs **Parking:** 4

This attractive farmhouse stands on a 120-acre arable and sheep farm on Cannock Chase, part of the Shugborough Estate. The large, attractively furnished bedrooms have a host of extras such as fresh flowers, fruit, tea facilities and shortbread. Large fluffy towels are provided in the luxury bathrooms. Breakfast, using local produce, is served in the lounge-dining room. The area is a paradise for walkers and cyclists, and you can fish for carp and other coarse fish in the lake.

Recommended in the area

Shugborough Estate (NT); Wedgwood Museum; Alton Towers; Trentham Gardens

Entrance to Thor's Cave in the Manifold Valley

SUFFOLK

Seaside living at Aldeburgh, Suffolk

The Chantry

★★★★ GUEST ACCOMMODATION

Address 8 Sparhawk Street, BURY ST EDMUNDS, IP33 1RY
Tel: 01284 767427
Fax: 01284 760946
Email: chantryhotel1@aol.com
Website: www.chantryhotel.com
Map ref: 4 TL86 **Directions:** From cathedral S onto Crown St, left onto Sparhawk St
Rooms: 14 en suite (1 fmly) (1 GF)
S £69-£85 D £89-£115
Notes: Wi-fi **Parking:** 16

A delightful Grade II listed building where parking for each room is provided via a 19th-century carriage access. Bedrooms are decorated in period style, and the spacious superior double rooms have antique beds. There is a cosy lounge bar, and breakfast and dinner are served in the restaurant. Dishes are home cooked and prepared from the freshest of ingredients.

Recommended in the area

Abbey Gardens and ruins; Theatre Royal (NT); Ickworth House, Park & Gardens (NT)

Clarice House

★★★★★ ❀ GUEST ACCOMMODATION

Address Horringer Court, Horringer Road,
BURY ST EDMUNDS, IP29 5PH
Tel: 01284 705550
Fax: 01284 716120
Email: bury@claricehouse.co.uk
Website: www.claricehouse.co.uk
Map ref: 4 TL86
Directions: 1m SW from town centre on A143 towards Horringer
Rooms: 13 en suite S £70-£85 D £110-£150
Notes: ⊗ ⋈ 5yrs **Parking:** 85 **Closed:** 24-26 Dec & 31 Dec-1 Jan

This large neo-Jacobean mansion is set in 20 acres of landscaped grounds just a short drive from Bury St Edmunds. The family-run residential spa, with superb leisure facilities, has spacious, well-equipped bedrooms. Public rooms include a smart lounge bar, an intimate restaurant offering quality food and a changing menu, a further lounge and a conservatory.

Recommended in the area

Bury St Edmunds; Abbey Gardens; Ickworth House, Park and Gardens (NT)

Valley Farm

★★★★★ BED & BREAKFAST

Address Bungay Road, HOLTON, IP19 8LY
Tel: 01986 874521 & 07971 669270
Email: mail@valleyfarmholton.co.uk
Website: www.valleyfarmholton.co.uk
Map ref: 4 TM47
Directions: A144 onto B1123 to Holton, left at fork in village, left at school, 500yds on left
Rooms: 2 en suite (1 fmly) **S** £70-£90
D £70-£90 **Notes:** Wi-fi ⊗ **Parking:** 15

The owners of Valley Farm are keen advocates of green tourism, and this is reflected in many aspects of the charming red brick farmhouse situated in a peaceful rural location, a short drive or walk from the small market town of Halesworth. The individually decorated en suite bedrooms are tastefully appointed with many thoughtful touches. Breakfast, featuring locally sourced and home-grown produce, is served at a large communal table in the smart dining room. The property also boasts two and a half acres of lovely landscaped grounds and an indoor heated swimming pool.

Recommended in the area

Southwold; Minsmere RSPB sanctuary; The Cut arts centre

Sandpit Farm

★★★★ BED & BREAKFAST

Address Bruisyard, SAXMUNDHAM, IP17 2EB
Tel: 01728 663445
Email: smarshall@aldevalleybreaks.co.uk
Website: www.aldevalleybreaks.co.uk
Map ref: 4 TM36
Directions: 4m W of Saxmundham. A1120 onto B1120, 1st left for Bruisyard, house 1.5m on left
Rooms: 2 en suite **S** £40-£60 **D** £65-£80
Notes: Wi-fi **Parking:** 4 **Closed:** 24-26 Dec

This delightful Grade II listed farmhouse set in 20 acres of grounds, with the River Alde meandering along the boundary of the gardens, is well located for visiting the many places of interest in Suffolk. The en suite bedrooms are well-equipped and enjoy lovely country views; one is located in its own wing of the house. There is also a cosy sitting room for relaxing, as well as a secret garden, a wild-flower orchard and a hard tennis court. Breakfast features quality local and home-made produce as well as freshly laid free-range eggs.

Recommended in the area

Framlingham; Minsmere RSPB reserve; Sutton Hoo (NT)

Sutherland House

★ ★ ★ ★ ★  RESTAURANT WITH ROOMS

Address 56 High Street, SOUTHWOLD, IP18 6DN
Tel: 01502 724544
Email: enquiries@sutherlandhouse.co.uk
Website: www.sutherlandhouse.co.uk
Map ref: 4 TM57 **Directions:** A1095 into Southwold,
on High St on left after Victoria St
Rooms: 4 en suite (1 fmly) **S** £140-£200 **D** £140-£250
Notes: Wi-fi ⊗ **Parking:** 1

This delightful 15th-century house is at the heart of the bustling town centre. Alongside its wealth of period character, such as oak beams, exposed brickwork and open fireplaces, guests will find rich contemporary furnishings and sumptuous fabrics. The stylish en suite bedrooms come with king-sized beds, flat-screen TVs and DVD players with a choice of films. Public rooms include a large restaurant with a regularly changing menu based on locally sourced ingredients.

Recommended in the area

Southwold Railway; Walberswick; Electric Picture Palace

The Case Restaurant with Rooms

★ ★ ★ ★  RESTAURANT WITH ROOMS

Address Further Street, Assington, SUDBURY,
CO10 5LD
Tel: 01787 210483 **Fax:** 01787 211725
Email: restaurant@
thecaserestaurantwithrooms.co.uk
Website: www.thecaserestaurantwithrooms.co.uk
Map ref: 4 TL84 **Directions:** Exit A12 at Colchester
onto A134 to Sudbury. 7m from Colchester on left
Rooms: 7 en suite (2 fmly rooms) (7 GF) **S** £65-£89
D £85-£135 **Notes:** Wi-fi ⊗ **Parking:** 25

There's no mistaking that The Case Restaurant with Rooms is a family-run business where the owners really care about good hospitality. The boutique-style accommodation is stylish and furnished to the highest standards. Some rooms come with corner Jacuzzis and private patios, while all have power showers and lots of thoughtful touches like full-length mirrors with power sockets nearby, heated towel rails in the bathrooms and luxury toiletries. Home-cooked dishes are served in the restaurant.

Recommended in the area

Gainsborough's House, Sudbury; Colchester Zoo; Constable Country

Sunrise at Puttenham

Bentley Mill

★ ★ ★ ★ ★ BED & BREAKFAST

Address	Gravel Hill Road, Bentley, FARNHAM, GU10 5JD
Tel:	01420 23301 & 07768 842729
Fax:	01420 22538
Email:	ann.bentleymill@supanet.com
Website:	www.bentleymill.com
Map ref:	3 SU84

Directions: Off A31 (Farnham-Alton road), opp Bull Inn, turn left onto Gravel Hill Rd
Rooms: 2 en suite (1 GF)
Notes: Wi-fi ⊗ ⚁ 8yrs Parking: 6

David and Ann welcome you to their lovely home, a former corn mill beside the River Wey and set in five acres of beautiful grounds. The two spacious suites are former mill rooms with original beams; each has its own private entrance that is separate from the main house. They have countryside and river views and feature antiques, luxurious beds and deep sofas. A full breakfast is cooked on the Aga.
Recommended in the area
Jane Austen's House, Chawton; The Watercress Line, Alresford; Portsmouth Historic Dockyard

The Crown Inn

★ ★ ★ ★ ★ INN

Address	The Green, Petworth Road, CHIDDINGFOLD, GU8 4TX
Tel:	01428 682255
Fax:	01428 683313
Email:	enquiries@thecrownchiddingfold.com
Website:	www.thecrownchiddingfold.com

Map ref: 3 SU93 Rooms: 8 en suite
S £100 D £125-£200 Notes: Wi-fi ⊗ Parking: 15

The Crown Inn is an idyllic English pub, nestled in a quiet corner of the picture-perfect village green at Chiddingfold. Beautiful stained glass windows provide a stunning backdrop to the dining rooms, where traditional meals making the best use of seasonal ingredients are served, complemented by a selection of over 40 wines and real ales. The eight bedrooms, including four with four-posters, have been completely refurbished whilst retaining their ancient beams and quirky sloping floors. All have superb en suite bathrooms with REN toiletries, supremely comfortable beds, flat-screen TVs, DVD players and clock-radios with iPod docks.
Recommended in the area
Goodwood; Petworth House & Park (NT); Ramster Gardens

Asperion Hillside

★★★★ 🍽 GUEST ACCOMMODATION

Address	Perry Hill, Worplesdon,
	GUILDFORD, GU3 3RF
Tel:	01483 232051
Fax:	01483 237015
Email:	info@thehillsidehotel.com
Website:	www.asperionhillside.com
Map ref:	3 SU94

Rooms: 15 en suite (6 GF) S £65 D £90-£120
Notes: Wi-fi ⊗ Parking: 15 Closed: 21 Dec-7 Jan

Located just a short drive from central Guildford, this high-quality guest accommodation, which uses organic and Fairtrade produce, is popular with both business and leisure travellers. The en suite bedrooms are comfortable and equipped with good facilities, including free Wi-fi; one suite has a king-size, four-poster bed. There is a lounge bar and a bistro-style restaurant. The gardens feature a Koi carp pond and guest terrace. Asperion Hillside specialises in intimate high quality weddings, parties and small conferences.

Recommended in the area

St Mary's Church, Worplesdon; RHS Garden, Wisley; Clandon Park (NT)

Footpath through West Warren woods on the North Downs Way at Compton

EAST SUSSEX

Walkers take in the dramatic view from the South Downs Way

Five

★ ★ ★ ★ GUEST ACCOMMODATION
Address 5 New Steine, BRIGHTON, BN2 1PB
Tel: 01273 686547
Fax: 0871 5227472
Email: info@fivehotel.com
Website: www.fivehotel.com
Map ref: 3 TQ30
Directions: On A259 towards E, 8th turn
on left into square
Rooms: 10 en suite
Notes: Wi-fi ⊗

Five, a period town house overlooking a classic Regency square, has far-reaching views and is only a few steps from the beach. The contemporary rooms are comfortable and well-equipped, and benefit from crisp white linen, luxurious duvets, TVs with DVD players, Wi-fi, tea and coffee facilities and, in some cases, i-Pod docks. Some triple and family rooms are available. Breakfast, which includes organic bacon, eggs, mushrooms and fresh berries, is served in the bay-fronted dining room.
Recommended in the area
Brighton Pier; Brighton Pavilion; shopping in The Lanes

New Steine

★ ★ ★ ★ ≜ ⊜ GUEST ACCOMMODATION
Address 10-11 New Steine, BRIGHTON, BN2 1PB
Tel: 01273 695415 & 681546
Fax: 01273 622663
Email: reservation@newsteinehotel.com
Website: www.newsteinehotel.com
Map ref: 3 TQ30
Directions: A23 to Brighton Pier, left onto Marine
Parade, New Steine on left after Wentworth St
Rooms: 20 (16 en suite) (4 fmly rooms)
S £24.50-£59 D £49.50-£135 Notes: Wi-fi 🐾 4yrs

Elegant and fashionable, this five-storey Georgian townhouse in central Brighton is favoured by both business and leisure guests. Decorated in a contemporary style in shades of chocolate, cream and red, the chic bedrooms are equipped with free Wi-fi, desk space, hairdryers, flat-screen LCD TVs, tea- and coffee-making facilities and luxury toiletries. French cuisine, prepared from local produce, is served in the New Steine Bistro. There's a 24-hour concierge service, and conference rooms are available.
Recommended in the area
The Royal Pavilion; Devil's Dyke; Brighton Museum & Art Gallery

The Twenty One

★ ★ ★ ★ GUEST ACCOMMODATION

Address   21 Charlotte Street, Marine Parade,
           BRIGHTON, BN2 1AG
Tel: 01273 686450
Email: enquiries@thetwentyone.co.uk
Website: www.thetwentyone.co.uk
Map ref: 3 TQ30 Directions: From Brighton Pier turn left
onto Marine Parade, 16th turning on left
Rooms: 8 en suite (1 fmly) S £50-£60 D £90-£149
Notes: Wi-fi ⊗

Located in a quiet residential side street in the lively and
cosmopolitan Kemp Town area of Brighton, this stylishly
refurbished Regency townhouse is nevertheless within easy reach of the town's major attractions,
clubs, bars and restaurants and is just a few steps from the famous seafront. Within the house, guests
can relax in the refurbished, elegantly furnished and comfortable bedrooms, which have either smart
and modern en suite shower rooms or bathrooms. Each room has an abundance of thoughtful extras,
such as flat-screen TVs with Freeview, DVD players, digital radio alarms, towelling bathrobes and
slippers, well-stocked hospitality trays, mini-bars with complimentary mineral water, and iPod docking
stations. Some of the rooms have oblique sea views, and one of these, a large high-ceilinged double
with a brass bed and the original cornicing intact, has bay windows and its own private balcony. A
family room is also available. The smart dining room is the setting for an extensive buffet breakfast
comprising a choice of cereals, fresh fruit, yoghurt, croissants, fruit smoothies and freshly brewed
coffee, in addition to a freshly cooked hot breakfast, with a vegetarian alternative available. Locally
sourced ingredients are used as far as possible.

Recommended in the area

Brighton Pier; The Lanes; Brighton Marina

Tovey Lodge

★ ★ ★ ★ ★ GUEST ACCOMMODATION
Address Underhill Lane, DITCHLING, BN6 8XE
Tel: 08456 120544 **Fax:** 08456 120533
Email: info@sussexcountryholidays.co.uk
Website: www.sussexcountryholidays.co.uk
Map ref: 3 TQ31 **Directions:** From Ditchling village,
N on Beacon Rd. After 0.5m left onto Underhill Ln,
100yds 1st drive on left
Rooms: 5 en suite (4 fmly rooms) (2 GF)
D £80-£155 **Notes:** Wi-fi **Parking:** 28

Set within three acres of garden and enjoying great views of the South Downs, Tovey Lodge provides guests with an indoor swimming pool, sauna and jacuzzi. The bedrooms and en suite bathrooms are spacious and stylishly decorated and come with extras such as Wi-fi and plasma-screen TVs with DVD players. Three rooms are suitable for families, and two rooms are on the ground floor. There is also a spacious guest lounge, which backs onto a patio offering additional space to relax and features a 50-inch plasma-screen TV. A cooked or continental breakfast can be enjoyed in the dining room.
Recommended in the area
South Downs National Park; Wings Place; St Margaret's Church

Bodiam Castle

The Manse B&B

★★★★★ BED & BREAKFAST

Address   7 Dittons Road,
          EASTBOURNE, BN21 1DW
Tel: 01323 737851
Email: anne@themansebb.com
Website: www.themansebb.com
Map ref: 4 TV69
Directions: A22 to town centre railway station,
onto Old Orchard Rd, right onto Arlington Rd
Rooms: 3 en suite S £55-£60 D £80-£92
Notes: Wi-fi Parking: 2

Originally built in 1906 as a Presbyterian manse, this character property in the Arts and Crafts style retains many of its original features, such as stained-glass windows, oak panelling and oak floors. The property benefits from a quiet location, yet is just a five-minute stroll from Eastbourne's lively town centre, with its many shops, theatres, pubs and restaurants. The start of the South Downs is within a 10-minute stroll and there are many lovely walks and places to visit in the nearby area. Inside, the spacious, beautifully decorated en suite bedrooms provide armchairs, digital TVs, DVD/CD players, Wi-fi access, hospitality trays and fridges. Guests can enjoy a good night's sleep in king- or super-king-size beds with deep pocket-sprung mattresses. The wide selection of breakfast options, many of them locally sourced, homemade, and free-range and/or organic, is served in the south-facing dining room, which has French doors leading to the rear garden. Guests can relax in the garden if the weather is fine, or otherwise there's a comfortable sitting room. Off-street and unrestricted street parking is available.

Recommended in the area

South Downs and Beachy Head; Charleston (home of the Bloomsbury Group); Michelham Priory

Ocklynge Manor

★★★★★ BED & BREAKFAST

Address Mill Road, EASTBOURNE, BN21 2PG
Tel: 01323 734121 & 07979 627172
Email: ocklyngemanor@hotmail.com
Website: www.ocklyngemanor.co.uk
Map ref: 4 TV69
Directions: From Eastbourne Hospital follow town centre/seafront sign, 1st right onto Kings Av, Ocklynge Manor at top of road
Rooms: 3 (2 en suite) (1 pri facs) **S** £45-£60
D £80-£100 **Notes:** Wi-fi ⊗ ⚑ 16yrs **Parking:** 3

Instantly inviting, this 300-year-old house is set in extensive grounds, making it hard to imagine that you are just 10 minutes' walk from the centre of Eastbourne. The manor is on land that was previously occupied by a monastery, and this was also the site of a 12th-century Commandery of the Knights of St John of Jerusalem. According to a blue plaque, the house was also once the home of the renowned children's book illustrator Mabel Lucie Atwell. Today, David and Wendy Dugdill welcome guests to the manor, providing a charming personal touch to every aspect of the place. The bedrooms, all accessed via the main staircase, are spacious and sunny, with views across the garden from the large windows. The decor and furnishings are comfortable and elegant, and top quality Egyptian cotton bed linen and towels are provided. Fresh flowers, a TV, DVD player, radio, hairdryer and plenty of lamps are among the extra touches that so enhance a stay here. The bathrooms are modern and luxurious, and two adjoining rooms can be used as a suite which sleeps three. The public rooms include an elegant drawing room with grand piano, and the beautiful garden is a lovely place to stroll on a summer evening. A full English breakfast is served in the dining room.

Recommended in the area

South Downs Way; Beachy Head; Great Dixter; Bodiam Castle (NT); Bateman's

Parkside House

★★★★ GUEST ACCOMMODATION

Address 59 Lower Park Road,
HASTINGS, TN34 2LD
Tel: 01424 433096
Email: bkentparksidehse@aol.com
Map ref: 4 TQ80
Directions: A2101 to town centre, right at rdbt,
1st right
Rooms: 5 (4 en suite) (1 pri facs) (1 fmly)
S £35-£50 D £60-£70
Notes: Wi-fi ⊗

Parkside House is in a quiet conservation area opposite Alexandra Park, with its lakes, tennis courts and bowling green, yet is only a 15-minute walk from the seafront. The rooms are stylishly furnished, with many antique pieces, and generously equipped with video recorders, hairdryers, styling tongs, bathrobes and beverage trays. A good range of breakfast options – English or continental – is served at individual tables in the elegant dining room, and there is also an inviting lounge.

Recommended in the area

Battle Abbey; Bodiam Castle (NT); Michelham Priory

Holly Grove

★★★★ BED & BREAKFAST

Address Little London, HEATHFIELD, TN21 0NU
Tel: 01435 863375 & 07811 963193
Email: joedance@btconnect.com
Website: www.hollygrovebedandbreakfast.co.uk
Map ref: 4 TQ52 **Directions:** A267 to Horam, turn
right at Little London garage, proceed to bottom of
lane **Rooms:** 3 (2 en suite) (1 pri facs) (1 fmly) (2 GF)
S £50-£70 D £60-£85
Notes: Wi-fi **Parking:** 5

Holly Grove is in a quiet rural location in the heart of East Sussex, yet has easy access to many attractions. Set in over two acres of garden, it offers use of the heated outdoor swimming pool from May to October. Inside guests will enjoy the luxury, comfort and warm welcome offered by the Christie family. The bedrooms are appointed to a very high standard, with flat-screen TVs and many thoughtful extras. There is a separate lounge with open fire and a games room for the sole use of guests. Breakfast is served in the dining room or on the terrace.

Recommended in the area

Bentley Wildfowl and Motor Museum; Glyndebourne; Bateman's

Brighton Pier at dusk

Cleavers Lyng Country House

★ ★ ★ ★ GUEST ACCOMMODATION

Address   Church Road, HERSTMONCEUX,
          BN27 1QJ
Tel: 01323 833644
Email: cleaverslyng@btinternet.com
Website: www.cleaverslyng.co.uk
Map ref: 4 TQ61
Directions: A271 at Herstmonceux, turn onto Chapel
Row leading onto Church Rd, 1.5m on right
Rooms: 4 en suite (1 fmly)
S £50-£90 D £75-£110 Notes: Wi-fi Parking: 10

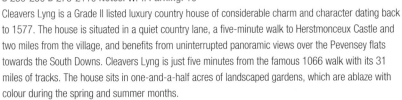

Cleavers Lyng is a Grade II listed luxury country house of considerable charm and character dating back to 1577. The house is situated in a quiet country lane, a five-minute walk to Herstmonceux Castle and two miles from the village, and benefits from uninterrupted panoramic views over the Pevensey flats towards the South Downs. Cleavers Lyng is just five minutes from the famous 1066 walk with its 31 miles of tracks. The house sits in one-and-a-half acres of landscaped gardens, which are ablaze with colour during the spring and summer months.

Recommended in the area

Sussex Weald; South Downs; local beaches

Wild flowers growing at Ditchling

The Blacksmiths Arms

★ ★ ★ ★ ⬭ INN

Address   London Road, Offham,
           LEWES, BN7 3QD
Tel: 01273 472971
Email: blacksmithsarms@shineadsl.co.uk
Website: www.theblacksmithsarms-offham.co.uk
Map ref: 3 TQ41
Directions: 1m N of Lewes. On A275 in Offham
Rooms: 4 en suite S £50-£90 D £65-£100
Notes: Wi-fi ⊗ Parking: 22

Nestled beneath the Sussex Downs just outside Lewes, this charming 18th-century inn is in an Area of Outstanding Natural Beauty, and is a great base for touring the south coast. Each of the high-quality, comfortable double bedrooms at the Blacksmiths Arms features an en suite bathroom, flat-screen TV and tea- and coffee-making facilities. All have been refurbished and are stylishly decorated. Downstairs, open log fires and a warm, relaxed atmosphere welcome you to the cosy bar, where excellent dinners and hearty breakfasts are freshly cooked to order. Evening diners can choose from the inventive brasserie-style menu, which draws from only the best local produce wherever possible, including fresh fish and seafood landed at local ports. Dishes here are much more than pub food, and might include roast local estate free-range venison, wild sea bass fillets on a seafood risotto with a lobster velouté drizzle, or 'Auntie Kate's fresh crispy roast duckling'. Bernard Booker, the owner and chef, has won awards for his seafood dishes. Award-winning, locally brewed Harveys Sussex Bitter is properly served in superb condition; another indication that they like to do things properly here.

Recommended in the area

Brighton; South Downs Way; Sheffield Park Gardens; Bluebell Railway; Glyndebourne Opera House

Nightingales

★ ★ ★ ★ GUEST ACCOMMODATION
Address The Avenue, Kingston, LEWES, BN7 3LL
Tel/Fax: 01273 475673
Email: nightingalesbandb@gmail.com
Website: www.nightingalesbandb.co.uk
Map ref: 3 TQ41
Directions: 2m SW of Lewes. A23 onto A27
to Lewes, at Ashcombe rdbt 3rd exit for Kingston,
under rail bridge, 2nd right into The Avenue, house
2nd from end on right
Rooms: 2 en suite (2 GF) **Notes:** ⊗ 🐾 **Parking:** 2

A spacious bungalow with a light and airy feel, Nightingales is set in a tree-lined avenue in the village of Kingston, with off-street parking provided. A footpath from the gardens leads directly to the South Downs Way, so it is a perfect base from which to explore this lovely area. Bedrooms are furnished with comfortable beds and equipped with flat-screen TVs and tea- and coffee-making facilities. Aga-cooked breakfasts are prepared from locally sourced produce, with eggs from the household hens.
Recommended in the area
Lewes Castle; Anne of Cleves House; Charleston; Glyndebourne Opera

Manor Farm Oast

★ ★ ★ ★ ★ 🏠 ☕ GUEST ACCOMMODATION
Address Windmill Lane, ICKLESHAM, TN36 4WL
Tel/Fax: 01424 813787
Email: manor.farm.oast@lineone.net
Website: www.manorfarmoast.co.uk
Map ref: 4 TQ92 **Directions:** 4m SW of Rye. A259
W past Icklesham church, left at x-rds onto Windmill
Ln, after sharp left bend left into orchards
Rooms: 3 (2 en suite) (1 pri facs) (1 fmly)
S £65-£90 **D** £105
Notes: Wi-fi ⊗ 🐾 11yrs **Parking:** 7 **Closed:** 23 Dec-15 Jan

Built in 1860 and surrounded by a working orchard on the edge of Icklesham, Manor Farm Oast is ideal for a quiet break. The oast house has been converted to keep the unusual original features both inside and out – the double bedroom in one tower is completely round. Your host Kate Mylrea provides a very friendly welcome. Kate is passionate about food: as well as a traditional English breakfast or a healthier alternative, she can prepare a top quality five-course dinner by arrangement on Fridays and Saturdays.
Recommended in the area
Battle Abbey; historic Rye; Ellen Terry's House (NT)

Strand House

★ ★ ★ ★ 🏨 🍽 GUEST ACCOMMODATION

Address   Tanyards Lane, Winchelsea,
             RYE, TN36 4JT
Tel: 01797 226276 **Fax:** 01797 224806
Email: info@thestrandhouse.co.uk
Website: www.thestrandhouse.co.uk
Map ref: 4 TQ92
Directions: M20 junct 10 onto A2070 to Lydd.
Follow A259 through Rye to Winchelsea, 2m past Rye
Rooms: 13 (9 en suite) (1 pri facs)
(4 fmly rooms) (3 GF) **S** £55-£120 **D** £65-£135 **Notes:** Wi-fi 🐾 10yrs **Parking:** 15

Strand House provides a calm retreat from the stresses of modern living, with elegant rooms set in a historic Tudor house full of period detail, such as low, oak-beamed ceilings, winding stairs and inglenook fireplaces in the large lounge. Bedrooms are full of quality furniture and include thoughtful extras such as hand-made biscuits. Sussex breakfasts are provided. Afternoon tea, packed lunches and evening meals are all available – using organic local meat, fish from the boats at Rye Bay, plus home-made cakes.

Recommended in the area

Great Dixter; Sissinghurst; Romney Hythe and Dymchurch Railway

Remains of Battle Abbey

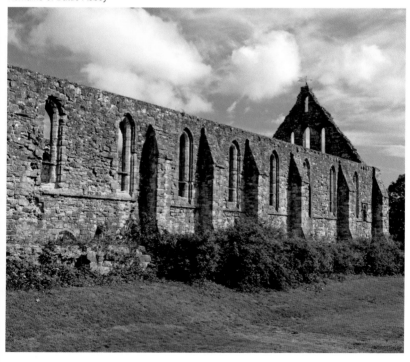

Ab Fab Rooms

★ ★ ★ ★ 🛏 BED & BREAKFAST

Address	11 Station Road, Bishopstone, SEAFORD, BN25 2RB
Tel:	01323 895001 & 07053 603204
Fax:	0870 127 1624
Email:	stay@abfabrooms.co.uk
Website:	www.abfabrooms.co.uk
Map ref:	3 TV49
Rooms:	3 en suite S £55-£65 D £70-£80
Notes:	Wi-fi ⊗ Parking: 2

Situated in Bishopstone, close to the train station and on the outskirts of the pretty Sussex town of Seaford, Ab Fab Rooms is just a short walk from sandy beaches and the South Downs, making it an ideal base for visiting local sights and attractions. The stylish, contemporary en suite bedrooms enjoy stunning views of the end of Seaford Bay and on to the ferry port of Newhaven and beyond. Each room offers a superior level of comfort and amenities, such as fluffy towels, TV/DVDs and well-stocked hospitality trays, which include such treats as home-baked biscuits and cakes. One room has a chocolate brown leather bed and tub chairs in which to relax. Breakfast, served in the garden conservatory, is a special feature and includes home-made jams and marmalade alongside local Sussex produce. Sunsets in this part of the world are spectacular, and the friendly owners are happy to provide sunset picnic baskets, packed with delicious home-made food, for guests to sit back and enjoy on the beach. They'll even chill the wine beforehand. Guest parking is available.

Recommended in the area

Brighton & Hove; Glyndebourne; Charleston Farmhouse

The Avondale

★ ★ ★ GUEST ACCOMMODATION
Address   Avondale Road, SEAFORD, BN25 1RJ
Tel: 01323 890008
Fax: 01323 490598
Email: avondalehotel@btconnect.com
Website: www.theavondale.co.uk
Map ref: 3 TV49
Directions: In town centre, off A259 behind
war memorial
Rooms: 14 (8 en suite) (4 fmly rooms)
Notes: Wi-fi ⊗

The Avondale is conveniently positioned for both the town centre and the seafront, with Seaford
Leisure Centre close by and Brighton, Eastbourne, the South Downs and many other places of interest
within easy reach. Guests frequently comment on how well they sleep in the spotlessly clean bedrooms.
The beds are certainly comfortable, but the friendly service, relaxed atmosphere and fresh flowers also
play their part in the home-from-home experience. Jane and Martin Home and their experienced staff
spare no effort in making your stay relaxing and enjoyable, offering a perfect blend of modern comforts
and traditional courtesy and service. All bedrooms are accessible by stair-lift and eight rooms have en
suite facilities. Each room has free Wi-fi access, a hospitality tray, complimentary toiletries, radio and
TV, with a DVD player on request. An inviting lounge is available during the day for guests' use, and
breakfast is served at individual tables in the spacious dining room. Guests appreciate the quality and
choice at breakfast, and dinners and hot/cold buffets featuring home-cooked local produce can be
provided by arrangement. There are also plenty of good pubs and restaurants serving food in the area.
Recommended in the area
Beachy Head Countryside Centre; Firle Place; Alfriston Clergy House (NT)

Arundel Castle

Angmering Manor

★★★★ ⇔ GUEST ACCOMMODATION

Address   High Street, ANGMERING, BN16 4AG
Tel: 01903 859849 Fax: 01903 783268
Email: angmeringmanor@
            thechapmansgroup.co.uk
Website: www.relaxinnz.co.uk
Map ref: 3 TQ00 Directions: Follow A27 towards
Portsmouth, exit A280, follow signs for Angmering
Rooms: 17 en suite (3 fmly rooms)
Notes: Wi-fi ⊗ Parking: 25

Situated in the heart of Angmering village, Angmering Manor offers luxurious rooms and excellent food in a tranquil setting. The manor is within easy reach of Brighton, Chichester and Arundel, and an ideal base for visitors to Goodwood racecourse. Originally built in the 16th century, Angmering Manor has been recently refurbished to a high standard, with 17 exquisite en suite bedrooms, all well-equipped with flat-screen televisions and Wi-fi. The restaurant offers fine dining at affordable prices, while other facilities include a heated indoor pool, mini gym and on-site beauty therapist.

Recommended in the area

Brighton; Arundel Castle & Cathedral; The South Downs

The Townhouse

★★★★ ❀❀ RESTAURANT WITH ROOMS

Address   65 High Street, ARUNDEL, BN18 9AJ
Tel: 01903 883847
Email: enquiries@thetownhouse.co.uk
Website: www.thetownhouse.co.uk
Map ref: 4 TQ00 Directions: Follow A27 to Arundel,
onto High Street, establishment on left at top of hill
Rooms: 4 en suite S £70-£95 D £95-£130
Notes: Wi-fi ⊗ Closed: 2wks Feb & 2wks Oct

The Townhouse, occupying a prime position opposite Arundel Castle, is an elegant Grade II listed building dating from around the 1800s. The spectacular carved ceiling in its dining room, however, is much older than the rest of the house; it originated in Florence and is a beautiful example of late Renaissance architecture. All of the en suite bedrooms here are sympathetically and tastefully decorated, and all benefit from TV, hairdryer and tea- and coffee-making facilities. The restaurant, too, is stylish, though informal, with owner/chef Lee Williams offering a diverse menu based on local produce and featuring fresh bread made on the premises, earning The Townhouse two AA Rosettes.

Recommended in the area

Glorious Goodwood; Arundel Castle; Chichester Theatre

Rooks Hill

★★★★★ ☻ GUESTHOUSE

Address	Lavant Road, Lavant, CHICHESTER, PO18 0BQ
Tel:	01243 528400
Email:	enquiries@rookshill.co.uk
Website:	www.rookshill.co.uk
Map ref:	3 SU80
Rooms:	6 en suite (2 GF)
Notes:	Wi-fi ⊗ 🐾 12yrs
Parking:	6

This charming grade II listed country house is situated on the edge of the Sussex Downs, and enjoys stunning views over Goodwood. Rooks Hill has been lovingly restored by Ron and Lin Allen, the friendly proprietors, and the tasteful result combines character and contemporary style. Accommodation is in the form of superbly finished, light and airy bedrooms, two of which are on the ground floor. All have pristine en suite bathrooms with power showers and White Company toiletries, as well as pocket-sprung mattresses and white cotton bed linen, LCD flat-screen televisions, hairdryers, hospitality trays and other thoughtful extras. Free Wi-fi is available. The excellent breakfast includes a choice of full English, fresh fruit, cereals, yoghurts, organic free-range eggs, freshly baked bread, and preserves made using organic fruit from the garden. This feast is served in the stylish oak-beamed breakfast room, with its log burner in cooler months. In warmer weather the French doors are opened on to a beautiful wisteria-clad courtyard. Guests may also enjoy afternoon tea in the courtyard, or relax in the cosy guest lounge, which is well stocked with books, magazines and newspapers. There are good pubs and restaurants in the vicinity for evening meals.

Recommended in the area

Chichester Festival Theatre and Cathedral; Goodwood Racecourse; West Wittering Beach

TYNE & WEAR

Souter Lighthouse at South Shields

The Stables Lodge

★★★★★ ⌂ GUESTHOUSE

Address South Farm, Lamesley,
GATESHEAD, NE11 0ET
Tel: 0191 492 1756
Fax: 0191 410 6192
Email: janet@thestableslodge.co.uk
Website: www.thestableslodge.co.uk
Map ref: 7 NZ26
Directions: From A1, take Team Valley/Retail World
slip road and turn off towards Lamesley/Kibblesworth
Rooms: 3 en suite (1 fmly) (1 GF) **Notes:** ⊗ **Parking:** 6

The Stables Lodge enjoys an easily accessible yet semi-rural setting not far from Newcastle, Gateshead and the A1, with the Metro Centre and the Angel of the North only minutes away. The establishment has been thoughtfully converted by experienced owners with a background in interior design, presenting a 'Hunting Lodge' theme throughout. Notable features include luxurious surroundings and excellent guest care – The Stables was the AA's Guest Accommodation of the Year for England in 2008–2009. Each of the en suite bedrooms has a unique character and provides a host of indulgent extras such as chocolates, satellite TV and DVD player, mini-fridge, towelling bathrobes, guest slippers and Molton Brown toiletries. The Red Room has its own spa bath, sauna and steam room, while the Garden Room has an outside seating area. Breakfast, taken in the main lounge, is an informal affair and majors on local, organic and Fairtrade ingredients. As well as lighter options, such as fresh fruit and freshly baked croissants, traditional full English breakfasts are prepared on the Aga, and a pre-ordered luxury option, featuring champagne and strawberries, scrambled eggs with smoked salmon, and creamed chestnut mushrooms with Wiltshire ham on toasted muffins, is also available.

Recommended in the area

Grey's Monument; The Angel of the North; Segedunum Roman Fort

WARWICKSHIRE

Warwick Castle and River Avon

Chapel House

★★★★★ ⊛ RESTAURANT WITH ROOMS

Address Friar's Gate, ATHERSTONE, CV9 1EY
Tel: 01827 718949
Fax: 01827 717702
Email: info@chapelhouse.eu
Website: www.chapelhouse.eu
Map ref: 3 SP39 **Directions:** A5 to town centre,
right onto Church St. Right onto Sheepy Rd & left
onto Friar's Gate **Rooms:** 12 en suite **Notes:** Wi-fi ⊗
Closed: Etr wk, Aug BH wk & Xmas wk

Peacefully set in the heart of a charming market town, this fine Georgian town house glows with a mellow ambience that befits its age. Built in 1728, it retains many original features and sits in a pretty walled garden. Each of the spacious bedrooms is individually designed, and all come with luxurious linens and en suite bathrooms with power showers. Wi-fi access is available. Dinner is a highlight, offering a menu of impressive dishes. Crisp white linen, fine silverware and candlelight add to the atmosphere in the dining room.

Recommended in the area

Twycross Zoo; National Exhibition Centre; Mallory Park

Fulready Manor

★★★★★ ⊜ BED & BREAKFAST

Address Fulready, ETTINGTON,
           Stratford-upon-Avon, CV37 7PE
Tel: 01789 740152
Fax: 01789 740247
Email: stay@fulreadymanor.co.uk
Website: www.fulreadymanor.co.uk
Map ref: 3 SP24
Directions: 2.5m SE of Ettington. 0.5m S off A422
at Pillerton Priors
Rooms: 3 en suite D £125-£140
Notes: Wi-fi ⊗ ⛛ 15yrs **Parking:** 6

Set in 125 acres, this luxury new home appears from afar to be a 16th-century castle. Full of character, the entrance hall has a stone fireplace and a floor-to-ceiling front window, while one of the en suite bedrooms has a four-poster bed with gold-embroidered muslin. The Manor offers old-fashioned comfort and the breakfasts are a feast.

Recommended in the area

Warwick Castle; Warwick; Royal Shakespeare Theatre, Stratford-Upon-Avon; The Cotswolds

Holly End Bed & Breakfast

★ ★ ★ ★ 🛏 BED & BREAKFAST

Address London Road, SHIPSTON ON STOUR,
CV36 4EP
Tel: 01608 664064
Email: hollyend.hunt@btinternet.com
Website: www.holly-end.co.uk
Map ref: 3 SP24
Directions: 0.5m S of Shipston on Stour on A3400
Rooms: 3 (2 en suite) (1 pri facs) (1 fmly)
S £60-£80 D £75-£110
Notes: Wi-fi ⊗ 🐾 9yrs **Parking:** 6

Holly End provides top-drawer accommodation on the edge of the Cotswolds, midway between Moreton-in-Marsh and Stratford-Upon-Avon. Whether your preferences lie with long country hikes and exploring quaint Cotswold villages, or discovering the history and culture of Shakespeare country, Holly End is suitably placed for both. This delightful family home, immaculately maintained and spotlessly clean, is just a short walk from the centre of Shipston on Stour. Shipston, once an important sheep market town, was also a major stopping point for coaches, and many of the inns in the High Street date from that era. Holly End's spacious, comfortable bedrooms – king-size, twin and double – with subtle soft furnishings and décor, have well-equipped bathrooms, while dormer windows add extra character. You can pamper yourself with the Sanctuary spa products provided in each room. Digital televisions and tea- and coffee-making facilities are also provided. A comprehensive freshly cooked English breakfast uses the best of local produce (organic wherever possible). Afternoon tea or sherry and snacks are offered on arrival. There is a beautiful sunny garden with a lawn and patio dotted with many container plants.

Recommended in the area

Stratford-Upon-Avon; Hidcote Manor (NT); Warwick Castle; Cotswold Falconry Centre; Cotswolds

Ambleside Guest House

★ ★ ★ ★ GUESTHOUSE

Address 41 Grove Road,
STRATFORD-UPON-AVON, CV37 6PB
Tel: 01789 297239
Fax: 01789 297239
Email: peter@amblesideguesthouse.com
Website: www.amblesideguesthouse.com
Map ref: 3 SP25 **Directions:** 250mtrs from town
centre on A4390 opposite Firs Gdns
Rooms: 7 (5 en suite) (2 pri facs) (2 fmly rooms) (2
GF) S £30-£38 D £60-£85 **Notes:** Wi-fi ⊗ ☜ 7yrs **Parking:** 8

Ambleside is a comfortable guest house in the heart of Stratford-Upon-Avon, where owners Ruth and Peter provide a warm welcome. A refurbishment has left the house in sparkling condition, and the accommodation can suit every need. Choose from the family rooms, one of which is situated on the ground floor, a double, twin or singles. Many rooms have shower rooms en suite, and each is equipped with a TV, hairdryer and hospitality tray. Ironing facilities are also available. Breakfast is served in the bright and spacious dining room, which looks out over the charming front patio garden. The menu offers plenty to suit all tastes and appetites, and the traditional full English and vegetarian alternative are always freshly cooked. Ambleside stands opposite the attractive gardens of Firs Park and is just a short stroll from the town centre, where there is a good choice of restaurants, cafés and inns. As well as the Shakespeare attractions, Stratford-Upon-Avon offers a wide range of shops, and there are town trails to help guide you around its many ancient buildings. Ambleside guests can also benefit from free on-site parking and Wi-fi.

Recommended in the area

Shakespeare's birthplace; The Royal Shakespeare, Swan and Courtyard theatres; Anne Hathaway's Cottage; Warwick Castle; Warwick

Arden Way Guest House

★ ★ ★ GUESTHOUSE

Address 22 Shipston Road, STRATFORD-UPON-AVON, CV37 7LP
Tel/Fax: 01789 205646
Email: info@ardenwayguesthouse.co.uk
Website: www.ardenwayguesthouse.co.uk
Map ref: 3 SP25 **Directions:** On A3400, S of River Avon, 100mtrs on left **Rooms:** 6 en suite (1 fmly) (2 GF) **S** £35-£55 **D** £56-£72
Notes: Wi-fi ⊗ **Parking:** 6

Arden Way is a friendly, family-run guest house close to all the amenities of the town centre and just a few minutes from the theatres. To the back of the house there is a large garden with a summer house, while at the front there is ample space for guests' cars. The bedrooms are attractively decorated and all have en suite facilities. All the rooms have Freeview flat-screen TVs, Wi-fi access and tea- and coffee-making equipment. A hearty breakfast is served in the dining room which overlooks the garden. Special diets are catered for on request.

Recommended in the area

Shakespeare properties; The Cotswolds; Warwick Castle

Victoria Spa Lodge

★ ★ ★ ★ GUESTHOUSE

Address Bishopton Lane, Bishopton, STRATFORD-UPON-AVON, CV37 9QY
Tel: 01789 267985
Fax: 01789 204728
Email: ptozer@victoriaspalodge.demon.co.uk
Website: www.victoriaspa.co.uk
Map ref: 3 SP25
Directions: A3400 1.5m N to junct A46, 1st left onto Bishopton Ln, 1st house on right
Rooms: 7 en suite (3 fmly rooms) **S** £50-£55 **D** £65-£70 **Notes:** Wi-fi ⊗ **Parking:** 12

An elegant Grade II listed building originally opened by Queen Victoria in 1837, Victoria Spa Lodge was also the home of cartoonist Bruce Bairnsfather. Overlooking the canal, it is only a 20-minute walk from the town. The beautifully appointed bedrooms offer space, comfort, quality furniture, stylish fabrics and thoughtful touches, as well as free Wi-fi. Expect a warm welcome and high standards of service.

Recommended in the area

Warwick Castle; Shakespeare theatres & properties; The Cotswolds

WILTSHIRE

The Westbury White Horse

The George & Dragon

★★★★ ◎◎ RESTAURANT WITH ROOMS

Address High Street, ROWDE,
Devizes, SN10 2PN
Tel: 01380 723053
Email: thegandd@tiscali.co.uk
Website: www.thegeorgeanddragonrowde.co.uk
Map ref: 2 ST96
Directions: 1.5m from Devizes on A350
towards Chippenham
Rooms: 3 (2 en suite) (1 pri facs) (1 fmly)
D £55-£105
Notes: ⊗ **Parking:** 15

A 16th-century coaching inn, the George & Dragon retains many original features, including exposed beams with the carved Tudor rose and large open fireplaces. Wooden floors, antique rugs and candlelit tables create a warm atmosphere in the bar and restaurant. The inn is located on the village high street in Rowde which is only a couple of miles from Devizes and not far from the Caen Hill lock flight on the Kennet & Avon Canal. Accommodation is provided in individually designed bedrooms, furnished with large double beds made up with luxurious linens. Two of the bedrooms are en suite while the third has its own private bathroom. All are equipped with flat-screen televisions with DVD players, iPod stations and tea- and coffee-making facilities. The inn has two AA Rosettes for its food, so dining in the bar or restaurant should not be missed. The house speciality is fresh fish delivered daily from Cornwall, but a full a la carte is offered featuring local produce, meats and game and is available in both the restaurant and bar. Events are held throughout the year, including the likes of summer barbecues, wine and cheese tastings, games nights and charity quizzes.

Recommended in the area

Bowood House & Gardens; Roman Baths & Pump Room; Stonehenge

The Old House

★★★★ GUEST ACCOMMODATION

Address   161 Wilton Road,
          SALISBURY, SP2 7JQ
Tel: 01722 333433
Fax: 01722 335551
Map ref: 3 SU12
Directions: 1m W of city centre on A36
Rooms: 7 en suite (1 fmly)
S £40-£70 D £65-£75
Notes: ⊗ ⚑ 7yrs Parking: 10

Charming accommodation is offered at this 17th-century house that is within walking distance of Salisbury city centre. Ground-floor areas are beautifully furnished in-keeping with the building's period character. The mature gardens are a lovely surprise, with three distinct areas providing privacy on summer evenings. Bedrooms have been tastefully decorated and equipped with modern facilities, including bath or shower rooms en suite. There are two rooms at ground-floor level and one room with a sleigh bed. All the bedrooms are equipped with hairdryers and hospitality trays.

Recommended in the area

Stourhead (NT); Heale Garden; Wilton House

The Manor

★★★★ RESTAURANT WITH ROOMS

Address   SHREWTON,
          SP3 4HF
Tel: 01980 620216
Email: info@rollestonemanor.com
Website: www.rollestonemanor.com
Map ref: 3 SU04
Rooms: 7 en suite (3 fmly rooms) (1 GF)
S £45-£115 D £45-£130
Notes: Wi-fi ⊗ Parking: 40

The Manor is a Grade II listed building dating back to the 13th century, only two minutes away from historic Stonehenge. Each room has its own individual character along with 21st century comforts such as free Wi-fi, iPod docking station, flat-screen TV with built in DVD, and tea- and coffee-making facilities. If you're looking to really treat yourself, there's a luxurious room with a four-poster bed and roll-top bath, and you can order champagne and strawberries on arrival, with a bucks fizz breakfast to complete the occasion. Children aged 12 and under can sleep in a family room at an additional £15 per night.

Recommended in the area

Stonehenge; Old Sarum; Salisbury Cathedral

Stonehenge

Ardecca

★★★★ GUEST ACCOMMODATION

Address Fieldrise Farm, Kingsdown Lane,
Blunsdon, SWINDON, SN25 5DL

Tel: 01793 721238 & 07791 120826

Email: chris-graham.ardecca@fsmail.net

Website: www.ardecca-bedandbreakfast.co.uk

Map ref: 3 SU18

Directions: Off A419 onto B4019 to Blunsdon/
Highworth then onto Turnpike Rd at Cold Harbour
pub, then left down Kingsdown Ln

Rooms: 4 (4 pri facs) (1 fmly) (4 GF) **S** £40 **D** £60

Notes: Wi-fi ⊗ 🐾 6yrs **Parking:** 5

Ardecca (the name is an amalgamation of the names Rebecca and Richard, the owners' children) has been the family home of Chris and Graham Horne for over 25 years. The large modern bungalow is immaculate inside and out and sits in 16 acres of pastureland on the edge of Blunsdon village. It's a quiet rural setting, within easy reach of Swindon and Cirencester, the Cotswolds and the Marlborough Downs. The bungalow offers spacious first-class accommodation in a friendly and relaxed atmosphere created by Chris and Graham. The bedrooms are larger than average and equipped with modern amenities including Wi-fi access, TV, hairdryer, radio alarm and tea- and coffee-making facilities. A full English breakfast is provided and freshly cooked evening meals are available by arrangement. Alternatively, your hosts will be happy to point you in the direction of one of the many good pubs and restaurants in the area. During your stay you can relax on the patio in the garden, explore the immediate area on public footpaths leading through the meadows, or perhaps take part in an on-site arts and crafts workshop. Ample parking is available. Please note that credit cards are not accepted.

Recommended in the area

Cotswold Water Park; STEAM (Museum of the Great Western Railway); Avebury; Stonehenge

The Pear Tree Inn

★★★★★ ◎◎ RESTAURANT WITH ROOMS

Address Maypole Group, Top Lane,
WHITLEY, SN12 8QX
Tel: 01225 709131
Fax: 01225 702276
Email: peartreeinn@maypolehotels.com
Website: www.maypolehotels.com
Map ref: 2 ST86
Rooms: 8 en suite (2 fmly rooms) (4 GF)
S £70 **D** £90 **Notes:** Wi-fi **Parking:** 45

This delightful country inn, located just outside Bath, provides cosy, luxurious accommodation and good food. The chic en suite bedrooms, some housed in an adjoining annexe, combine English and French influences. The restaurant draws visitors from a wide area thanks to the interesting menu, which features organic meats, free-range chicken, locally grown vegetables and healthy children's dishes, as well as the rustic atmosphere and the friendliness of the hosts. Food may be eaten outside, weather permitting. Real ales, a good wine list and roaring log fires complete the picture.

Recommended in the area

Lacock Abbey; Avebury (NT); Silbury Hill

A narrow boat on the Kennet and Avon Canal

The Bell Tower in Evesham

Cowley House

★★★★ GUEST ACCOMMODATION

Address Church Street, BROADWAY, WR12 7AE
Tel: 01386 858148
Email: cowleyhouse.broadway@tiscali.co.uk
Website: www.the-cotswolds.com
Map ref: 3 SP03
Directions: Follow signs for Broadway. Church St adjacent to village green, 3rd on left
Rooms: 7 (6 en suite) (1 pri facs) (1 fmly rooms) (2 GF) **Notes:** Wi-fi **Parking:** 7

Cowley House is an archetypal mellow Cotswold stone building in the heart of picture-postcard Broadway. The 18th century house is full of old-world charm, with original stone floors, oak and elm beams, and an Elizabethan four-poster bed in one of the six bedrooms. The accommodation is full of character and furnished to a high standard. A hearty Cotswold breakfast is served in the elegant dining room, and there's a delightful garden, plus under-cover storage for bicycles. Your friendly hosts, Joan and Peter, will be happy to arrange activities and advise on places to visit.

Recommended in the area

Cotswolds Area of Outstanding Natural Beauty; Cotswold Way; Broadway shopping

View of Bredon Hill

The Boot Inn

★★★★ ⬭ INN

Address   Radford Road, FLYFORD FLAVELL,
Worcester, WR7 4BS
Tel: 01386 462658
Fax: 01386 462547
Email: enquiries@thebootinn.com
Website: www.thebootinn.com
Map ref: 2 SO95
Directions: In village centre, signed from A422
Rooms: 5 en suite (2 GF) S £55-£70 D £70-£100
Notes: Wi-fi Parking: 30

An inn has occupied this site since the 13th century, though 'The Boot' itself, as it is called locally, dates from the Georgian period. It provides an ideal base for anyone wishing to explore Stratford-Upon-Avon, the Cotswolds or the Malvern Hills. The award-winning inn has undergone modernisation, yet it has managed to retain much of its historic charm. The comfortable bedrooms in the converted coach house, furnished in antique pine, are equipped with practical extras such as tea- and coffee-making facilities, trouser press and radio-alarm clock, and all have modern bathrooms. Two rooms have disabled access. Guests can relax and indulge in the range of options available at this family-run pub, which prides itself on its friendly staff and lively atmosphere. Traditional ales and an extensive wine list complement the varied and imaginative menus, which are adapted according to availability of ingredients, with everything from sandwiches to bar meals to full carte on offer. The excellent food here, made from fine local produce, can be enjoyed in the cosy public areas, which include an attractive restaurant, a light and airy conservatory and a shaded patio area especially suited to summer dining.

Recommended in the area

Worcester Cathedral; Stratford-Upon-Avon; Evesham

The Dell House

★ ★ ★ ★ BED & BREAKFAST

Address Green Lane, Malvern Wells,
MALVERN, WR14 4HU

Tel: 01684 564448

Fax: 01684 893974

Email: burrage@dellhouse.co.uk

Website: www.dellhouse.co.uk

Map ref: 2 SO74

Directions: 2m S of Great Malvern on A449. Turn
left off A449 onto Green Ln. House at top of road on
right, just below old church

Rooms: 3 en suite Notes: Wi-fi ⊗ 🐾 10yrs Parking: 3

The Dell House was built around 1820 when one of Malvern's famous healing springs was diverted to
its grounds. Ian and Helen Burrage offer spacious, individually styled bedrooms where period elegance
is combined with homely comforts and Wi-fi access; two rooms have wonderful views to the Cotswolds.
Breakfast is served in the impressive morning room with superb views over the Severn Valley.

Recommended in the area

Malvern Hills; Malvern Theatre; Three Counties Showground; Malvern Springs & Wells

Dawn at the Worcestershire Beacon, Great Malvern, in the Malvern Hills

The lighthouse at Flamborough Head from the coastal path

Burton Mount Country House

★★★★★ 🏠 GUEST ACCOMMODATION

Address Malton Road, Cherry Burton, BEVERLEY, HU17 7RA
Tel: 01964 550541
Email: pg@burtonmount.co.uk
Website: www.burtonmount.co.uk
Map ref: 8 TA03 **Directions:** 2m NW of Beverley. B1248 for Malton, 2m right at x-rds, house on left
Rooms: 3 en suite
Notes: Wi-fi ⊗ 🐾 12yrs **Parking:** 20

Burton Mount is a charming country house three miles from Beverley, set in delightful gardens. The en suite bedrooms are well equipped with TVs, hairdryers, tea- and coffee-making facilities and bathrobes. An excellent, Aga-cooked Yorkshire breakfast is served in the morning room, and includes smoked bacon, free-range eggs, home-made preserves and fresh bread. In summer, guests can relax on the outdoor terrace, while in the cooler months log fires blaze in the elegant drawing room and the comfortable sitting room. Owners, the Greenwood family, are renowned for their warm hospitality.

Recommended in the area

Beverley Minster; Bishop Burton Horse Trials; Wilberforce House

The River Ouse in the centre of York

Druid's Writing Desk, Brimham Rocks, Yorkshire Dales National Park

Shallowdale House

★ ★ ★ ★ ★ 🏠 ☕ GUEST ACCOMMODATION

Address West End, AMPLEFORTH, YO62 4DY
Tel: 01439 788325
Fax: 01439 788885
Email: stay@shallowdalehouse.co.uk
Website: www.shallowdalehouse.co.uk
Map ref: 8 SE57 **Directions:** Off A170 at
W end of village, on turn to Hambleton
Rooms: 3 (2 en suite) (1 pri facs)
S £78.75-£90 **D** £97.50-£120 **Notes:** Wi-fi ⊗ 🏃
12yrs **Parking:** 3 **Closed:** Xmas & New Year

Owned by Anton van der Horst and Phillip Gill, Shallowdale House is in a stunning location overlooking an Area of Outstanding Natural Beauty. The spacious south-facing bedrooms have huge picture windows and lovely views, and the atmosphere is relaxed and friendly. The four-course dinners are a highlight, featuring local and seasonal produce, and equal care is taken with breakfast, which can feature Whitby kippers and local sausages, as well as home-made preserves.

Recommended in the area

Castle Howard; Rievaulx Abbey; Nunnington Hall (NT)

Brookhouse Guest House

★ ★ ★ ★ ☕ GUESTHOUSE

Address Station Road, CLAPHAM,
Lancaster, LA2 8ER
Tel: 015242 51580
Email: admin@brookhouseclapham.co.uk
Website: www.brookhouse-clapham.co.uk
Map ref: 6 SD76 **Directions:** Off A65 into village
Rooms: 3 (2 en suite) (1 pri facs) (1 fmly)
Notes: Wi-fi ⊗

Situated in a pretty conservation village beside Clapham Beck, this well-maintained guest house offers comfortable accommodation and good food. Meals are based on locally sourced ingredients and cooked to a high standard by chef-proprietor, Alan Whitmore, who has over 20 years experience. Dinner is taken in the licensed restaurant, which attracts many non-residents and has a roaring log fire for the winter months. The thoughtfully furnished en suite bedrooms, including a family room, provide a home-from-home, with fluffy towels and bathrobes, TVs with Freeview, complimentary Wi-fi, hospitality trays, hairdryers and radio alarms. There is also a quiet lounge to relax in.

Recommended in the area

Ingleborough Cave; Ingleton Waterfalls trail; Settle to Carlisle Railway

The Flask Inn

★ ★ ★ INN
Address Fylingdales, WHITBY, YO22 4QH
Tel: 01947 880305
Email: admin@theflaskinn.com
Website: www.theflaskinn.com
Map ref: 8 NZ81 **Directions:** On A171, 7m S from
Whitby **Rooms:** 6 en suite (2 fmly rooms)
S £45 D £75 **Parking:** 20

Set amid the unspoilt landscape of the North York
Moors National Park and a short drive from the coast, this is an appealing 17th-century inn offering a
range of cosy, traditional-style rooms, each with en suite bathroom. It's a friendly, family-run place,
with a regular clientele of locals enjoying the hand-pulled ales and adding to the ambience in the bar in
the evenings. The menu is diverse and everything is based on high quality, locally sourced ingredients.
The Sunday lunch carvery is particularly popular, and breakfasts will certainly set you up for a day of
busy sightseeing. Children are well catered for, with family rooms, cots and highchairs, a
children's menu and play area.
Recommended in the area
Whitby; Robin Hood's Bay; North Yorkshire Heritage Coast

Ashfield House

★★★★★ ▧ ◴ GUEST ACCOMMODATION
Address Summers Fold, GRASSINGTON,
Skipton, BD23 5AE
Tel: 01756 752584
Fax: 07092 376562
Email: sales@ashfieldhouse.co.uk
Website: www.ashfieldhouse.co.uk
Map ref: 7 SE06
Directions: B6265 to village centre, main street, left
onto Summers Fold
Rooms: 8 en suite S £47.50-£85 D £75-£120 **Notes:** Wi-fi ⊗ ◨ 5yrs **Parking:** 8

This well-maintained Grade II listed 17th-century house is tucked away down a private lane with its
own walled gardens. Ashfield House was once a row of miners' cottages, but today it provides luxurious
accommodation. There are smart furnishings throughout, from the well equipped en suite bedrooms
to the cosy lounges with honesty bar. Guests dine in style, at breakfast time with home-made yoghurt,
marmalade, granola, and own-recipe sausages, or from imaginative evening menus.
Recommended in the area
Skipton Castle; Bolton Abbey; Pennine boat trips

The Kings Head at Newton

★ ★ ★ ★ GUEST ACCOMMODATION

Address   The Green, NEWTON-UNDER-ROSEBERRY,
          Nr Great Ayton, TS9 6QR
Tel: 01642 722318
Fax: 01642 724750
Email: info@kingsheadhotel.co.uk
Website: www.kingsheadhotel.co.uk
Map ref: 8 NZ61
Directions: A171 towards Guisborough, at rdbt
onto A173 to Newton under Roseberry, under
Roseberry Topping landmark
Rooms: 8 en suite (1 fmly) (2 GF) S £62.50-£87.50 D £77.50-£115
Notes: Wi-fi ⊗ Parking: 100 Closed: 25 Dec & 1 Jan

This family-owned establishment offers stylish, thoughtfully equipped bedrooms. The restaurant, next-door, offers quality food with produce sourced from the local area. A full English or continental breakfast is served in the glass-roofed breakfast area with unspoiled views of Roseberry Topping.

Recommended in the area

Cleveland Way; North York Moors National Park; Whitby

The Grafton

★ ★ ★ ★ GUEST ACCOMMODATION

Address   1-3 Franklin Mount,
          HARROGATE, HG1 5EJ
Tel: 01423 508491 Fax: 01423 523168
Email: enquiries@graftonhotel.co.uk
Website: www.graftonhotel.co.uk
Map ref: 8 SE35 Directions: Follow signs to
International Centre, onto Kings Rd with Centre on
left, Franklin Mount 450yds on right
Rooms: 14 en suite (1 fmly room) (1 GF)
S £50-£75 D £70-£120 Notes: Wi-fi ⊗ Parking: 1 Closed: 15 Dec-6 Jan

This chic townhouse B&B is just a few minutes' walk from the centre of Harrogate. It has a stylish, elegant decor, friendly and efficient service and a warm and homely atmosphere. There are 14 comfortable, well-equipped en suite bedrooms, including several superior rooms which have been recently refurbished in a more contemporary style. There's a cosy lounge bar with an open fire, plenty of free parking, and the home-cooked breakfasts are superb.

Recommended in the area

Harrogate spa and shopping; Yorkshire Dales National Park; Fountains Abbey

Shelbourne House

★ ★ ★ ★ GUEST ACCOMMODATION
Address 78 Kings Road, HARROGATE, HG1 5JX
Tel: 01423 504390
Email: sue@shelbournehouse.co.uk
Website: www.shelbournehouse.co.uk
Map ref: 8 SE35 **Directions:** Follow signs to
International Centre, over lights by Holiday Inn,
premises on right **Rooms:** 8 en suite (2 fmly rooms)
Notes: ⊗ **Parking:** 1

Shelbourne House is a Victorian family home which has been transformed into a beautiful boutique
style B&B. Located in the heart of town, it's an ideal base for exploring Harrogate and the Yorkshire
Dales. Only the finest quality locally sourced Yorkshire produce is served each morning at breakfast,
while packed lunches and evening bites can be provided on request. Relax in the lavish baroque guest
lounge in front of a real fire. Owners, Sue and Neil, have created a homely atmosphere at Shelbourne
House, making it the perfect place to leave you refreshed, recharged and ready to face the hectic pace
of modern life again.

Recommended in the area

Harrogate Turkish Baths and Spa; Fountains Abbey & Studley Royal Estate; Harlow Carr

The New Inn Motel

★ ★ ★ GUEST ACCOMMODATION
Address Main Street, HUBY, York, YO61 1HQ
Tel/Fax: 01347 810219
Email: enquiries@newinnmotel.freeserve.co.uk
Website: www.newinnmotel.co.uk
Map ref: 8 SE56 **Directions:** Off A19 E into village
centre, motel on left **Rooms:** 8 en suite (3 fmly
rooms) (8 GF) S £40-£55 D £70-£80
Parking: 8 **Closed:** mid Nov-mid Dec & part Feb

Located behind the New Inn, this modern family-run motel-style establishment occupies a quiet
location in the village of Huby, 9 miles north of York, and is in an ideal spot for visiting the historic city
and surrounding countryside. The comfortable en suite chalet bedrooms, all on the ground floor, are
spacious and neatly furnished, with TVs and tea- and coffee-making facilities. Full English breakfasts,
made from locally sourced dry-cured bacon, black pudding and sausages, are served in the cosy dining
room. The reception area hosts an array of maps and tourist information, and the resident owners
provide a friendly and helpful service.

Recommended in the area

Beningbrough Hall and Gardens (NT); Sutton Bank Visitor Centre; City of York

Newton House

★ ★ ★ ★ ☰ GUEST ACCOMMODATION

Address 5-7 York Place,
KNARESBOROUGH, HG5 0AD
Tel: 01423 863539
Fax: 01423 869748
Email: newtonhouse@btinternet.com
Website: www.newtonhouseyorkshire.com
Map ref: 8 SE35
Directions: On A59 in Knaresborough, 200yds
from town centre
Rooms: 11 (10 en suite) (1 pri facs) (3 fmly rooms) (3 GF) Notes: Wi-fi Parking: 10 Closed: 1wk Xmas

This delightfully elegant, Grade II listed former coaching inn is only a short walk from the river, castle and market square. Owners Mark and Lisa Wilson place the emphasis on relaxation, informality and comfort, and the very well equipped bedrooms include four-posters and king-size doubles, as well as family and interconnecting rooms. There is a comfortable lounge too. Breakfasts include eggs Benedict, poached smoked haddock, and porridge with sultanas in malt whisky, as well as the traditional full English.

Recommended in the area

Fountains Abbey; Yorkshire Dales; Newby Hall; RHS Harlow Carr Gardens

Capple Bank Farm

★ ★ ★ ★ ★ BED & BREAKFAST

Address West Witton, LEYBURN, DL8 4ND
Tel: 01969 625825 & 07836 645238
Email: julian.smithers@btinternet.com
Website: www.capplebankfarm.co.uk
Map ref: 7 SE19 Directions: A1 to Bedale. Turn
off onto A684 to Leyburn. Continue towards Hawes
through Wensley, take 1st left in West Witton. Up hill,
round left bend, gates straight ahead Rooms: 2 en
suite S £50 D £80 Notes: ⊗ ✴ 10yrs Parking: 6

Ideal for exploring the Yorkshire Dales National Park, or just enjoying the peace and quiet, this spacious house, which commands extensive views of Wensleydale, has recently been converted and refurbished. The en suite bedrooms have been finished to a high standard, with quality bed linen and a range of home comforts, and guests have use of a charming lounge with a real fire lit on cooler days. Breakfast, made from fresh local produce and featuring kedgeree and fish cakes as well as full English and continental options, is served at a beautiful table in the open-plan kitchen and impressive dining room.

Recommended in the area

Bolton Castle; Wensleydale; Aysgarth Falls

Lake Gormire, North York Moors National Park

River House

★★★★ 🏠 🍽 GUESTHOUSE

Address   MALHAM, Skipton, BD23 4DA
Tel: 01729 830315
Email: info@riverhousehotel.co.uk
Website: www.riverhousehotel.co.uk
Map ref: 7 SD96
Directions: Off A65, N to Malham
Rooms: 8 en suite (1 GF) S £45-£65 D £60-£75
Notes: Wi-fi 🐾 9yrs Parking: 5

Dating in parts back to 1664, this attractive guest house makes a great base for exploring the Yorkshire Dales. The house combines modern comfort with period elegance, as seen in the bright, comfortable en suite bedrooms, all of which have luxury Scottish toiletries, big fluffy towels and Wi-fi. Some rooms have stunning views of the dales. Public areas include a cosy lounge bar with wood-burning stove and a large, well-appointed dining room. Excellent breakfasts and evening meals offer choice and quality local produce, plus packed lunches are available. Walkers can make use of the drying room to hang wet clothes, as well as the laundry room. There is also secure bike storage available.

Recommended in the area

Gordale Scar; Settle to Carlisle Railway; Skipton Castle

Roslyn House

★★★ GUEST ACCOMMODATION

Address   9 King St, PATELEY BRIDGE, HG3 5AT
Tel: 01423 711374
Fax: 01423 715995
Email: enquiries@roslynhouse.co.uk
Website: www.roslynhouse.co.uk
Map ref: 7 SE16
Directions: B6165 into Pateley Bridge, end of High St turn right at newsagents onto King Street, house 200yds on left
Rooms: 6 en suite (1 fmly room) S £49-£55 D £69-£75 Notes: Wi-fi ⊗ 🐾 3yrs Parking: 6

Roslyn House is a well appointed, comfortable and charming period guest house located in the centre of Pateley Bridge. It has a pleasant lounge, an attractive café-style breakfast room, and six beautifully refurbished en suite bedrooms. The owners, Lawrence and Liz Glynn, place great emphasis on a warm welcome, good food and first-class service. There's a wide choice at breakfast and everything is prepared from fresh local produce.

Recommended in the area

Fountains Abbey; Newby Hall; Brimham Rocks

St George's Court

★★★★ 🏠 FARMHOUSE

Address   Old Home Farm, Grantley,
          RIPON, HG4 3PJ
Tel: 01765 620618
Email: info@stgeorgescourt.co.uk
Website: www.stgeorges-court.co.uk
Map ref: 7 SE37 **Directions:** B6265 W from Ripon,
up hill 1m past Risplith sign & next right, 1m on right
Rooms: 5 en suite (1 fmly room) (5 GF) S £45-£55
D £70-£80 **Notes:** Wi-fi **Parking:** 12

This family-run bed and breakfast in a renovated farmhouse sits in 20 acres of secluded farmland, making it the ideal restful retreat. Originally a working pig farm, the owners now keep a small number of sheep, cattle, pigs and chickens, plus three dogs, a cat, a pony and a pet peacock called Peter. There is a fishing lake within the grounds and plenty of opportunities for country walks. St George's Court has five recently upgraded en suite rooms arranged around a pretty courtyard. Imaginative breakfasts are served in the new breakfast room, which, along with the guest lounge, has lovely countryside views.

Recommended in the area

Fountains Abbey; Harrogate; Yorkshire Dales National Park

The Moorings

★★★★ GUEST ACCOMMODATION

Address   3 Burniston Road,
          SCARBOROUGH, YO12 6PG
Tel: 01723 373786
Email: post@scarboroughmoorings.co.uk
Website: www.scarboroughmoorings.co.uk
Map ref: 8 TA08 **Directions:** 300mtrs from North
Bay Beach, next to the Peasholm Park entrance
Rooms: 12 en suite (2 fmly rooms) (1 GF)
S £35 D £66-£80
Notes: Wi-fi ⊗ **Parking:** 12 **Closed:** 2wks Xmas

The Moorings is well placed to take advantage of the developments in Scarborough's North Bay. It offers well maintained, individually designed rooms with modern furnishings, flat-screen TVs and free Wi-fi access. Some have their own private lounges and some come with fridges. There is a garden to relax in and a bedroom on the ground floor for wheelchair users. Top quality ingredients go into making The Moorings' excellent breakfasts.

Recommended in the area

Open air theatre; Peasholm Park; Sealife Centre

Low Skibeden House

★ ★ ★ FARMHOUSE

Address Harrogate Road, SKIPTON, BD23 6AB
Tel: 01756 793849
Website: www.lowskibeden.co.uk
Map ref: 7 SE35 **Directions:** 1m E of Skipton on right before A59/A65 rdbt, set back from road
Rooms: 4 (2 en suite) (2 fmly rooms)
S £40-£56 D £60-£68
Notes: ⊗ ☜ 14yrs **Parking:** 4

Surrounded by open countryside, on the edge of the Yorkshire Dales National Park and enjoying fine views, Low Skibeden House is an attractive stone-built 16th-century farmhouse. It is located just a mile from Skipton, which has many amenities. Guests are greeted with tea or coffee and cake, before settling into the traditionally furnished bedrooms (all en suite). Family accommodation is available, and there is also a spacious and comfortable visitors' lounge with TV where guests are invited to enjoy evening drinks. A separate dining room is the setting for hearty farmhouse breakfasts.

Recommended in the area

Bolton Abbey; Harrogate; York

Sunset over Wensleydale, Yorkshire Dales National Park

The Blackwell Ox Inn

★★★★ ⊛ INN

Address Huby Road, SUTTON-ON-THE-FOREST,
YO61 1DT
Tel: 01347 810328
Fax: 01347 812738
Email: enquiries@blackwelloxinn.co.uk
Website: www.blackwelloxinn.co.uk
Map ref: 8 SE56
Directions: A1237 onto B1363 to Sutton-on-the-
Forest. Left at T-junct, 50yds on right
Rooms: 7 en suite S £65 D £95-£110
Notes: Wi-fi ⊗ **Parking:** 18

A picturesque village just seven miles from the centre of York is the location of this friendly, renovated inn, which dates back to around 1823 and is named after a memorable 2,278lb, 6ft-tall (at the shoulders) animal that was bred locally. The finest local meat and produce still figures prominently in the inn's renowned restaurant, where Head Chef Tom Kingston and his team create serious gastro-pub food. There's a separate area where you can relax with an aperitif and browse the menu before being served in the traditional-style dining room. For less formal eating, a selection from the restaurant menu is also available in the bar, where logs blaze in an open fireplace in winter and fine, hand-pulled ales are kept in top condition (children are allowed in the bar until 8pm). There's also a pleasant terrace for alfresco dining on warm summer days. Accommodation at the inn offers stylish en suite bedrooms which have been individually designed – you can opt for a four-poster room with a big, claw-foot bathtub right in the bedroom, and perhaps upgrade to the Champagne Break for a really romantic stay. All of the rooms include a television with DVD player and the bathrooms have Molton Brown toiletries.

Recommended in the area

Sutton Park and Gardens; the City of York; Beningbrough Hall (NT)

Spital Hill

★ ★ ★ ★ ★ 🏠 ☕ GUEST ACCOMMODATION

Address   York Road, THIRSK, YO7 3AE
Tel: 01845 522273
Fax: 01845 524970
Email: spitalhill@spitalhill.entadsl.com
Website: www.spitalhill.co.uk
Map ref: 8 SE48
Directions: 1.5m SE of town, set back 200yds from A19, driveway marked by 2 white posts
Rooms: 5 (4 en suite) (1 pri facs) (1 GF)
S £64-£69 D £100-£110 Notes: Wi-fi ⊗ ✿ 12yrs Parking: 6

Robin and Ann Clough are passionate about offering their guests genuine hospitality at their beautiful home set in gardens and surrounded by open countryside. Ann produces an excellent set dinner each evening as an optional extra, using good fresh produce; usually the couple will join their guests at the table. Breakfast is also a highlight. Bedrooms are furnished with quality and style, and thoughtfully equipped with many extras; there is no tea-making equipment as Ann prefers to offer tea as a service.

Recommended in the area

Herriott Centre, Thirsk; Byland Abbey; Rievaulx Abbey

Corra Lynn

★ ★ ★ ★ GUEST ACCOMMODATION

Address   28 Crescent Avenue, WHITBY, YO21 3EW
Tel: 01947 602214
Fax: 01947 602214
Map ref: 8 NZ81
Directions: Corner A174 & Crescent Av
Rooms: 5 en suite (1 fmly) D £68
Notes: ⊗ Parking: 5 Closed: 21 Dec-14 Feb

Bruce and Christine Marot have a passion for what they do, mixing traditional values of cleanliness, comfort and friendly service with a modern style. The house is set in a prominent corner position on the West Cliff within easy walking distance of the town of Whitby and its picturesque harbour. The bedrooms are thoughtfully equipped with colour TV, radio-alarm and hospitality tray, and are individually furnished and colourfully decorated. The delightful dining room, with a corner bar and a wall adorned with clocks, really catches the eye. Breakfasts at Corra Lynn are hearty, with a vegetarian option, and the menu changes with the seasons. There is off-street parking.

Recommended in the area

Whitby Abbey; Captain Cook Memorial Museum; Robin Hood's Bay

Limestone pavement, above Malham Cove, Yorkshire Dales National Park

Beach huts at Scarborough's North Bay

Estbek House

★★★★ ◉◉ ⬔ RESTAURANT WITH ROOMS

Address East Row, Sandsend, WHITBY, YO21 3SU
Tel: 01947 893424
Fax: 01947 893625
Email: info@estbekhouse.co.uk
Website: www.estbekhouse.co.uk
Map ref: 8 NZ81
Directions: From Whitby take A174. In Sandsend, left into East Row
Rooms: 4 (3 en suite) (1 pri facs)
Notes: Wi-fi ⊗ ⛐ 14yrs **Parking:** 6

Estbek House, a beautiful Georgian establishment located in a small coastal village north-west of Whitby, is a restaurant with rooms that specialises in seafood. Here, diners can indulge themselves in the first-floor restaurant while listening to the relaxing sound of breaking waves from the nearby Yorkshire Moors coastline. Chef/co-proprietor Tim Lawrence has nearly 30 years' experience of seafood cookery and he and his team present a range of mouth-watering dishes, including non-fish alternatives, on daily-changing menus. Over 100 wines – many available by the glass – are offered on the blackboard, including a large Australian contingent. Surroundings in the restaurant are modern and stylishly simple – airy and bright by day, thoughtfully lit in the evenings. When the weather allows, diners may eat outside in the flower-bordered courtyard. On the ground floor is a small bar and breakfast room, while above are the individually decorated and luxurious bedrooms. Each has its own name – such as Florence or Eva – and character, and comes with a wealth of thoughtful extras including flat-screen TV, CD/radio-alarm, hairdryer, tea- and coffee-making facilities and complimentary guest pack.

Recommended in the area

Mulgrave castles; Mulgrave woods; Cleveland Way

Netherby House

★★★★ 🏠 🍽 GUEST ACCOMMODATION

Address	90 Coach Road, Sleights, WHITBY, YO22 5EQ
Tel:	01947 810211
Fax:	01947 810211
Email:	info@netherby-house.co.uk
Website:	www.netherby-house.co.uk

Map ref: 8 NZ81 **Directions:** In village of Sleights, off A169 (Whitby-Pickering road)
Rooms: 11 en suite (1 fmly) (5 GF)
S £39-£49.50 **D** £78-£99 **Notes:** Wi-fi ⊗ 🐾 2yrs **Parking:** 17 **Closed:** 25-26 Dec

For owners Lyn and Barry Truman their bed and breakfast business is a labour of love; the beautifully kept gardens and the delightful day rooms and bedrooms, all contribute to a restful stay. Hospitality is another strength of Netherby House, and imaginative evening meals using fresh garden produce are served in the candlelit dining room. There are twin, double and family rooms, and a four-poster room adds that extra touch of luxury. There is a lounge-bar with Sky TV and a conservatory for relaxing in.

Recommended in the area

Historic Whitby; North Yorkshire Moors National Park; North Yorkshire Moors Railway

Ripon Cathedral

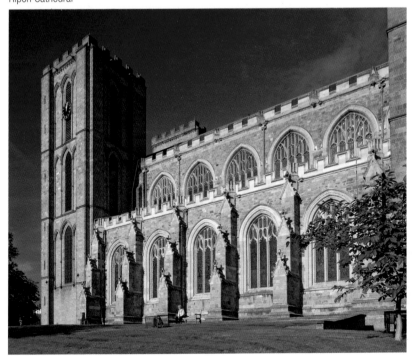

Ascot House

★★★★ GUEST ACCOMMODATION

Address   80 East Parade, YORK, YO31 7YH
Tel: 01904 426826
Fax: 01904 431077
Email: admin@ascothouseyork.com
Website: www.ascothouseyork.com
Map ref: 8 SE65
Directions: 0.5m NE of city centre. Off A1036
Heworth Green onto Mill Ln, 2nd left
Rooms: 12 en suite (3 fmly rooms) (2 GF)
S £55-£80 D £70-£80 Notes: Wi-fi Parking: 13 Closed: 21-28 Dec

This Victorian villa was built for a prominent family in 1869 close to the city centre. The owners have retained many original features, yet they have improved the building to provide modern standards of comfort. Most of the spacious rooms on the ground and first floors have period furniture and four-poster or canopy beds. The top-floor rooms have now been completely refurbished and come with superb bathrooms; all rooms have hospitality trays, hairdryers, radio-alarms and TVs. The curved stained-glass window on the landing is a particularly attractive feature. There is a spacious and comfortable lounge where you can relax, watch television or enjoy a drink from the Butler's Pantry. Tea and coffee are also served in the lounge throughout the day. Delicious traditional, vegetarian and continental breakfasts are served in the dining room; the generous portions are sure to set you up for the day. Ascot House is a welcoming property that can be reached from the city by bus in just a few minutes, or by a short brisk walk. It has an enclosed car park, and the public park next door has two tennis courts and two bowling greens. A nearby pub serves good food, and there are also many restaurants, wine bars and theatres within walking distance.

Recommended in the area

Jorvik Viking Centre; National Railway Museum; York Minster

The Heathers Guest House

★★★★ GUEST ACCOMMODATION

Address 54 Shipton Rd, Clifton-Without, YORK, YO30 5RQ
Tel: 01904 640989
Fax: 01904 640989
Email: aabbg@heathers-guest-house.co.uk
Website: www.heathers-guest-house.co.uk
Map ref: 8 SE65 **Directions:** N of York on A19, halfway between A1237 ring road & York city centre
Rooms: 6 (4 en suite) (2 pri facs) (2 fmly rooms)
S £52-£126 **D** £56-£130 **Notes:** Wi-fi ⊗ 🐾 10yrs **Parking:** 9 **Closed:** Xmas

Remodelling and refurbishment at this large 1930s house has resulted in a most comfortable and welcoming establishment. Heather and Graham Fisher have designed each room individually using quality fabrics and decor and there is a feeling of luxury in the bedrooms, all of which have en suite or private facilities and benefit from TV, Wi-fi and well-stocked tea- and coffee-making facilities. The light and airy breakfast room looks out onto a well-tended garden area, and off-street parking is guaranteed.

Recommended in the area

North York Moors; Castle Howard; Ryedale Folk Museum

Ribblehead Viaduct, Yorkshire Dales National Park

Goit Stock Falls in heart of Goit Stock Wood

The Huddersfield Central Lodge

★★★★ GUEST ACCOMMODATION

Address   11/15 Beast Market,
           HUDDERSFIELD, HD1 1QF
Tel: 01484 515551
Fax: 01484 432349
Email: angela@centrallodge.com
Website: www.centrallodge.com
Map ref: 7 SE11
Directions: In town centre off Lord St, signs for
Beast Market from ring road
Rooms: 22 en suite (2 fmly rooms) S £52-£58 D £68 Notes: Free Wi-fi Parking: 50

This friendly, family-run operation is located in the town centre, close to amenities and transport links. Some of the smart, spacious bedrooms are in the main building, while others, many with kitchenettes, are situated across a courtyard. All are well equipped, with Freeview TVs. Public rooms include a bar with a plasma-screen TV and a conservatory. Breakfasts are based on local and organic produce. For evening meals, ask about Woks Cooking. There are smoking rooms available and children and pets are welcome.

Recommended in the area

Galpharm Stadium; Holmfirth; The National Coal Mining Museum for England

View of Stoodley Pike on Pennine Way

CHANNEL ISLANDS

St Ouen's Bay, Jersey

Harbour View

★★★★ GUESTHOUSE

Address	Le Boulevard, ST AUBIN,
	St Brelade, JE3 8AB
Tel:	01534 741585
Email:	harbourview@localdial.com
Website:	www.harbourviewjersey.com

Map ref: 13 Rooms: 16 en suite (4 fmly rooms) (2 GF)
S £50-£55 D £100-£110
Notes: Wi-fi Parking: 8 Closed: Dec-Feb

This charming family-run guest house overlooks picturesque St Aubin harbour, with stunning views from most bedrooms, as well as from the sun terrace. The house was originally built in 1709 and has been sympathetically restored and refurbished over the years to provide luxury accommodation with all mod-cons, including hairdryers, satellite TV and en suite bathrooms. There are two suites available, one on the top floor with amazing sea views, and a newly built garden suite on the ground floor. A continental or English breakfast buffet is included in your stay, as is parking and Wi-fi access.

Recommended in the area

St Aubin beach; Durrell Wildlife Conservation Trust; Jersey War Tunnels

Seymour Tower, La Rocque

The Panorama

★ ★ ★ ★ ★ ♨ GUEST ACCOMMODATION

Address	La Rue du Crocquet,
	ST AUBIN, JE3 8BZ
Tel:	01534 742429
Fax:	01534 745940
Email:	info@panoramajersey.com
Website:	www.panoramajersey.com
Map ref:	13
Directions:	In village centre
Rooms:	14 en suite (3 GF) S £44-£70 D £88-£140
Notes:	Wi-fi ⊗ ✗ 18yrs
Closed:	mid Oct-mid Apr

The Panorama is aptly named indeed, with its spectacular views across St Aubin's Bay. A long established favourite with visitors, not least because of the genuinely warm welcome, it is situated on a pretty seafront street. Inside are antiques aplenty, including a number of elegant fireplaces, and a collection of over 500 teapots. A feature of the recently upgraded bedrooms is the luxurious pocket-sprung beds, most well over six feet long. The breakfasts, each individually cooked to order, are another draw, with dishes such as 'grand slam' and 'elegant rarebit' among the inventive choices on the lengthy menu. For lunch or dinner there are many restaurants in close proximity, providing ample opportunity to sample the best produce that Jersey has to offer. Many are within walking distance, and the owners will happily make recommendations. The Panorama makes a good base for walking, cycling (a cycle track along the promenade leads to St Helier) or travelling around the island by bus. Day trips by boat are available to the neighbouring islands of Guernsey, Herm and Sark, and also to St Malo in Brittany. The accommodation is unsuitable for children.

Recommended in the area

Picturesque village of St Aubin; Railway Walk to Corbière; Beauport and Les Creux Country Park

Corbiére Lighthouse

SCOTLAND

Loch Katrine, Loch Lomond and the Trossachs National Park

Callater Lodge Guest House

★★★★ GUESTHOUSE

Address 9 Glenshee Road, BRAEMAR, AB35 5YQ
Tel: 013397 41275
Email: info@hotel-braemar.co.uk
Website: www.callaterlodge.co.uk
Map ref: 12 NO19
Directions: Next to A93, 300yds S of Braemar centre
Rooms: 6 en suite (1 fmly)
S £40-£80 **D** £75-£150
Notes: Wi-fi ⊗ **Parking:** 6 **Closed:** Xmas

A warm welcome is assured at Callater Lodge which stands in spacious, attractive grounds. Sink into deep leather chairs after a day spent walking, climbing, golfing, cycling, fishing or skiing. The individually-styled, en suite bedrooms have lovely soft furnishings, TV, and tea- and coffee-making facilities. A wide choice is offered at breakfast, and later, soup of the day, snacks and sandwiches are served. Surrounded by fine hills, Braemar Castle can be reached via a pretty walk, and a number of local trails includes the Whisky Trail. There is a drying room, plus storage for bicycles, golf clubs and skis for guests.

Recommended in the area

Balmoral Castle; Cairngorm National Park; Glenshee Ski Centre, Cairnwell

Glenburnie House

★★★★ GUESTHOUSE

Address The Esplanade, OBAN, PA34 5AQ
Tel: 01631 562089
Fax: 01631 562089
Email: graeme.strachan@btinternet.com
Website: www.glenburnie.co.uk
Map ref: 9 NM82
Directions: On Oban seafront. Follow signs for Ganavan
Rooms: 12 en suite (2 GF) **S** £45-£50 **D** £80-£100
Notes: Wi-fi ⊗ ⛔12yrs **Parking:** 12 **Closed:** Nov-Feb

This impressive Victorian house, which sits on Oban's seafront just a few minutes' stroll from the town centre, has breathtaking views over the bay down to the Sound of Lorn. Inside, it has been lovingly restored to a high standard. The en suite bedrooms (including a four-poster room and a mini-suite) are beautifully decorated and very well equipped. There is also a cosy ground-floor lounge and an elegant dining room, where hearty traditional breakfasts, which include home-made preserves, are served.

Recommended in the area

McCaig's Tower; Dunstaffnage Castle; Trips to the Isle of Mull

Craigadam

★ ★ ★ ★ 🛏 ☕ GUESTHOUSE

Address Craigadam, CASTLE DOUGLAS, DG7 3HU
Tel: 01556 650233 & 650100
Fax: 01556 650233
Email: inquiry@craigadam.com
Website: www.craigadam.com
Map ref: 5 NX76 **Directions:** From Castle Douglas
E on A75 to Crocketford. In Crocketford turn left on
A712 for 2m. House on hill **Rooms:** 10 en suite
(2 fmly rooms) (7 GF) **S** £45-£80 **D** £90
Notes: Wi-fi **Parking:** 12 **Closed:** Xmas & New Year

A relaxed, peaceful stay is guaranteed at this elegant country house on a working farm. Large en suite bedrooms are housed in a converted 18th-century farmstead, with antique furnishings and French windows opening out onto a courtyard. Public areas include a lounge with a log fire and a snooker room with comprehensive honesty bar. The dining room features a magnificent 15-seater table, the setting for Celia Pickup's delightful home-cooking using ingredients from Craigadam estate and smokehouse.

Recommended in the area

Henry Moore/Roden statues; Drumlandrig Castle; Threave Gardens

Wallamhill House

★ ★ ★ ★ BED & BREAKFAST

Address Kirkton, DUMFRIES,
DG1 1SL
Tel: 01387 248249
Email: wallamhill@aol.com
Website: www.wallamhill.co.uk
Map ref: 5 NX97 **Directions:** 3m N of Dumfries.
Off A701 signed Kirkton, 1.5m on right
Rooms: 3 en suite (1 fmly) **S** £38 **D** £60
Notes: Wi-fi ⊗ **Parking:** 6

Hospitality is a real strength at Wallamhill House, where you are always assured a warm welcome. An attractive house set in well-tended gardens and peaceful countryside three miles from Dumfries, the large bedrooms are extremely well-equipped and there is a drawing room and a mini health suite with sauna, steam shower and gym equipment. The area offers great walking, cycling, or mountain biking in the Ae and Mabie forests, and there is an abundance of wildlife.

Recommended in the area

Nithsdale; Sweetheart Abbey, New Abbey; Caerlaverock Castle

Bonnington Guest House

★★★★ GUESTHOUSE
Address 202 Ferry Road, EDINBURGH, EH6 4NW
Tel: 0131 554 7610
Email: booking@thebonningtonguesthouse.com
Website: www.thebonningtonguesthouse.com
Map ref: 10 NT27
Directions: On A902, near corner of Ferry Rd & Newhaven Rd
Rooms: 7 (5 en suite) (2 pri facs) (4 fmly rooms) (1 GF)
S £50-£70 **D** £66-£104 **Notes:** Wi-fi ⊗ **Parking:** 9

An impressive three-storey property, this guest house is situated just 10 minutes from Edinburgh city centre, with its own off-road parking and good public transport links. Built in 1840, the house backs onto Victoria Park and is close to Leith and the Botanical Gardens. The individually furnished bedrooms are located on two floors. All are equipped with fridges, bottled water, a decanter of sherry, tea- and coffee-making facilities and TVs with Freeview; Wi-fi access is also available. A substantial breakfast is served in the dining room.
Recommended in the area
Edinburgh Castle; Dynamic Earth; Museum of Scotland

Elmview

★★★★★ ☷ GUEST ACCOMMODATION
Address 15 Glengyle Terrace, EDINBURGH, EH3 9LN
Tel: 0131 228 1973
Email: nici@elmview.co.uk
Website: www.elmview.co.uk
Map ref: 10 NT27
Directions: 0.5m S of city centre. Off A702 Leven St onto Valleyfield St, one-way to Glengyle Ter
Rooms: 3 en suite (3 GF) **S** £70-£100 **D** £90-£120
Notes: Wi-fi ⊗ ⚬ 15yrs **Closed:** Dec-Feb

Elmview is situated in the heart of Edinburgh in a delightful Victorian terrace within easy walking distance of Edinburgh Castle and Princes Street. The spacious and quiet en suite bedrooms have been furnished to include everything a guest could want. Fresh flowers, complimentary sherry and elegant furnishings all add to the feeling of a personal home. Elmview overlooks a large urban park, which includes a free, 36-hole pitch and putt golf course. The highlight of a stay is the excellent breakfast taken at one large table.
Recommended in the area
Edinburgh Castle; Edinburgh Old Town; Museum of Scotland; Royal Mile

Kew House

★ ★ ★ ★ ★ GUEST ACCOMMODATION

Address 1 Kew Terrace, Murrayfield,
EDINBURGH, EH12 5JE
Tel: 0131 313 0700
Fax: 0131 313 0747
Email: info@kewhouse.com
Website: www.kewhouse.com
Map ref: 10 NT27
Directions: 1m W of city centre A8
Rooms: 6 en suite (1 fmly) (2 GF)
S £75-£90 **D** £85-£165
Notes: Wi-fi ⊗ **Parking:** 6

Kew House forms part of a listed Victorian terrace dating from 1860, located a mile west of the city centre, convenient for Murrayfield Rugby Stadium, and just a 15-minute walk from Princes Street. Regular bus services from Princes Street pass the door. The house is ideal for both business travellers and holidaymakers, with secure private parking. While many period features have been retained, the interior design is contemporary, and the standards of housekeeping are superb. Expect complimentary sherry and chocolates on arrival, and you can order supper in the lounge. Full Scottish breakfast with an alternative vegetarian choice is included in the room tariff, and light snacks, with room service, are available all day. Bedrooms, including some on the ground floor, are en suite and well-equipped with remote control TV with digital channels, direct-dial telephones, modem points, hairdryers, trouser presses, fresh flowers and tea- and coffee-making facilities. The superior rooms also have their own fridge. Kew House also offers a luxurious serviced apartment accommodating up to three people.

Recommended in the area

Edinburgh Castle; Edinburgh International Conference Centre; Murrayfield Rugby Stadium

23 Mayfield

★★★★ 🏛 GUEST ACCOMMODATION

Address 23 Mayfield Gardens,
EDINBURGH, EH9 2BX
Tel: 0131 667 5806
Fax: 0131 667 6833
Email: info@23mayfield.co.uk
Website: www.23mayfield.co.uk
Map ref: 10 NT27

Directions: A720 bypass S, follow city centre signs.
Left at Craigmillar Park, 0.5m on right
Rooms: 9 en suite (2 fmly rooms) (2 GF) **S** £50-£75 **D** £70-£160 **Notes:** Wi-fi ⊗ **Parking:** 10

A great location just a mile from the city centre adds to the appeal of this family-run guest house. It occupies a detached Victorian villa that retains many original features, and has spacious, individually and stylishly designed rooms. The Four Poster Room boasts a huge, hand-carved mahogany bed, Egyptian cottons, flat-screen TV and Bose sound system. Other amenities include free Wi-fi, an elegant lounge and an exceptional breakfast menu, which includes, of course, Scottish smoked salmon.

Recommended in the area

Edinburgh Castle; Holyrood Palace; Princes Street

Southside Guest House

★★★★ 🏛 GUESTHOUSE

Address 8 Newington Road, EDINBURGH, EH9 1QS
Tel: 0131 668 4422 **Fax:** 0131 667 7771
Email: info@southsideguesthouse.co.uk
Website: www.southsideguesthouse.co.uk
Map ref: 10 NT27 **Directions:** E end of Princes St onto North
Bridge to Royal Mile, continue S, 0.5m, house on right
Rooms: 8 en suite (2 fmly rooms) (1 GF)
S £65-£90 **D** £80-£140 **Notes:** Wi-fi ⊗ 🐾 10yrs

Built in 1865, Southside Guest House is an elegant Victorian sandstone terraced house in the centre of Edinburgh, only a few minutes from Holyrood Park. The Owners, Lynne and her Italian husband Franco, have been involved in the hospitality trade for many years. They offer individually designed, stylish, well-equipped accommodation with direct-dial telephones, DVD players and free wireless internet access. Two rooms have four-poster beds and comfortable sofas, and there's also a new self-contained apartment. Breakfast is served at individual tables in the attractive dining room.

Recommended in the area

Edinburgh Castle; The Palace of Holyroodhouse; Princes Street shops and gardens

The Spindrift

★★★★ ⬠ ⬡ GUESTHOUSE

Address	Pittenweem Road,
	ANSTRUTHER, KY10 3DT
Tel:	01333 310573
Fax:	01333 310573
Email:	info@thespindrift.co.uk
Website:	www.thespindrift.co.uk
Map ref:	10 NO50

Directions: Enter town from W on A917, 1st building on left

Rooms: 8 (7 en suite) (1 pri facs) (2 fmly rooms) **S** £40-£70 **D** £64-£80

Notes: Wi-fi ⛄ 10yrs **Parking:** 12 **Closed:** Xmas-late Jan

A unique feature of this house is the top-floor Captain's Room, made to resemble a shipmaster's cabin by the original owner – the east-facing window looks towards Anstruther harbour. All the individually furnished, spacious bedrooms are brightly decorated and have a wide range of extras. The lounge has an honesty bar for a pre-dinner drink, and enjoyable, home-cooked fare is served in the dining room.

Recommended in the area

Scottish Fisheries Museum; St Andrews; East Neuk coastal villages

Distillery Guest House

★★★★ GUESTHOUSE

Address	Nevis Bridge, North Road,
	FORT WILLIAM, PH33 6LR
Tel:	01397 700103
Email:	disthouse@aol.com
Website:	www.stayinfortwilliam.co.uk

Map ref: 12 NN17 **Directions:** A82 from Fort William towards Inverness, on left after Glen Nevis rdbt

Rooms: 10 en suite (1 fmly) (1 GF)

Notes: ⊗ **Parking:** 20

Distillery House is a conversion of three former workers' cottages built for the old Glenlochy Distillery, the shell of which stands at the foot of Ben Nevis on the banks of the River Nevis. It's an idyllic spot, just a stone's throw from the end of the West Highland Way. At Distillery House you can be assured of the very best of Highland hospitality, which begins with complimentary whisky and shortbread served in the cosy reading lounge. The en suite bedrooms are tastefully furnished, with king-size beds, flat-screen TVs and upgraded toiletries in the new superior rooms.

Recommended in the area

Ben Nevis; Ben Nevis Distillery tour; Jacobite Steam Train

Flanders Moss in the Trossachs

The Ghillies Lodge

★ ★ ★ ★ 🛏 BED & BREAKFAST

Address 16 Island Bank Road,
INVERNESS, IV2 4QS
Tel: 01463 232137
Email: info@ghillieslodge.com
Website: www.ghillieslodge.com
Map ref: 12 NH64
Directions: 1m SW from town centre on B862, pink
house facing river
Rooms: 3 en suite (1 GF) **S** £40-£50 **D** £60-£72
Notes: Wi-fi **Parking:** 3

Built in 1847 as a fisherman's lodge, the Ghillies Lodge lies on the River Ness with fine views over the Ness Islands and just a mile from Inverness centre, making it an ideal base for touring the Highlands. The attractive and peaceful en suite bedrooms (including one on the ground floor) are individually styled and well-equipped, and wireless internet connection is available. There is a comfortable lounge-dining room and a conservatory overlooks the river.

Recommended in the area

Loch Ness; Speyside distilleries; Isle of Skye

Trotternish on the Isle of Skye

Moyness House

★★★★ GUEST ACCOMMODATION

Address 6 Bruce Gardens, INVERNESS, IV3 5EN
Tel: 01463 233836
Fax: 01463 233836
Email: stay@moyness.co.uk
Website: www.moyness.co.uk
Map ref: 12 NH64
Directions: Off A82 (Fort William road), almost opp Highland
Regional Council headquarters
Rooms: 6 en suite (1 fmly) (2 GF)
S £65-£80 **D** £68-£100
Notes: Wi-fi ⊗ ✿ 5yrs **Parking:** 10

Built in 1880 this gracious villa, once the home of acclaimed Scottish author Neil Gunn, has been sympathetically restored to its full Victorian charm by Jenny and Richard Jones, and has many fine period details. The six stylish en suite bedrooms, named after Gunn's novels, are enhanced by contemporary amenities and thoughtful extra touches. Breakfasts served in the elegant dining room include a wide range of delicious Scottish dishes, as well as vegetarian and healthy options, using fresh local produce. The inviting sitting room overlooks the garden to the front, and a pretty walled garden to the rear is a peaceful retreat in warm weather. Free wireless internet connection is available throughout the house. Moyness House has ample parking within the grounds, and is well located in a quiet residential street, less than 10 minutes' walk from the city centre where there are several highly recommended restaurants, the Eden Court Theatre and delightful riverside walks. Jenny and Richard are happy to advise on local restaurants and to make dinner reservations for their guests. They will also be glad to provide touring advice and help guests make the most of their stay in the beautiful Highlands.

Recommended in the area

Culloden Battlefield; Loch Ness and the Caledonian Canal; Urquhart Castle and Cawdor Castle

Trafford Bank

★ ★ ★ ★ ★ 🏛 GUESTHOUSE

Address 96 Fairfield Road,
INVERNESS, IV3 5LL
Tel: 01463 241414
Email: enquiries@
invernesshotelaccommodation.co.uk
Website: www.traffordbank.co.uk
Map ref: 12 NH64 **Directions:** Off A82 at Kenneth St, Fairfield
Rd 2nd left, 600yds on right
Rooms: 5 en suite (2 fmly rooms)
S £70-£95 **D** £90-£120
Notes: Wi-fi ⊗ **Parking:** 10

Luxurious accommodation and Highland hospitality go hand-in-hand at this guest house, run by Lorraine and Koshal Pun. This multilingual pair can welcome you in Italian, French, Hindi and Swahili. Located within walking distance of the city centre and the Caledonian Canal, Trafford Bank, built in 1873, was once the local bishop's home. Lorraine's flair for interior design has produced a pleasing mix of antique and contemporary; some furnishings she has designed herself. The dining room chairs are a special feature, and there is unusual lighting and original art throughout the house. The bright bedrooms are individually themed; all are en suite and have enticing extras like Arran Aromatics products and organic soap from the Strathpeffer Spa Soap Company. Each bedroom is superbly decorated with fine bed linen, hairdryers, Fairtrade tea and coffee, flat-screen digital TVs, DVD players, CD/radio alarms, iPod docking stations and silent fridges. Breakfast is prepared using the best Highland produce and served on Anta pottery in the stunning conservatory. There are two spacious lounges and the house is surrounded by mature gardens that guests are welcome to enjoy. Wi-fi is available throughout the house.

Recommended in the area

Cawdor Castle; Culloden Battlefield (NTS); Loch Ness; Moniack Castle (Highland Winery)

Craiglinnhe House

★★★★ GUESTHOUSE

Address Lettermore, BALLACHULISH,
PH49 4JD
Tel: 01855 811270
Email: info@craiglinnhe.co.uk
Website: www.craiglinnhe.co.uk
Map ref: 9 NN05
Directions: From village A82 onto A828,
Craiglinnhe 1.5m on left
Rooms: 5 en suite **S** £45-£64 **D** £60-£85
Notes: Wi-fi ⊗ ☇ 13yrs **Parking:** 5 **Closed:** 24-26 Dec

Situated overlooking Loch Linnhe, Craiglinnhe House was built in 1885 and, while retaining its Victorian style and character, it has been modernised to provide the utmost comfort with stylish, well-equipped bedrooms. This is the perfect base for walking, climbing, skiing and exploring the West Highlands. The elegant lounge has stunning views of Loch Linnhe and is a lovely place to relax, while the dining room provides a fine setting for the superb meals cooked by owner David Hughes. A fine selection of single malts whiskies is available.

Recommended in the area

Glencoe; Fort William; Whisky distillery

Portland Arms

★★★★ ⬷ INN

Address Main Street, LYBSTER, KW3 6BS
Tel: 01593 721721
Fax: 01593 721722
Email: manager@portland-arms.co.uk
Website: www.portlandarms.co.uk
Map ref: 12 ND23
Directions: On A99, 4m N of Thurso junct
Rooms: 23 en suite (4 fmly rooms) (4 GF) **S** £50-£70
D £80-£140 **Notes:** Wi-fi ⊗ **Parking:** 72

The Portland Arms sits on the outskirts of the small fishing village of Lybster, only half-a-mile from the dramatic North Sea coastline with its unspoilt beaches and abundant birdlife. It was built in 1856 as a coaching inn and has been providing excellent food and comfortable lodgings for travellers from all over the world ever since. The present day owners pride themselves in continuing that great tradition, and offer a warm Highland welcome with friendly service and good, home-style cooking using fresh local produce. The aim at the Portland Arms is to create a home from home feel for all guests.

Recommended in the area

Unspoilt beaches; coastal walks; bird watching

Corriechoille Lodge

★ ★ ★ ★ 🛏 GUESTHOUSE

Address SPEAN BRIDGE, PH34 4EY
Tel: 01397 712002
Website: www.corriechoille.com
Map ref: 12 NN28
Directions: Off A82 signed Corriechoille, 2.5m, left at fork (10mph sign). At end of tarmac, turn right up hill & left
Rooms: 4 en suite (2 fmly rooms) (1 GF)
S £42-£48 D £64-£76
Notes: Wi-fi ⊗ 🐕 7yrs **Parking:** 7 **Closed:** Nov-Mar

Standing above the River Spean, Corriechoille Lodge is an extensively renovated former fishing lodge near Spean Bridge. There are magnificent views of the Nevis range and surrounding mountains from the comfortable first-floor lounge and some of the bedrooms. Guest rooms are spacious and well-appointed, with en suite facilities, TVs and tea-and-coffee facilities. Enjoy traditional breakfasts, with evening meals available by arrangement. The house is licensed and stocks many single malt whiskies.

Recommended in the area

Glenfinnan Monument; Viaduct & Station Museum; Ben Nevis footpath/Glen Nevis; Creag Meagaidh

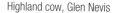

Highland cow, Glen Nevis

Tigh Na Leigh Guesthouse

★★★★★ 🏠 ☕ GUEST ACCOMMODATION

Address 22-24 Airlie Street, ALYTH, PH11 8AJ
Tel: 01828 632372
Fax: 01828 632279
Email: bandcblack@yahoo.co.uk
Website: www.tighnaleigh.co.uk
Map ref: 10 NO24
Directions: In town centre on B952
Rooms: 5 en suite (1 GF) **S** £48 **D** £97-£122.50
Notes: Wi-fi 🐾 12yrs **Parking:** 5 **Closed:** Dec-Feb

Previous winner of the AA 'Guest Accommodation of the Year for Scotland' award, this guest house in the heart of the country town of Alyth is an absolute delight. Tigh Na Leigh is Gaelic for 'the house of the doctor or physician', and although it may look rather sombre from the outside, the property is superbly modernised and furnished with an eclectic mix of modern and antique furniture. The large, luxurious and individually decorated bedrooms, one of which is on the ground floor, are very well equipped. All rooms have spa baths as well as TV/DVD players, tea- and coffee-making facilities, hairdryer and bathrobes. For extra luxury, one room has a grand four-poster, while the suite has its own lounge with a very comfortable sofa. The public rooms comprise three entirely different lounges, one with a log fire for cooler evenings, another a large TV lounge, and the third a reading room with brochures, maps and guides detailing the activities available in the area. Wi-fi is available throughout the house. The superb home-cooked dinners have an international flavour and, like the hearty breakfasts, are all made from the best of Scottish produce – vegetables come from the kitchen garden or surrounding organic farms where possible. Meals are served in the huge conservatory/dining room overlooking the spectacular landscaped garden.

Recommended in the area

Scone Palace; Glamis Castle; Dunkeld Cathedral

Gilmore House

★ ★ ★ ★ 🛏 BED & BREAKFAST

Address	Perth Road, BLAIRGOWRIE, PH10 6EJ
Tel:	01250 872791
Fax:	01250 872791
Email:	jill@gilmorehouse.co.uk
Website:	www.gilmorehouse.co.uk
Map ref:	10 NO14
Directions:	On A93 S
Rooms:	3 en suite D £60-£70
Notes:	Wi-fi **Parking:** 3 **Closed:** Xmas

Built in 1899, this deceptively spacious late-Victorian detached house is the perfect base from which to explore all that Perthshire has to offer, being conveniently located for Glamis Castle, Scone Palace and Dunkeld. The three comfortable en suite rooms include a cosy king, a twin and a very spacious super-king. There are two beautiful lounges for guests' use, with plenty of reading material to plan your activities. A full Scottish breakfast or a lighter option is served in the elegant dining room overlooking the front garden, and the owners pride themselves on the relaxed, warm and friendly ambience.

Recommended in the area

Glamis Castle; Blair Castle; Perth races

Crailing Old School

★ ★ ★ ★ 🛏 🍽 GUESTHOUSE

Address CRAILING, Nr Jedburgh, TD8 6TL
Tel: 01835 850382
Email: jean.player@virgin.net
Website: www.crailingoldschool.co.uk
Map ref: 10 NT62
Directions: A698 onto B6400 signed Nisbet, Crailing Old School also signed
Rooms: 4 (2 en suite) (1 pri facs) (1 GF)
S £38.50-£45 D £60-£80
Notes: Wi-fi 🐾 9yrs **Parking:** 6 **Closed:** 24 Dec-2 Jan, 1wk Feb & 2wks Autumn

This delightful Victorian village school has been imaginatively renovated to combine original features with modern comforts. Jean Leach-Player has been a runner-up in the AA's 'Landlady of the Year' award on three occasions. This is a good area for outdoor pursuits including fishing, walking and golf. Breakfasts (and dinner by arrangement) are served in the stylish lounge/dining room and the best local ingredients are used. The lodge annexe, 10 metres from the house, offers ground floor access.

Recommended in the area

St Cuthbert's Way; The Teviot and Tweed Rivers; Roxburghe Championship Golf Course

Fauhope House

★ ★ ★ ★ ★ 🏠 GUESTHOUSE

Address Gattonside, MELROSE, TD6 9LU
Tel: 01896 823184
Fax: 01896 823184
Email: info@fauhopehouse.com
Map ref: 10 NT53 **Directions:** 0.7m N of Melrose
over River Tweed. N off B6360 at Gattonside 30mph
sign (E) up long driveway
Rooms: 3 en suite **S** £70-£110 **D** £90-£110
Notes: ⊗ **Parking:** 10

Fauhope House is a fine example of the Arts and Crafts style of architecture of the 1890s, designed by Sidney Mitchell, who was also responsible for Edinburgh's much-admired Ramsey Gardens property. It is perched high on a hillside on the north-east edge of the village of Gattonside, and provides the kind of breathtaking views of the River Tweed and the Eildon Hills that have inspired artists and writers down the years. It offers discerning guests comfortable seclusion and the space to relax, yet is just a ten-minute walk from the Borders town of Melrose, with its shops, restaurant and small theatre. A short drive will take you to Abbotsford, home of Sir Walter Scott, and the Robert Adam-designed Mellerstain House. The hospitality provided by experienced host Sheila Robson is first-class, and the delightful country house boasts a splendid interior, furnished and decorated to the highest possible standard. Stunning floral displays enhance the overall interior design, and lavish drapes and fine furniture grace the drawing room and the magnificent dining room, where full Scottish or a continental breakfast is served. The generously sized bedrooms are luxurious and superbly equipped, each with individual furnishings and thoughtful extras. Fauhope House was named AA 'Guest Accommodation of the Year for Scotland' 2008/2009.

Recommended in the area

Melrose Abbey; Roxburghe Golf Course; River Tweed; Fantastic walks

Daviot House

★★★★ GUESTHOUSE

Address 12 Queens Terrace, AYR, KA7 1DU
Tel: 01292 269678
Email: daviothouse@hotmail.com
Website: www.daviothouse.com
Map ref: 9 NS32
Directions: Off A719 onto Wellington Sq & Bath Place, turn right
Rooms: 6 (5 en suite) (1 pri facs) (1 fmly) (1 GF)
S £30-£40 **D** £50-£60
Notes: Wi-fi ⊗

In a peaceful residential area, a short distance from the beach and town centre, Daviot House is a comfortable Victorian terrace home that retains many original features. Bedrooms are bright and modern, and equipped with thoughtful extras. In the dining room, guests congregate around one big table to start the day with a hearty, cooked Scottish breakfast. The hosts are happy to book a round of golf for guests on the local municipal courses.

Recommended in the area

Burns Cottage; Royal Troon & Turnberry golf courses; Culzean & Country Park

Rissons at Springvale

★★★ ☻ RESTAURANT WITH ROOMS

Address 18 Lethame Road,
 STRATHAVEN, ML10 6AD
Tel: 01357 521131 & 520234 **Fax:** 01357 521131
Email: rissons@msn.com
Website: www.rissonsrestaurant.co.uk
Map ref: 9 NS74
Directions: A71 into Strathaven, W of town centre off Townhead St **Rooms:** 9 en suite (1 fmly) (1 GF) **S** £42.50-£55 **D** £75
Notes: Wi-fi ⊗ **Parking:** 10 **Closed:** 1st wk Jan

A small family-run restaurant with rooms, Rissons at Springvale is a little gem in the heart of the quiet village of Strathaven. The restaurant has a warm and friendly atmosphere, and is the setting for co-proprietor Scott Baxter's simple but accomplished Scottish cooking. You can dine in the stylish restaurant or the adjoining conservatory. Scott and Anne Baxter have refurbished Rissons at Springvale in recent years, and the result is 10 well-equipped and tastefully furnished bedrooms.

Recommended in the area

Glasgow; Edinburgh; Ayrshire coast; Clyde Valley

Arden House

★ ★ ★ ★ 🛎 GUEST ACCOMMODATION

Address Bracklinn Road, CALLANDER,
FK17 8EQ
Tel: 01877 330235
Email: ardenhouse@onetel.com
Website: www.ardenhouse.org.uk
Map ref: 9 NN60
Directions: Off A84 Main St onto Bracklinn Rd,
house 200yds on left
Rooms: 6 en suite (2 GF) **S** £40-£70 **D** £70-£80
Notes: Wi-fi ⊗ 🐾 14yrs **Parking:** 10 **Closed:** Nov-Mar

This is the fictional home of Doctors Finlay and Cameron and is peacefully located in the town's most beautiful setting. Ian and William offer guests a genuine welcome with tea and home-made cakes in their stylish sitting room on arrival. The house has been tastefully and lovingly refurbished to reflect its Victorian heritage. Beautifully presented Scottish breakfasts, prepared using locally sourced produce and supplemented by daily specials, are the perfect start to the day.

Recommended in the area

Loch Lomond & Trossachs National Park; Stirling Castle; Loch Katrine; The Falkirk Wheel

Belsyde House

★ ★ ★ ★ 🛎 GUEST ACCOMMODATION

Address Lanark Road, LINLITHGOW, EH49 6QE
Tel: 01506 842098
Fax: 01506 842098
Email: info@belsydehouse.com
Website: www.belsyde.com
Map ref: 10 NS97
Directions: 1.5m SW on A706, 1st left over
Union Canal
Rooms: 3 en suite (1 fmly) **S** £35-£48
D £70-£90 **Notes:** Wi-fi ⊗ 🐾 12yrs **Parking:** 10 **Closed:** Xmas

A tree-lined driveway leads to this welcoming 18th-century farmhouse, peacefully situated in attractive grounds with horse and sheep pastures and views of the Ochil Hills beyond. Close to the Union Canal and halfway between Glasgow and Edinburgh, it makes a good touring base. Inside, well-proportioned bedrooms are individually furnished and well-equipped, with complimentary Wi-fi. The breakfast includes a vegetarian menu. Belsyde has also won a Green Tourism award.

Recommended in the area

Hopetoun House; Linlithgow Palace; The Falkirk Wheel, Falkirk

WALES

Pembrokeshire Coast Path - looking back along Maen Bachau near St Justinian's

Sarnau Mansion

★★★★ GUEST ACCOMMODATION

Address   Llysonnen Road,
          CARMARTHEN, SA33 5DZ
Tel/Fax: 01267 211404
Email: d.fernihough@btinternet.com
Website: www.sarnaumansion.co.uk
Map ref: 1 SN42
Directions: 5m W of Carmarthen. Off A40 onto
B4298 & Bancyfelin road, Sarnau on right
Rooms: 4 (3 en suite) (1 pri facs) S £50 D £70-£80
Notes: ⊗ ⛄ 5yrs Parking: 10

This fine Grade II listed country house, built in 1765, is set in the heart of the Carmarthen countryside, in 16 acres of grounds, which include a tennis court. It's not far from here to the many attractions and beaches of south and west Wales, and it is a delightful place to return to each evening. Many original features have been retained and the public areas are both comfortable and elegant. Bedrooms are large and nicely decorated, and all of the rooms have stunning rural views.

Recommended in the area

National Botanic Garden of Wales; Aberglasney Gardens; Dylan Thomas Boathouse, Laugharne

Carreg Cennen Castle

Allt Y Golau Farmhouse

★ ★ ★ ★ ≙ FARMHOUSE

Address Allt Y Golau Uchaf, FELINGWM UCHAF, SA32 7BB
Tel: 01267 290455
Email: alltygolau@btinternet.com
Website: www.alltygolau.com
Map ref: 1 SN52
Directions: A40 onto B4310, N for 2m. 1st on left after Felingwm Uchaf
Rooms: 3 (2 en suite) (1 pri facs) (2 GF)
S £45 D £68
Notes: ⊗ **Parking:** 3 **Closed:** 20 Dec-2 Jan

Beautifully renovated by owners Colin and Jacquie Rouse, this Georgian stone farmhouse offers the epitome of gracious country living and a welcome that earned Jacquie a place in the finals of the AA 'Friendliest Landlady of the Year' Awards in 2008. The owners are knowledgeable about the heritage and nature of the area, and are always happy to advise guests on how to get the best out of their visit. The setting of the farmhouse, with views over the Tywi Valley towards the Black Mountain, is glorious, and the two acres of gardens include a fine orchard. Snowdrops, daffodils and bluebells carpet the ground in spring, and ducks, geese, turkeys, and the hens that provide the breakfast eggs roam free here. Inside the house there are cosy sofas and easy chairs around the lovely old fireplace in the lounge. The traditional dining room features one big elm table and an eclectic display of antiques, including a stately grandfather clock. Breakfast here is a real highlight, with home baking and the finest local produce accompanying those fresh eggs. The bright, comfortable bedrooms are in traditional style, with pine furniture and patchwork quilts.

Recommended in the area

National Botanic Garden of Wales; Aberglasney Gardens; Dynefwr Castle and Park

Coedllys Country House

★★★★★ BED & BREAKFAST

Address   Coedllys Uchaf, Llangynin,
          ST CLEARS, SA33 4JY
Tel: 01994 231455
Fax: 01994 231441
Email: coedllys@btinternet.com
Website: www.coedllyscountryhouse.co.uk
Map ref: 1 SN21
Directions: A40 St Clears rdbt, take 3rd exit, at lights
turn left. After 100yds turn right, 3m to Llangynin,
pass village sign. 30mph sign on left, turn immediately down track (private drive)
Rooms: 4 en suite D £90-£100 Notes: Wi-fi ☜ 12yrs Parking: 6 Closed: Xmas

Set in 11 acres of grounds, Coedllys is the ultimate country hideaway, tucked away in a tranquil spot and surrounded by farmland with far-reaching views and a pretty woodland dell. Guests are invited to amble around and enjoy the abundant wildlife. Owners Valerie and Keith Harber are serious about conservation and nature and they provide a refuge for countless animals, including sheep, donkeys and ponies. Inside, this large, beautiful house has been tastefully restored to provide elegant bedrooms with antique furniture and luxurious fabrics, as well as a host of thoughtful extras such as chocolates, fruit, flowers and magazines alongside soft bathrobes, slippers, flat-screen TV/DVD, free Wi-fi, iPod dock, comfortable sofas and large, inviting antique beds – all of which combine to make a stay here truly memorable. Energetic guests are welcome to make use of the fitness suite, or they can simply relax in the hydro swimming pool (available April–September only) and sauna. An extensive breakfast menu, from lighter choices through to a full breakfast, uses the finest local produce, including free-range eggs from Coedllys' own chickens.

Recommended in the area

Dylan Thomas Boathouse, Laugharne; Millennium Coastal Path; National Botanical Gardens

Woodland walk around Dinas Rock, near Ystradffin

The Kinmel Arms

★★★★★ ◉◉ RESTAURANT WITH ROOMS

Address   The Village, St George, ABERGELE, LL22 9BP
Tel: 01745 832207
Fax: 01745 822044
Email: info@thekinmelarms.co.uk
Website: www.thekinmelarms.co.uk
Map ref: 5 SH97
Directions: From A55 junct 24a to St George. E on A55, junct
25. 1st left to Rhuddlan, then 1st right into St George. Take 2nd
right
Rooms: 4 en suite (2 GF) **Notes:** ⊗ 🚼 16yrs **Parking:** 8
Closed: 25 Dec & 1 Jan

This delightful restaurant with rooms is the perfect place to rest, eat and explore. It's in a wonderfully
peaceful spot, surrounded by stunning countryside, yet only a few hundred metres from the A55 North
Wales Expressway, with ready access to the coast, mountains and cwms of beautiful North Wales.
The inn dates from the 17th century and has been lovingly renovated and extended by Lynn Cunnah-
Watson and husband Tim to create a truly luxurious hideaway. The stylish, contemporary restaurant,
decorated with Tim's artworks, serves buzzy brasserie-style lunches and relaxed evening meals,
complemented by an excellent wine list. Good, fresh food is at the heart of The Kinmel Arms, with as
much produce as possible sourced from North Wales and North West England, and everything made
in-house. The lively bar is popular for its traditional cask ales, with a different guest ale every week. The
four luxurious guest suites are individually designed and furnished with Tim's striking artworks. All have
handmade, super-king-size oak and maple beds, porcelain bathrooms and locally crafted Welsh green
oak balconies, while the upper rooms feature lofty ceilings and skylights.

Recommended in the area

Snowdonia National Park; Bodnant Gardens; Championship golf courses

Cwmanog Isaf Farm

★★★★ FARMHOUSE

Address Fairy Glen, BETWS-Y-COED, LL24 0SL
Tel: 01690 710225 & 07808 421634
Email: h.hughes@btinternet.com
Website: www.cwmanogisaffarmholidays.co.uk
Map ref: 5 SH75
Directions: 1m S of Betws-y-Coed off A470 by Fairy Glen Hotel, 500yds on farm lane
Rooms: 3 (2 en suite) (1 pri facs) (1 GF)
S £45-£60 **D** £60-£70
Notes: ⊗ ⛔ 15yrs **Parking:** 4 **Closed:** 15 Nov-1 Mar

Hidden away, yet only a 20-minute stroll from the Victorian village of Betws-y-Coed, Cwmanog Isaf, a 200-year-old house on a working livestock farm, is set in 30 acres of undulating land, including the renowned Fairy Glen, and has stunning views of the surrounding countryside. It provides comfortably furnished and well-equipped bedrooms (one on the ground floor), and serves wholesome Welsh farmhouse cuisine using home-reared and local organic produce, home-made bread and preserves.

Recommended in the area

Bodnant Garden (NT); Fairy Glen; Portmeirion

Mynydd y Dref, or Conwy Mountain, looking towards Penmaenbach

Llynau Mymbyr near Capel Curig, Snowdonia National Park

Penmachno Hall

★★★★★ ⬬ GUEST ACCOMMODATION

Address Penmachno, BETWS-Y-COED, LL24 0PU
Tel: 01690 760410
Fax: 01690 760410
Email: stay@penmachnohall.co.uk
Website: www.penmachnohall.co.uk
Map ref: 5 SH75 **Directions:** 4m S of Betws-y-Coed. A5 onto
B4406 to Penmachno, over bridge, right at Eagles pub signed
Ty Mawr. 500yds at stone bridge
Rooms: 3 en suite D £80-£95
Notes: Wi-fi ⊗ **Parking:** 5 **Closed:** Xmas & New Year

Penmachno Hall, a lovingly restored Victorian rectory, is situated
in over two acres of mature grounds in the secluded Glasgwm Valley in Snowdonia National Park. With
its breathtaking views and quiet forest tracks leading to waterfalls, the valley is a haven of tranquillity
within easy reach of bustling Betws-y-Coed. This is an establishment that prides itself on catering
for the visitor's every need. Stylish decor and quality furnishings highlight the many original features
throughout the ground-floor areas, while the bedrooms come with a wealth of thoughtful extras, and
each benefits from panoramic views. The spacious morning room has comfortable sofas and large
bay windows overlooking the garden; it houses a large collection of books, maps, walking guides and
tourist information, as well as games and puzzles. The slightly more formal dining room is the venue
for evening meals, served dinner-party style around a central table. Supper is available from Tuesday to
Friday (£15 per person), with a five-course set dinner on Saturdays (£35 per person), based on guests'
preferences and using only the finest, fresh local produce. An extensive wine list complements the
meal, and expert advice is available to help guests select the most appropriate bottle.

Recommended in the area

Snowdon; Bodnant Garden (NT); Portmeirion

The Groes Inn

★★★★★ 🏵 INN

Address Tyn-y-Groes, CONWY, LL32 8TN
Tel: 01492 650545 **Fax:** 01492 650855
Email: enquiries@thegroes.com
Website: www.groesinn.com
Map ref: 5 SH77 **Directions:** A55, over Old Conwy
Bridge, 1st left through Castle Walls on B5106
(Trefriw Road), 2m on right **Rooms:** 14 en suite (1
fmly) (6 GF) **S** £85-£160 **D** £105-£180 **Notes:** Wi-fi
Parking: 100 **Closed:** 25 Dec

The Groes Inn continues to welcome travellers four centuries after it first opened its doors. The inn is full of old-world charm, with roaring log fires and lots of little nooks and crannies. There's a lovely garden, airy conservatory and intimate restaurant, where the accomplished home-cooking is complemented by real ales and fine wines. The 14 stylish bedrooms combine the features of the 16th century inn with the requirements of the modern guest. Some have terraces or balconies, and all have magnificent countryside views.

Recommended in the area

Conwy Castle; Bodnant Garden; Rhug Estate

Conwy Castle and Telford's suspension bridge

The Glyders at dawn, from the south

Abbey Lodge

★ ★ ★ ★ GUESTHOUSE

Address   14 Abbey Road,
            LLANDUDNO,
            LL30 2EA

Tel: 01492 878042

Email: enquiries@abbeylodgeuk.com

Website: www.abbeylodgeuk.com

Map ref: 5 SH78

Directions: A546 to N end of town, onto Clement Av, right onto Abbey Rd

Rooms: 4 en suite S £40 D £70-£75

Notes: Wi-fi ⊗ **Parking:** 4 **Closed:** Dec-1 Mar

Built in 1840 and set in a quiet leafy avenue within easy walking distance of the promenade, Abbey Lodge retains all the charm of a Victorian townhouse. This Grade II listed building is under the personal supervision of Dennis and Janet, who welcome guests with a complimentary pot of tea or coffee in the comfortable lounge; they will even meet you from the train. The pretty walled garden that shelters beneath the Great Orme is the perfect place to relax. The charming en suite bedrooms are well-equipped with hospitality trays, hairdryers, TV, magazines, books, towels and bathrobes. Free wi-fi is available throughout the house. A collection of local interest books and maps is available to help guests plan excursions. Breakfast is mostly sourced from the farmers' market, and packed lunches can be ordered. Abbey Road is quiet, yet only five minutes' walk from the pier and the Victorian High Street with a good choice of shops, cafés and a variety of restaurants.

Recommended in the area

Bodnant Garden (NT); Conwy Castle; Snowdonia Mountains

St Hilary Guest House

★★★★ GUEST ACCOMMODATION

Address	The Promenade, 16 Craig-y-Don Parade, LLANDUDNO, LL30 1BG
Tel:	01492 875551
Fax:	01492 877538
Email:	info@sthilaryguesthouse.co.uk
Website:	www.sthilaryguesthouse.co.uk

Map ref: 5 SH78 Directions: 0.5m E of town centre. On B5115 seafront road near Venue Cymru
Rooms: 9 en suite (2 fmly rooms) (1 GF) S £45-£71
D £63-£80 Notes: Wi-fi ⊗ Closed: end Nov-early Feb

This elegant Grade II listed Victorian seafront guest house has spectacular views of Llandudno's sweeping bay and the Great and Little Orme headlands. Proprietors Anne-Marie and Howard provide you with a welcoming and friendly atmosphere. Delicious breakfasts, tastefully decorated, comfortable bedrooms with flat-screen TV, a well stocked drinks tray, free Wi-fi, and little extras make your stay special. For the theatre, or for conference delegates, Venue Cymru is only a five-minute walk.

Recommended in the area

The Great Orme Country Park; Conwy Castle; Snowdonia

Llandudno Bay from Great Orme

View down the Roman Steps towards Cwm Bychan in the Rhinogs, Snowdonia National Park

Plas Rhos

★★★★★ 🔔 GUEST ACCOMMODATION

Address Cayley Promenade,
RHOS-ON-SEA, LL28 4EP
Tel: 01492 543698
Fax: 01492 540088
Email: info@plasrhos.co.uk
Website: www.plasrhos.co.uk
Map ref: 5 SH88
Directions: A55 junct 20 onto B5115 for Rhos-on-
Sea, right at rdbt onto Whitehall Rd to promenade
Rooms: 8 en suite **S** £50-£70 **D** £80-£100
Notes: Wi-fi ⊗ 🐾 12yrs **Parking:** 4 **Closed:** 21 Dec-Jan

A yearning to live by the sea and indulge their passion for sailing brought Susan and Colin Hazelden to the North Wales coast. Running a hotel in Derbyshire for many years was the ideal preparation for looking after guests at their renovated Victorian home. Built as a gentleman's residence in the late 19th century, Plas Rhos is situated on Cayley Promenade, where it enjoys panoramic views over the bay, beach and coast. Breakfast, a particularly memorable meal, is taken overlooking the pretty patio garden. It consists of cereals, fresh fruit, juices and yoghurt followed by free-range eggs cooked to your liking with Welsh sausage, local back bacon, tomato, mushrooms, beans and fried bread or your choice of a number of other hot options including kippers or scrambled eggs with smoked salmon. The two sumptuous lounges have spectacular sea views, comfy chairs and sofas, and interesting memorabilia, while the modest-size bedrooms are individually decorated and have plenty of thoughtful extras. One period room is furnished with a romantic half-tester and antiques, and enjoys those same stunning views. Wi-fi access is available in all rooms – just bring your laptop.

Recommended in the area

Conwy Castle; Bodnant Garden (NT); Snowdonia National Park

Offa's Dyke footpath at Sebury near Chepstow

Castle House

★★★★★ BED & BREAKFAST

Address Bull Lane (Love Lane), DENBIGH, LL16 3LY
Tel: 01745 816860
Fax: 01745 817214
Email: stay@castlehouseBandB.co.uk
Website: www.castlehouseBandB.co.uk
Map ref: 5 SJ06
Directions: A55 junct 27 onto A525 to Denbigh. From Vale St take 1st exit at rdbt, pass supermarket, 1st left to T-junct then right. 20yds on left onto unmarked drive
Rooms: 3 en suite **S** £60-£67.50 **D** £120-£135
Notes: Wi-fi ⊗ **Parking:** 6 **Closed:** 20-30 Dec

Located within Denbigh's medieval town walls, this substantial Grade II listed former gentleman's residence dates back to 1820. As well as enjoying magnificent views across the Clwyd Valley towards the Clwydian range of mountains, designated an Area of Outstanding Natural Beauty, it enjoys prime position within the tranquil grounds of Plas Castell Estate, with two acres of landscaped gardens at guests' disposal, including a croquet lawn and fish pond. Also within the grounds is the 16th-century Leicester's Church, an unfinished cathedral built by the nobleman Robert Dudley. Inside Castle House, with its grand entrance reception hall and feature mirror lending a sense of days gone by, all has been lovingly restored to provide high standards of comfort and facilities. Spacious, individually themed and evocatively named bedrooms are equipped with quality furnishings, a wealth of thoughtful extras and smart, efficient en suite bathrooms with floor lighting and underfloor heating. There is also a romantic lounge and a formal dining room with ornate ceiling plasterwork and log fires in winter, where guests can enjoy delicious breakfasts through to scrumptious afternoon teas and candlelit dinners.

Recommended in the area

Offa's Dyke; Loggerheads Country Park; Snowdonia

Lake Llyn Idwal and Carnedd Dyfydd, Snowdonia National Park

Pentre Mawr Country House

★ ★ ★ ★ ★ ⇔ GUEST ACCOMMODATION

Address   LLANDYROG, LL16 4LA
Tel: 01824 790732
Fax: 01824 790441
Email: info@pentremawrcountryhouse.co.uk
Website: www.pentremawrcountryhouse.co.uk
Map ref: 5 SJ16
Directions: From Denbigh follow signs to Bodfari/
Llandyrnog. Left at rdbt to Bodfari, after 50yds
turn left onto country lane, follow road and
Pentre Mawr on left
Rooms: 8 en suite (4 GF) S £80-£160 D £100-£180 Notes: Wi-fi 🐾 13yrs Parking: 8

This property, owned by the same family for 400 years, is a unique destination, bursting with character. Tucked away in an unspoilt corner of North Wales, in an Area of Outstanding Natural Beauty, this former farmhouse is set in nearly 200 acres of meadows, park and woodland. A true Welsh country house, it features well-appointed en suite bedrooms and suites, some with hot tubs and all very spacious and thoughtfully equipped. As well as large drawing rooms, there is also a formal dining room, ideal for family gatherings and special occasions, and a less formal dining area in the conservatory by the saltwater swimming pool in the walled garden. The daily-changing menu includes carefully sourced local meats and cheeses as well as homemade breads and sorbets. Full Welsh breakfasts with Buck's fizz are served in the morning room. Influenced by a love of the outdoors and Africa, owners Bre and Graham have introduced a number of luxurious canvas safari lodges to bring guests closer to nature without compromising on comfort; all are fully heated, have super-king-size beds, oak floors and decks with hot tubs, plus bathrooms with free-standing baths and showers.

Recommended in the area

Snowdonia National Park; Denbigh Castle; Moel Fammau mountain walk

Swallow Falls waterfall at Betws-y-Coed, Snowdonia National Park

Firgrove Country House B&B

★★★★★ 🏠 🍴 BED & BREAKFAST

Address Firgrove, Llanfwrog, RUTHIN, LL15 2LL
Tel: 01824 702677
Fax: 01824 702677
Email: meadway@firgrovecountryhouse.co.uk
Website: www.firgrovecountryhouse.co.uk
Map ref: 5 SJ15 **Directions:** 0.5m SW of Ruthin.
A494 onto B5105, 0.25m past Llanfwrog church on
right **Rooms:** 3 en suite (1 GF) **S** £55-£70 **D** £70-
£100 **Notes:** Wi-fi ⊗ ✂ **Parking:** 4 **Closed:** Dec-Jan

This Grade II listed building sits in a delightful garden and has inspiring views across the Vale of Clwyd.
The well-proportioned bedrooms retain many original features whilst being well-equipped with modern
comforts, including smart bathrooms. One of the bedrooms has an attractive four-poster bed, while
another is a self-contained ground-floor suite with an open fire, small kitchen and a private sitting
room. Home-made and locally sourced produce features in the splendid breakfasts, and evening meals
can be enjoyed by prior arrangement.

Recommended in the area

Offa's Dyke Path; Bodnant Garden (NT); Chester

Denbigh Castle

Tan-Yr-Onnen Guest House

★★★★★ GUESTHOUSE

Address	Waen, ST ASAPH,
	LL17 0DU
Tel:	01745 583821
Fax:	01745 583821
Email:	tanyronnenvisit@aol.com
Website:	www.northwalesbreaks.co.uk
Map ref:	5 SJ07
Directions:	W on A55 junct 28, turn left in 300yds
Rooms:	6 en suite (1 fmly) (4 GF)
Notes:	Wi-fi **Parking:** 8

Set in the heart of North Wales, in the verdant Vale of Clwyd, Patrick and Sara Murphy's guest house, Tan-Yr-Onnen, is perfectly located for exploring this beautiful area and nearby Chester. Now awarded the AA's highest B&B rating, quality is the keyword here, with very high standards throughout.

The house has been extensively refurbished and the separately accessed bedrooms newly constructed; all are modern and well-equipped. The en suite ground-floor rooms feature king-size beds and some have French doors opening onto the patio, while those on the first floor offer suite accommodation.

All provide home comforts such as bathrobes, fluffy towels, comfy beds, flat-screen TVs (with Freeview and DVD players), and tea- and coffee-making facilities, plus little touches to make your stay feel extra special. Free Wi-fi is available. The hearty breakfast table will set you up for a day's exploration and features fruit juices, fresh fruit salad, yoghurts, cereals, home-baked bread and a full Welsh breakfast. Adjacent to the dining room is the lounge and large conservatory. Here you can enjoy a cool glass of wine in the evening as you admire the grounds and gardens at the foot of the Clwydian range. Private parking is available.

Recommended in the area

St Asaph; Bodelwyddan Castle; Offa's Dyke Path

Harlech Castle

Llwyndu Farmhouse

★★★★ 🛏 GUEST ACCOMMODATION

Address   Llanaber, BARMOUTH,
          LL42 1RR
Tel: 01341 280144
Email: intouch@llwyndu-farmhouse.co.uk
Website: www.llwyndu-farmhouse.co.uk
Map ref: 5 SH61
Directions: A496 towards Harlech where street lights
end, on outskirts of Barmouth, take next right
Rooms: 7 en suite (2 fmly rooms) D £96-£120
Notes: Wi-fi Parking: 10 Closed: 25-26 Dec

This converted 16th-century farmhouse stands overlooking Cardigan Bay in Llanaber, near Barmouth and the Mawddach Estuary, in an area of Outstanding Natural Beauty. Llwyndu has been drawing in customers with its fine ale and warm hospitality since 1600, and today it maintains that tradition by providing good food, wines and local beers as well as comfortable accommodation. Many attractive elements of the original building have also survived the centuries, including inglenook fireplaces, exposed beams and timbers. Bedrooms offer all modern comforts, with en suite facilities, televisions and tea- and coffee-making equipment, while some have a more old-world feel with four-poster beds. The bedrooms are split between the main house and the converted granary. There is a cosy lounge in the main house, where you might socialise with fellow guests and plan trips out. The restaurant is in the old hall – all inglenooks, beams and stone. Here, fresh ingredients are used to produce four to five choices at each course in a wonderfully atmospheric setting of flickering candles and lamps. A good choice is offered for breakfast too, including vegetarian dishes, while special diets can easily be catered for with prior notice.

Recommended in the area

RNLI Visitor Centre; Harlech Castle; Portmeirion Village

Tyddynmawr Farmhouse

★ ★ ★ ★ ★ FARMHOUSE
Address Cader Road, Islawrdref,
DOLGELLAU, LL40 1TL
Tel: 01341 422331
Website: www.wales-guesthouse.co.uk
Map ref: 2 SH71 **Directions:** From town centre left
at top of square, left at garage onto Cader Rd for 3m,
1st farm on left after Gwernan Lake
Rooms: 3 en suite (1 GF) D £70-£74
Notes: Wi-fi ⊗ ⛹ **Parking:** 8 **Closed:** Jan

Birdwatchers, ramblers, photographers and artists see these spectacular surroundings as a paradise.
Olwen Evans has been running Tyddynmawr as a five-star guesthouse for 25 years, and prides herself
on her home cooking and warm hospitality. Oak beams and log fires lend character to the stone house,
and bedrooms are spacious and furnished with Welsh oak furniture; one room has a balcony, and
a ground-floor room benefits from a patio. The en suites are large and luxurious. This breathtaking
mountain setting is about three miles from the historic market town of Dolgellau.
Recommended in the area
Walking – Cader Idris, Precipice walk, Mawddach Estuary walk; Steam railways; good local food

The Crown at Whitebrook

★ ★ ★ ★ ★ ⍟⍟ 🍽 RESTAURANT WITH ROOMS
Address WHITEBROOK, NP25 4TX
Tel: 01600 860254 **Fax:** 01600 860607
Email: info@crownatwhitebrook.co.uk
Website: www.crownatwhitebrook.co.uk
Map ref: 2 SO50 **Directions:** 4m from Monmouth
on B4293, left at sign to Whitebrook, 2m on
unmarked road, Crown on right **Rooms:** 8 en suite
S £90-£110 D £135-£160 **Notes:** Wi-fi ⊗ ⛹ 12yrs
Parking: 20 **Closed:** 23 Dec-7 Jan

In a secluded spot in the wooded valley of the River Wye, this former drover's cottage dates back
to the 17th century and boasts five acres of tranquil gardens. A restaurant with rooms, it boasts
contemporary accommodation with luxuries like walk-in power showers and double-ended baths, along
with outstanding views of the surrounding countryside. It's the smart, modern restaurant that lies at the
heart of the whole operation, however. Head chef James Sommerin's memorable cuisine is based on
excellent, locally sourced ingredients, and it's all accompanied by a seriously good wine list.
Recommended in the area
Brecon Beacons; Tintern Abbey; Offa's Dyke

Labuan Guest House

★★★★ GUESTHOUSE

Address	464 Chepstow Road, NEWPORT, NP19 8JF
Tel/Fax:	01633 664533
Email:	patricia.bees@ntlworld.com
Website:	www.labuanhouse.co.uk
Map ref:	2 ST38
Directions:	M4 junct 24, 1.5m on B4237
Rooms:	5 (3 en suite) (2 pri facs) (1 GF)
Notes:	Wi-fi **Parking:** 6

John and Patricia Bees have created a warm and friendly home-from-home atmosphere at their fine Victorian house with its lovely garden, set on the main road into Newport. Golfers will find kindred spirits in these keen players, who will arrange tee times for their guests at any of the 45 courses within a 40-minute drive; it's just a mile away from Celtic Manor Resort which hosted the 2010 Ryder Cup. After a day on the course or exploring the area, the high comfort levels in the stylish en suite bedrooms are very welcome indeed. Each good-sized room is well-equipped with TV/DVD, tea- and coffee-making facilities, hairdryers, fluffy bathrobes and Wi-fi. Bathrooms feature a wide range of extras. On the ground floor there is a twin room and a comfortable lounge where guests can relax, and in winter a log fire makes for a cosy atmosphere. There is a good choice from the menu for hearty breakfasts that include home-made bread and preserves, and are taken in the welcoming dining room. Evening meals can be arranged, as can lunches to go, packed in a cool bag. Labuan is just a few minutes drive from the M4, so it makes an ideal location for business people visiting Newport. Off-street parking is available.

Recommended in the area

Tredegar House; Caerleon Roman Site & History Museum; Newport Wetlands

St Justinian, near St David's

Erw-Lon Farm

★★★★★ ⌂ FARMHOUSE

Address	Pontfaen, FISHGUARD, SA65 9TS
Tel:	01348 881297
Email:	lilwenmcallister@btinternet.com
Website:	www.erwlonfarm.co.uk
Map ref:	1 SM93
Directions:	5.5m SE of Fishguard on B4313
Rooms:	3 en suite S £40-£45 D £64-£70
Notes:	⊗ ✕ 10yrs Parking: 5 Closed: Dec-Mar

This lovely old house is at the heart of a working sheep and cattle farm, and its landscaped gardens overlook the stunning Gwaun Valley towards Carningli, the Mountain of the Angels. Lilwen McAllister is an exceptional hostess, and the farmhouse has a very homely atmosphere. The lounge is a lovely place to relax, while the bedrooms are comfortable and well-equipped. Mrs McAllister's traditional farmhouse cooking uses fresh local produce and meals are served in generous portions. Erw–Lon Farm is well situated as a base to explore Pembrokeshire and Cardigan Bay.

Recommended in the area

Castell Henllys; Strumble Head; St David's Cathedral; Pembrokeshire Coastal Path

Crug-Glas Country House

★★★★★ ⌂ ⌷ GUESTHOUSE

Address	SOLVA, St David's, SA62 6XX
Tel:	01348 831302
Email:	janet@crugglas.plus.com
Website:	www.crug-glas.co.uk
Map ref:	1 SM82
Rooms:	7 en suite (1 fmly) (2 GF) S £70 D £100-£150
Notes:	Wi-fi ⊗ ✕ 12yrs Parking: 10
Closed:	24-27 Dec

Crug-Glas is a family-run country house situated about a mile inland from the breathtaking Pembrokeshire coast. On a dairy, beef and cereal farm of roughly 600 acres, this delightful property has a history dating back to the 12th century. Guests today can expect comfort, relaxation and flawless attention to detail. Each spacious bedroom has the hallmarks of assured design, with grand furnishings and luxury en suite bathrooms. One suite on the top floor provides great views. AA award-winning breakfasts and dinners use the finest local produce. The sunsets in the evening are stunning.

Recommended in the area

Abereiddy beach; Porthgain; St David's

The Anvil, near the village of Marloes in the Pembrokeshire Coast National Park

Ramsey House

★ ★ ★ ★ ★ 🏨 🛏 GUESTHOUSE

Address	Lower Moor, ST DAVID'S, Haverfordwest, SA62 6RP
Tel:	01437 720321 & 07795 575005
Email:	info@ramseyhouse.co.uk
Website:	www.ramseyhouse.co.uk
Map ref:	1 SM72

Directions: From Cross Sq in St David's towards Porthclais, house 0.25m on left

Rooms: 6 (5 en suite) (1 pri facs) (3 GF)

S £60-£110 D £90-£110 Notes: Wi-fi ⊗ 🐾 16yrs Parking: 10 Closed: Nov-13 Feb

Family-run by Suzanne and Shaun Ellison, Ramsey House is just a gentle stroll from the centre of Britain's smallest city, St David's, a place with a rich historical heritage surrounded by beautiful countryside, with the Pembrokeshire coastal path nearby. The Ellisons provide the ideal combination of professional hotel management and the warmth of a friendly guest house with a relaxed atmosphere. They are happy to advise guests on the many activities and places of interest nearby, and there are plenty of books and leaflets too, to help you plan your excursions. All bedrooms have been refurbished in a luxury boutique style; first-floor rooms have views out to sea, over countryside or towards the cathedral, and those on the ground-floor look out over the gardens. Accommodation includes a licensed bar, next to the dining room, secure bicycle storage, a wet room, light laundry facilities and ample off-street parking. Shaun is an accomplished chef who champions quality local produce, so you can expect a real flavour of Wales from your meals. Breakfast provides a choice of home-made items including breads and preserves, and a three-course dinner is served in the restaurant. Freshly prepared picnics can also be arranged for your day out.

Recommended in the area

Pembrokeshire islands; St David's Cathedral; Pembrokeshire Coast National Park

The Waterings

★★★★ BED & BREAKFAST

Address	Anchor Drive, High Street, ST DAVID'S, SA62 6QH
Tel:	01437 720876
Fax:	01437 720876
Email:	enquiries@waterings.co.uk
Website:	www.waterings.co.uk
Map ref:	1 SM72
Directions:	On A487 on E edge of St David's
Rooms:	5 en suite (4 fmly rooms) (5 GF)
Notes:	⊗ ⛄ 5yrs Parking: 20

The Waterings is set in an acre of beautiful landscaped grounds in a quiet location close to the Pembrokeshire Coast National Park Visitor Centre and only a short walk from St David's 800-year-old cathedral, which is the setting for an annual music festival at the end of May. The magnificent coastline with its abundance of birdlife is also within easy reach. The spacious en suite bedrooms are all on the ground floor and are set around an attractive courtyard. All the bedrooms are equipped with TV and have tea- and coffee-making facilities. The accommodation includes two family rooms with lounge, two double rooms with lounge and a double room with small sitting area. Breakfast, prepared from a good selection of local produce, is served in a smart dining room in the main house. Outside amenities at The Waterings include a picnic area with tables and benches, a barbecue and a croquet lawn. The nearest sandy beach is just a 15-minute walk away; other activities in the area include walking, boat trips to Ramsey Island, an RSPB reserve a mile offshore, sea fishing, whale and dolphin spotting boat trips, canoeing, surfing, rock climbing and abseiling.

Recommended in the area

Ramsey Island boat trips; Pembrokeshire Coast National Park; Whitesands Beach

Panorama

★ ★ ★ ★ 🏛 GUEST ACCOMMODATION

Address The Esplanade, TENBY, SA70 7DU
Tel: 01834 844976
Fax: 01834 844976
Email: mail@tenby-hotel.co.uk
Website: www.tenby-hotel.co.uk
Map ref: 1 SN10 **Directions:** A478 follow South Beach & Town Centre signs. Sharp left under railway arches, up Greenhill Rd, onto South Pde then Esplanade

Rooms: 8 en suite (1 fmly) **Notes:** ⊗ 🐾 5yrs **Closed:** 22-28 Dec

Right on the Esplanade overlooking Tenby's fine South Beach and across Carmarthen Bay, the friendly, family-run Panorama is part of a handsome terrace of Victorian properties. It provides the perfect location for exploring the Pembrokeshire coastline and the ancient town with its harbour and medieval wall. The well appointed bedrooms have been decorated and furnished to the highest standard, all en suite, with tea- and coffee-making facilities. A good selection of dishes is available at breakfast.

Recommended in the area

Caldy monastic island; Tudor Merchant's House; Tenby Museum & Art Gallery

Carn Llidi, looking over Whitesands with Ramsey in the background

Tretower Castle, Brecon Beacons National Park

The Coach House

★★★★★ ⌂ GUEST ACCOMMODATION

Address   Orchard Street,
BRECON, LD3 8AN
Tel: 01874 620043 & 07974 328437
Email: coachhousebrecon@gmail.com
Website: www.coachhousebrecon.com
Map ref: 2 SO02
Directions: From town centre W over bridge onto B4601, Coach
House 200yds on right
Rooms: 7 en suite **S** £50-£60 **D** £60-£90
Notes: Wi-fi ⊗ ⚒ 16yrs **Parking:** 7

Coach houses were traditionally warm and welcoming places,
and while a warm welcome is assured here in Brecon, this particular example is one of a new breed,
offering luxurious townhouse accommodation. The private garden of the Coach House is an oasis of
colour, and offers a retreat in which to relax, read a book or take a drink. Hosts Marc and Tony are
proud of their local knowledge, and offer advice on the best places to visit, whether by car, on foot or by
bicycle. There are also opportunities for sailing or pony-trekking in the area. The strong sense of place
evident in the photographs and maps of the Brecon Beacons on the walls, showing some of the most
unspoilt countryside in Wales, continues through to the Welsh-speciality breakfasts – try Eggs Brychan,
made with scrambled eggs, smoked salmon and laverbread for starters. Much thought has gone into
the contemporary design of the light, airy and well-equipped bedrooms, some of which come with DVD
players.

Recommended in the area

Brecon Beacons National Park; Dan yr Ogof Caves; Brecon Cathedral

Llanddetty Hall Farm

★★★★ FARMHOUSE

Address Talybont-on-Usk, BRECON, LD3 7YR
Tel: 01874 676415
Fax: 01874 676415
Map ref: 2 SO02
Directions: SE of Brecon. Off B4558
Rooms: 4 (3 en suite) (1 pri facs) (1 GF)
S £40 D £60-£70
Notes: ⊗ ⊮ 12yrs Parking: 6
Closed: 16 Dec-14 Jan

This listed farmhouse is part of a sheep farm in the Brecon Beacons National Park. The Brecon and Monmouth Canal flows through the farm at the rear, while the front of the house overlooks the River Usk. Bedrooms, including one on the ground floor, feature exposed beams and polished floorboards. Three rooms are en suite and one has a private bathroom – all have radio-alarms and tea- and coffee-making facilities. There is a lounge with a television, and a dining room where breakfast is served at an oak refectory table.

Recommended in the area

Brecon Beacons National Park; Hay-on-Wye; Aberglasney

Looking down onto Talybont Reservoir, Brecon Beacons National Park

Glangrwyney Court

★★★★★ BED & BREAKFAST

Address	CRICKHOWELL, NP8 1ES
Tel:	01873 811288
Fax:	01873 810317
Email:	info@glancourt.co.uk
Website:	www.glancourt.co.uk
Map ref:	2 SO21

Directions: 2m SE of Crickhowell on A40 (near county boundary)

Rooms:	10 en suite (1 fmly) (1 GF)
Notes:	Wi-fi Parking: 12

A privately-owned, Georgian Grade II listed country house, Glangrwyney Court offers delightful luxury accommodation. Forming part of a small country estate on the edge of the beautiful Brecon Beacons and the Black Mountains, it stands in four acres of walled gardens and makes an ideal base for touring this lovely area. The house throughout is tastefully decorated and furnished with period pieces. Guests are encouraged to relax in the cosy sitting room in front of a roaring log fire in the winter months. Glangrwyney Court has been home to the same family for the last 17 years, during which time the main house and the cottages have been sympathetically restored to provide excellent modern comforts. The accommodation comprises eight bedrooms in the main house, one ground-floor room in the garden courtyard, and three cottages which are available on a bed and breakfast basis or for self-catering. All rooms have TV and DVD players, hairdryers, clock radios, quality toiletries, fluffy bath towels and robes, plus tea- and coffee-making facilities.

Recommended in the area

Brecon Beacons National Park; Raglan Castle; Big Pit National Mining Museum of Wales

Guidfa House

★★★★★ 🏠 ☕ GUEST ACCOMMODATION

Address Crossgates, LLANDRINDOD WELLS,
LD1 6RF
Tel: 01597 851241
Fax: 01597 737269
Email: guidfa@globalnet.co.uk
Website: www.guidfa-house.co.uk
Map ref: 2 SO06 **Directions:** 3m N of Llandrindod
Wells, at junct of A483 & A44
Rooms: 6 en suite (1 GF) **S** £65-£90 **D** £80-£105
Notes: Wi-fi ⊗ 🚫 10yrs **Parking:** 10

Expect a relaxed stay at Anne and Tony Millan's charming Georgian house, set within picturesque gardens and located in the village of Crossgates, just north of Llandrindod Wells. All rooms come well-equipped with comfortable beds, fluffy towels, soft bathrobes and quality toiletries. The luxurious Coach House suite has a super-king double bed and a large, separate sitting room and spa bath. Breakfasts are a real treat, made from the very best local produce. Free Wi-fi is available.

Recommended in the area

Elan Valley RSPB Red Kite Feeding Station; Royal Welsh Showground; Builth Wells

Llangorse Lake, Brecon Beacons National Park

The Cammarch

★★★★ GUEST ACCOMMODATION

Address   LLANGAMMARCH WELLS,
           LD4 4BY

Tel: 01591 610802

Fax: 01591 610807

Email: mail@cammarch.com

Website: www.cammarch.com

Map ref: 2 SN94

Directions: Off A483 at Garth signed
Llangammarch Wells, opp T-junct

Rooms: 11 en suite (3 fmly rooms) **S** £59-£69 **D** £79-£89 Notes: Wi-fi **Parking:** 16

Kathryn Dangerfield took over The Cammarch in 2008 and has been busy ever since refurbishing and refining it to restore the Victorian building to its original elegance. Built in traditional Welsh stone, The Cammarch is surrounded by stunning countryside and is just a stone's throw from Builth Wells, with the Brecon Beacons National Park nearby and the coast and Aberystwyth just over an hour away. Kathryn offers all guests a warm and friendly welcome in a homely and comfortable environment. The high quality accommodation includes nine double or twin en suite bedrooms on the first two floors, and two excellent family suites with fully fitted kitchen/diner and a separate lounge on the top floor. There's a lovely residents' lounge with comfortable sofas, open fire, games and an honesty bar, while meals are taken in the attractive conservatory restaurant overlooking the garden. All the food is prepared from scratch using as much local produce as possible. The garden is a magical place, especially for children, with the river running around the edge – perfect for a paddle or a spot of fishing. For serious anglers, The Cammarch has fishing rights on the River Irfon.

Recommended in the area

Elan Valley Reservoir and Dams; Rhayader red kite feeding station; Royal Welsh Showground at Builth Wells

Caban Coch Reservoir bridge, Elan Valley

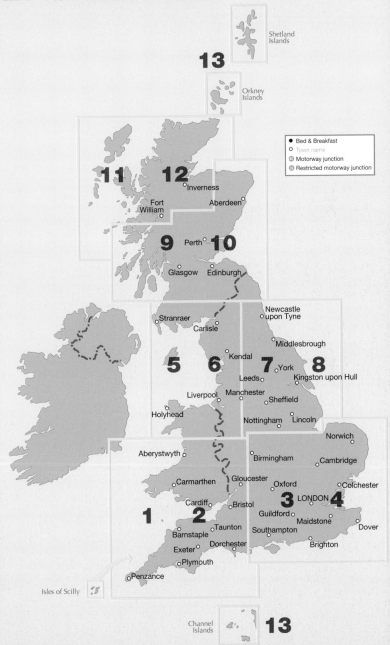

KEY TO ATLAS PAGES

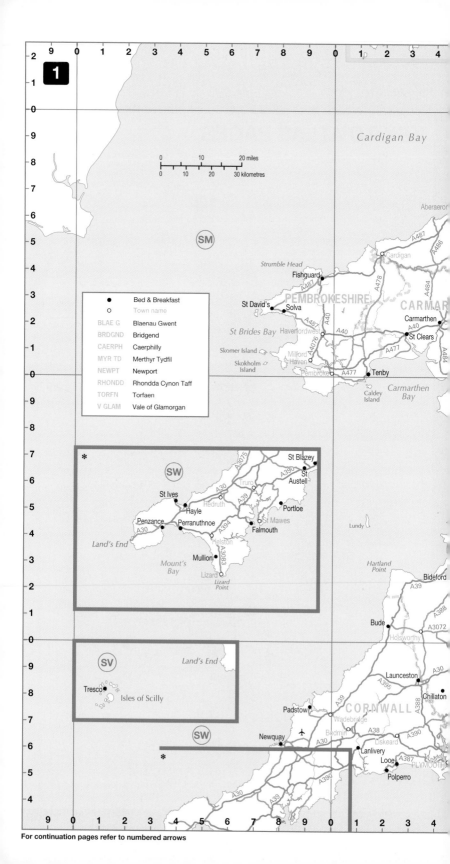

Legend

●	Bed & Breakfast
○	Town name
BLAE G	Blaenau Gwent
BRDGND	Bridgend
CAERPH	Caerphilly
MYR TD	Merthyr Tydfil
NEWPT	Newport
RHONDD	Rhondda Cynon Taff
TORFN	Torfaen
V GLAM	Vale of Glamorgan

1

Cardigan Bay

SM

Strumble Head
Fishguard
Cardigan
St David's Solva
PEMBROKESHIRE CARMAR
St Brides Bay Haverfordwest
Carmarthen
Skomer Island St Clears
Skokholm Milford Haven
Island Pembroke Tenby
Caldey Island
Carmarthen Bay

Aberaeror

0 — 10 — 20 miles
0 — 10 — 20 — 30 kilometres

*

SW

St Blazey
St Austell
Truro
St Ives Redruth
Hayle St Mawes
Penzance Perranuthnoe Portloe
Land's End Falmouth
Helston
Mullion
Mount's Bay Lizard
Lizard Point

Lundy

Hartland Point

Bideford

Bude
Holsworthy

SV Land's End
Tresco Isles of Scilly

Padstow
Wadebridge
CORNWALL
Bodmin
Newquay A30
Liskeard

Launceston
Chillaton

SW
*
Lanlivery
Looe
PLYMOUTH
Polperro

For continuation pages refer to numbered arrows

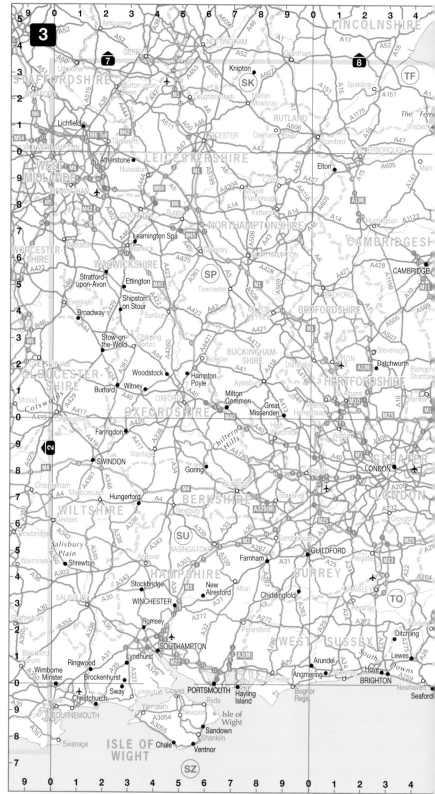

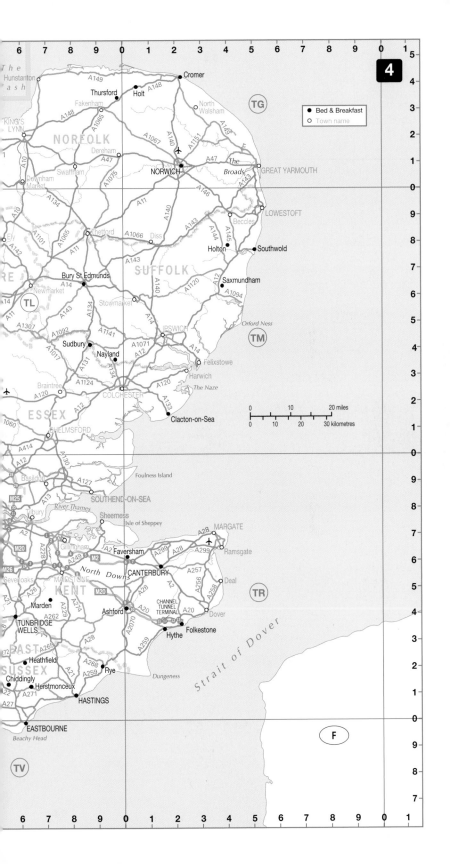

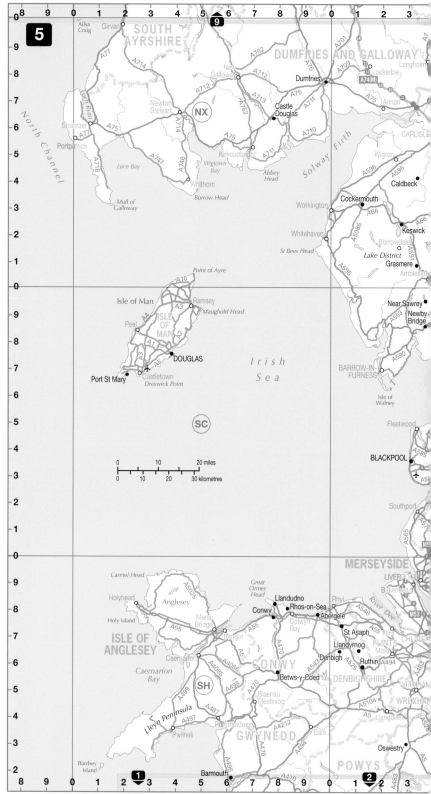

North Channel

SOUTH AYRSHIRE

Ailsa Craig
Girvan
A77
A714

DUMFRIES AND GALLOWAY
A701
A702
A709
Langholm
Lockerbie
A74(M)
Annan
A75
Dumfries
A76
A709
New Galloway
A712
A712
A713
Castle Douglas
A711
A710
Newton Stewart
NX
A762
Stranraer
A77
A75
Portpatrick
A716
A747
A746
Luce Bay
Kirkcudbright
A711
Wigtown Bay
Abbey Head
CARLISLE
Wigton
A596
A595
Caldbeck
Solway Firth
Whithorn
Burrow Head
Cockermouth
A66
Workington
A5086
A66
Keswick
Whitehaven
Borrowdale
St Bees Head
Lake District
A595
Grasmere
Ambleside
A591

Point of Ayre
A10
Isle of Man
Ramsey
A3
Maughold Head
Near Sawrey
A593
Newby Bridge
Peel
A4
ISLE OF MAN
A2
A590
A5
DOUGLAS
Port St Mary
A3
Castletown
Dreswick Point
BARROW-IN-FURNESS
Isle of Walney

Irish Sea

SC

Fleetwood
A585

0   10   20 miles
0   10   20   30 kilometres

BLACKPOOL
A585

Southport
A565
M5

MERSEYSIDE
LIVERPOOL
Birkenhead
M53
Carmel Head
Great Ormes Head
Llandudno
Rhyl
River Dee
A548
Holyhead
Anglesey
A5025
Conwy
Rhos-on-Sea
Abergele
A55
Flint
CHESTER
Holy Island
Menai Bridge
A55
Colwyn Bay
St Asaph
A55
FLINTS
ISLE OF ANGLESEY
A5
Bangor
A55
A470
Llandyrnog
Mold
A494
Caernarfon
A4086
CONWY
Denbigh
A525
Ruthin
A483
Caernarfon Bay
A4085
SH
A498
A470
Betws-y-Coed
DENBIGHSHIRE
WREXHAM
A499
Blaenau Ffestiniog
A5104
WREXHAM
Lleyn Peninsula
A487
Porthmadog
A4212
A5
Llangollen
A5
A497
Bala
GWYNEDD
Oswestry
Pwllheli
A494
Bardsey Island
A496
POWYS
Barmouth
A470
A483

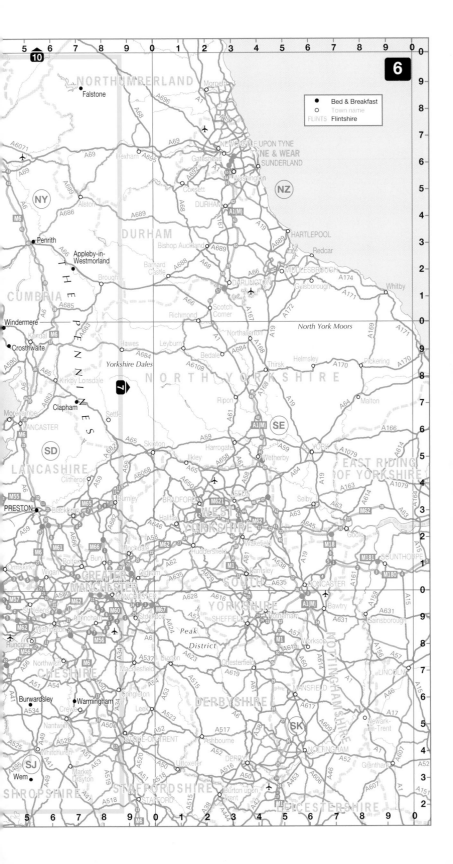

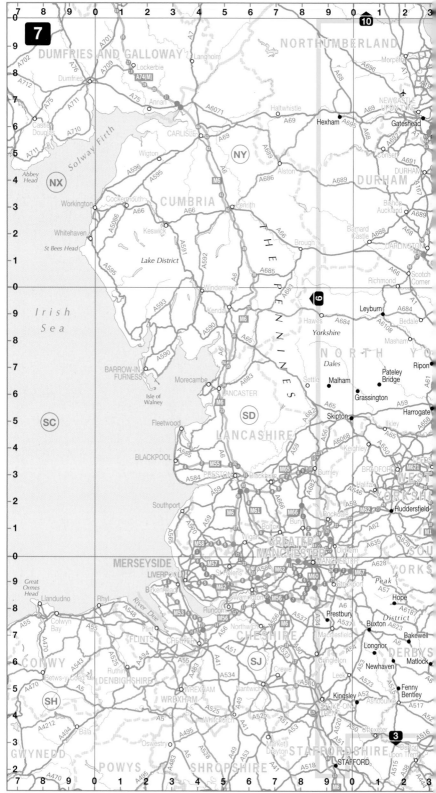

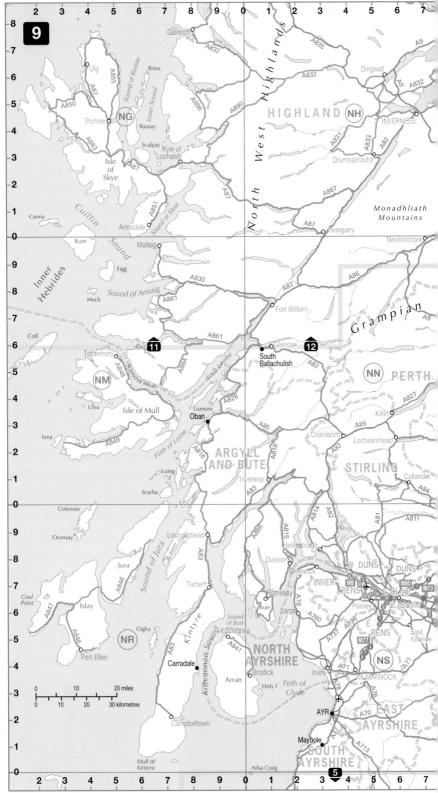

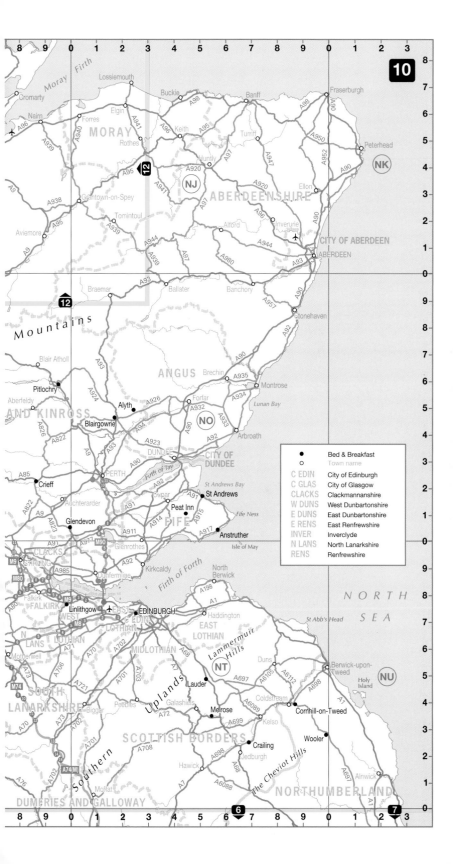

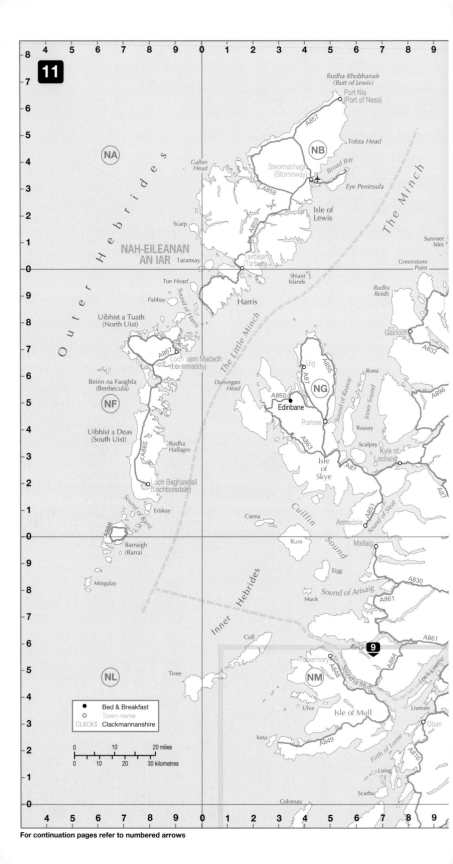

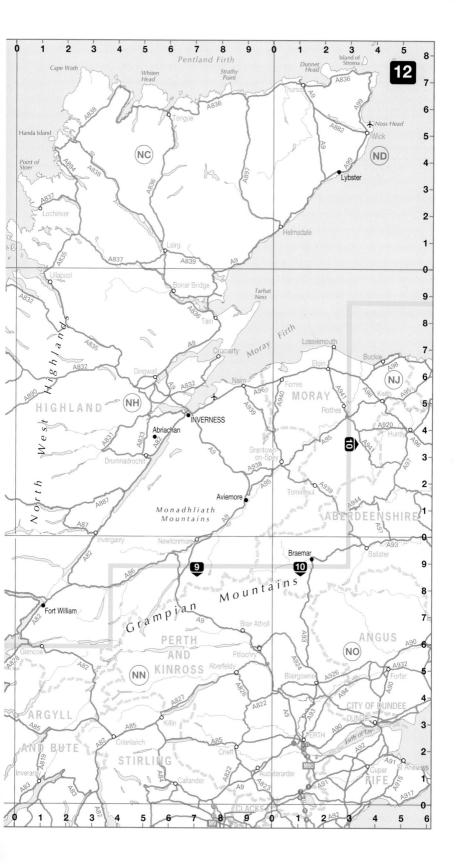

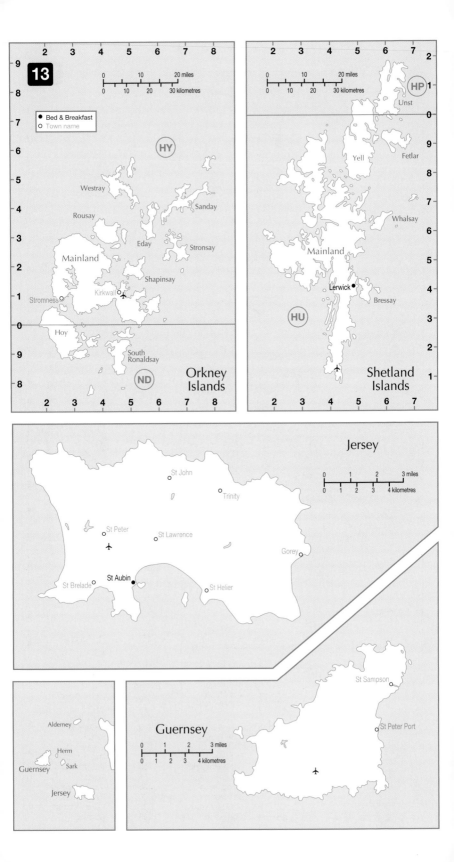

County Map

England

1	Bedfordshire
2	Berkshire
3	Bristol
4	Buckinghamshire
5	Cambridgeshire
6	Greater Manchester
7	Herefordshire
8	Hertfordshire
9	Leicestershire
10	Northamptonshire
11	Nottinghamshire
12	Rutland
13	Staffordshire
14	Warwickshire
15	West Midlands
16	Worcestershire

Scotland

17	City of Glasgow
18	Clackmannanshire
19	East Ayrshire
20	East Dunbartonshire
21	East Renfrewshire
22	Perth & Kinross
23	Renfrewshire
24	South Lanarkshire
25	West Dunbartonshire

Wales

26	Blaenau Gwent
27	Bridgend
28	Caerphilly
29	Denbighshire
30	Flintshire
31	Merthyr Tydfil
32	Monmouthshire
33	Neath Port Talbot
34	Newport
35	Rhondda Cynon Taff
36	Torfaen
37	Vale of Glamorgan
38	Wrexham

Location Index

Location Index

Location Index

Location Index

Bed & Breakfast Index

B&B Index

B&B Index

B&B Index

B&B Index

Credits

The Automobile Association would like to thank the following photographers, companies and picture libraries for their assistance in the preparation of this book.

Abbreviations for the picture credits are as follows: (t) top; (b) bottom; (l) left; (r) right; (c) centre; (AA) AA World Travel Library.

4 ; 5 Royalty Free Photodisc; 7 Bay View Farm; 8 Llwyndu Farmhouse; 10 Clive Restaurant with Rooms; 12 Moortown Lodge Hotel; 14/15 AA/M Jourdan; 16 AA/J Tims; 19 AA/J Tims; 20 AA/R Duke; 22 AA/M Moody; 24 AA/L Noble; 26 AA/C Jones; 28b AA/J Beazley; 29 AA/A Burton; 33b AA/A Burton; 35b AA/A Burton; 39b AA/J Wood; 42/43 AA/A Burton; 50b AA/J Wood; 53 AA/T Mackie; 58/59 AA/T Mackie; 63b AA/T Mackie; 65 AA/T Mackie; 67b AA/A J Hopkins; 71b AA/T Mackie; 72 AA/N Hicks; 73b AA/N Hicks; 74b AA/A Burton; 77b AA/G Edwardes; 78b AA/N Hicks; 80b AA/N Hicks; 82b AA/G Edwardes; 84/85 AA/G Edwardes; 96 AA/A Burton; 99b AA/M Jourdan; 105 AA/N Setchfield; 107 AA/H Palmer; 108b AA/D Hall; 110b AA/M Moody; 112 AA/D Hall; 114b AA/S Day; 115 AA/W Voysey; 118b AA/S Montgomery; 120/121 AA/A Burton; 122b AA/A Burton; 125 AA/H Palmer; 127 AA/M Moody; 128b AA/M Moody; 129 AA/V Bates; 130b AA/V Bates; 131 AA/A Burton; 132b AA/A Burton; 136 AA/L Noble; 139 AA/L Noble; 142 AA/D Clapp; 144 AA/D Clapp; 145 AA/J Tims; 146b AA/J Tims; 147 AA/J Tims; 148b AA/J Tims; 150 AA/N Setchfield; 153 AA/J Tims; 154 AA/T Mackie; 157 AA/T Mackie; 159 AA/R Coulam; 163 AA/J Hunt; 165 AA/J Tims; 167b AA/C Jones; 169 AA/D Hall; 170 AA/W Voysey; 172 AA/M Morris; 176 AA/C Jones; 178b AA/A Tryner; 180 AA/J Tims; 182b AA/C Jones; 186/187 AA/A Burton; 192 AA/C Jones; 195b AA/T Mackie; 196 AA/T Mackie; 200 AA/J Tims; 202b AA/J Tims; 203 AA/L Noble; 206b AA/L Noble; 210/211 AA/J Miller; 212b AA/J Miller; 215b AA/J Miller; 219 AA/L Noble; 221 AA/R Coulam; 223 AA/C Jones; 228 AA/M Moody; 231 AA/M Moody; 233b AA/M Moody; 234 AA/M Moody; 235b AA/D Hall; 237b AA/C Jones; 238 AA/D Clapp; 239b AA/D Clapp; 240 AA/T Mackie; 246/247 AA/M Kipling; 250 AA/T Mackie; 253 AA/T Mackie; 254/255 AA/J Hunt; 257b AA/T Mackie; 259b AA/T Mackie; 260 AA/J Tims; 261 AA/J Tims; 262 Jon Arnold Images Ltd/Alamy; 263b AA/S Abrahams; 265 Powered by Light/ Alan Spencer/Alamy; 266/267 AA/D W Robertson; 274/275 AA/S Day; 276b AA/S Whitehorne; 280b AA/S Whitehorne; 286/287 AA/C Warren; 288b AA/N Jenkins; 291 AA/N Jenkins; 293 AA/S Lewis; 294/295 AA/S Watkins; 297b AA/M Bauer; 298/299 AA/M Bauer; 301b AA/G Matthews; 302 AA/S Lewis; 304 AA/R Duke; 306 AA/M Bauer; 308/309 AA/N Jenkins; 310b AA/I Burgum; 312 AA/M Bauer; 316 AA/C Warren; 318 AA/C Warren; 321b AA/C Warren; 322 AA/D Santillo; 324b AA/D Santillo; 326b AA/N Jenkins; 328 AA/M Adelman;

Every effort has been made to trace the copyright holders, and we apologise in advance for any accidental errors. We would be happy to apply any corrections in the following edition of this publication.